KU-689-090

Malcolm Allison

Alan Ball

Gordon Banks

George Best

Derek Dougan

George Eastham

Pat Jennings

Howard Kendall

Peter Osgood

Bobby Robson

Peter Shilton

Bobby Smith

Mike Channon

Bobby Charlton

Brian Clough

Tommy Docherty

Denis Law

James McIlroy

Bobby Moore

Terry Neill

Mike Summerbee

Terry Venables

Ron Yeats

Alex Young

THE
SIXTIES
REVISITED

THE
SIXTIES
REVISITED

jimmy greaves
with
norman giller

RETRO CLASSICS

RETRO CLASSICS
is a collection of facsimile reproductions
of popular bestsellers from the 1980s and 1990s

The Sixties Revisited was first published in 1992
by Queen Anne Press

Re-issued in 2016 as a Retro Classic
by G2 Entertainment
in association with Lennard Publishing
Windmill Cottage
Mackerye End
Harpenden
Hertfordshire
AL5 5DR

Copyright © Jimmy Greaves and Norman Giller 1992

ISBN 978-1-909040-25-0

Edited by Caroline North

Printed and bound by Lightning Source

This book is a facsimile reproduction of the first edition of
The Sixties Revisited which was a bestseller in 1992.
No attempt has been made to alter any of the wording with
the benefit of hindsight, or to update the book in any way.

CONTENTS

KICK-OFF

This is the story of the greatest decade in the history of British football. I know because I was there and was lucky to play a small part in it. Our book is targeted at the generation of spectators who witnessed these seasons in the sun, and also at all those youngsters who want to know why their parents and grandparents are so nostalgic for a golden age when football was king. The swinging 'sixties were about rock 'n' roll, Beatlemania-, colourful fashion and a youth revolution, and it was all mirrored on the playing fields of England where footballers were transformed into folk heroes.

I have written this book in harness with Norman Giller, who reported from the press box throughout the 'sixties for the *Daily Herald* and then the *Daily Express.* The facts and figures of the book are his, but the feelings are mine. I have let him do all the work, and have then added my opinions. Some people say that is how I used to play my football, tapping the ball into the net after others had done all the hard work!

So as not to get in the way of history, I have confined comment on my personal contribution to football in the 'sixties to self-contained diary sections in each chapter. We revisit the 'sixties in processional season-by-season order, painting the picture of the decade by focusing on the great teams and outstanding players of the time. Hopefully we have captured most of the moments – the men and the matches – that mattered.

Norman and I dedicate this book to the memory of Cyril Knowles, my lovely old Tottenham team-mate of the 'sixties whose mixture of cheek, skill, power and eccentricity somehow epitomised the exciting age in which we played together.

Now join me in my time-machine. We are off to another world. Relax and enjoy the journey.

Come back with me to New Year's Eve, 31 December, 1959, to meet 100 of the main characters in the cast of thousands who were to make the 'sixties the most memorable decade in the history of British football. This is what they were doing at the dawn of the decade ...

THE CAST

MALCOLM ALLISON was recovering from an operation in which he had a lung removed after contracting tuberculosis. His League playing career was over and the 32-year-old former West Ham United and Charlton centre-half was now considering a move into management with non-League Bath City.

JIMMY ARMFIELD had completed his National Service with the King's Own Regiment, and was cementing his place at right-back in the Blackpool and England defences. Jimmy, who went to the same rugby-playing Arnold School as George Eastham, had chosen football ahead of a university education. He was studying journalism and every Sunday played the organ in his local church.

JEFF ASTLE was just starting out on his career down in the Third Division with Notts County, where he was getting lessons in how to head the ball from the recently retired master of the airways, Tommy Lawton. He had given up his job as an apprentice fitter at Eastwood Colliery to join the Meadow Lane groundstaff.

BERTIE AULD was halfway through his first full season with Celtic. He was a winger with a fiery temper, and Celtic were to sell him to Birmingham for a giveaway £15,000 before he matured and made a triumphant return to Celtic Park as one of the most influential midfield schemers of the 'sixties.

ALAN BALL was a 14-year-old pupil at a grammar school in Farnworth where his father, a former professional footballer, was managing the Rose and Crown pub. During the previous year Wolves had been reported to the Football Association for playing Ball in their junior side while he was unregistered. His local club, Bolton, were about to tell him that he was too small to make the grade as a professional. He was to kick off his career with Blackpool. His voice sounded as if it had yet to break.

GORDON BANKS had celebrated his 22nd birthday the day before. He was into his sixth month as Leicester City's goalkeeper, having joined them from Chesterfield after two years' National Service with the Royal Signals. His coal-bagging days were over.

JIM BAXTER was into his third season with Raith Rovers. Rangers were already sitting up and taking notice of the silken skills of the skinny 20-year-old wing-half. His days of having to double as a part-time footballer and a full-time pitworker would soon be behind him, and he would become an idol of Ibrox.

COLIN BELL was just about to be discovered by Bury while playing for Horden Colliery Welfare. He was preparing to start his last term at school and was wondering whether his future lay down the coal mines. Already his remarkable stamina was beginning to show, and he was a schoolboy running champion in his home-town area of Heselden.

GEORGE BEST was a 13-year-old pupil at Lisnasharragh Intermediate School in Belfast. His exceptional footballing talent was encouraged by his mother, a star player with the Queen Park Hockey Club. It was to be two years before he joined Manchester United as an apprentice professional.

DANNY BLANCHFLOWER was into his fifth year with Tottenham after skilled service with Glentoran, Barnsley and Aston Villa. He had been made Spurs skipper and was also captain of Northern Ireland.

JOHN BOND was playing at right-back and occasionally centre-forward for West Ham, where his powerful kicking had earned him the nickname 'Muffin the Mule'.

PETER BONETTI, the son of a Swiss-born restaurateur, was a junior with Chelsea, and was to make his League debut at the age of 17 while still the youth team goalkeeper at Stamford Bridge.

TONY BOOK was working as a bricklayer while playing as a part-time professional with Bath City. The 24-year-old right-back was about to be galvanised by the arrival at Bath of new manager Malcolm Allison.

BILLY BREMNER had just signed professional forms with Leeds United after finishing his apprenticeship at Elland Road. Leeds had got his signature despite competition from Arsenal, Chelsea and Celtic. During the current season he would make his League debut as a 17-year-old winger alongside the man who was soon to become his manager, Don Revie.

MATT BUSBY was just returning to full duties as Manchester United manager after recovering from injuries received in the horrific 1958 Munich air crash that cost the lives of eight 'Busby Babes'. Matt, with the help of right-hand man Jimmy Murphy, was busy building a team for the 'sixties after having battled with Wolves for a monopoly of the 'fifties.

JOHNNY BYRNE had just finished serving with the Army and was now conjuring up some magical stuff that was to push Crystal Palace to promotion from the Fourth Division. Nicknamed 'Budgie' because he never stopped talking, he later became the first Third Division player to be capped by England.

IAN CALLAGHAN decided to give up his apprenticeship as a central heating engineer to start a professional football career with Liverpool. He had been spotted playing as a wing-half with the Liverpool schools team, but Bill Shankly was to switch him to the wing.

NOEL CANTWELL was skipper of West Ham and the Republic of Ireland, and during

Johnny Haynes, the 'Brylcreem Boy' of football, took over from Ronnie Clayton as England captain in 1960. He skippered England in 22 matches, 12 of which were won, four drawn and six lost. In a run of six successive victories under his leadership England amassed 40 goals against eight. His international career was ended by a car smash six weeks after the 1962 World Cup finals.

the coming year he was to be transferred to Manchester United for £29,500 – a British record fee for a full-back.

HARRY CATTERICK was manager of Sheffield Wednesday, having made a name for himself at Rochdale. He was establishing Wednesday back in the First Division, having won the Second Division championship the previous season.

MIKE CHANNON was playing for the Wiltshire County youth side, and was also a regular in the Orcheston village team that played on the edge of the firing range on Salisbury Plain. Swindon and Southampton were on his trail. He was to choose The Saints and make his debut in the reserve team at The Dell at the age of 15.

BOBBY CHARLTON, a survivor of the Munich air crash, was bombing in goals from the left wing for Manchester United and England. He had a lovely head of blond hair.

JACK CHARLTON, two years older than Bobby at 24, was established at Leeds as centre-half successor to John Charles, but he was soon to be unsettled by a series of arguments with Don Revie about his approach to the game. After being put on the transfer list, his new boss was to tell him: 'If you will just get your attitude right you can join your brother in the England team'.

MARTIN CHIVERS, having attracted Southampton scouts to watch him play for Hampshire schoolboys, was invited along to The Dell for trials. Manager Ted Bates described him as an outstanding prospect, but Martin was tossing up whether to choose a career as a footballer or as an accountant. Football was to be the winner.

ALLAN CLARKE was a 13-year-old schoolboy whose performances for the South East Staffordshire team in the English Schools Trophy competition persuaded Aston Villa to invite him along for training. But they lost interest and he was to start his career as a groundstaff boy with Walsall.

RONNIE CLAYTON combined being captain of Blackburn Rovers and England with running a newsagent's shop, and every morning he delivered the newspapers himself.

BRIAN CLOUGH was banging in goals right, left and centre for his home-town club, Middlesbrough. It was to be 18 months before he was transferred to Sunderland, where his career was cruelly cut short by a knee injury. After this, at the age of 30, he was to become a manager...

GEORGE COHEN was established at right-back with Fulham, the club with which he spent his entire career. It was to be four years before he broke into the England team.

BOBBY COLLINS, the pocket battleship, was halfway through his second season with Everton after being bought from Celtic for £25,000 by Goodison manager Johnny Carey.

CHARLIE COOKE, a ball-playing wizard even at 17, had just signed for Aberdeen after he had been spotted playing for Renfrew Juniors.

RAY CRAWFORD was pumping in goals galore for Ipswich in the Second Division. Signed by Alf Ramsey from Portsmouth as a side-kick to Ted Phillips, he was to shoot

Ipswich to the Second and First Division titles in successive seasons.

PAT CRERAND had completed an apprenticeship as a welder while playing part-time with Duntocher Hibs, and was now purring away in midfield for Celtic. Manchester United were already on his trail.

TOMMY DOCHERTY was winding down his playing career with Arsenal before moving across London to Chelsea where he would become player-coach. At his interview he was to tell the Chelsea directors about one of his rivals for the job: 'If you appoint him you won't get a coach, you'll get a hearse'. It was the start of the Tommy Docherty Laugh-In.

DEREK DOUGAN was centre-forward with Blackburn Rovers and would help shoot them into the 1960 FA Cup final. On the morning of the final he posted a transfer request.

BRYAN DOUGLAS worked his market stalls and household equipment shops when he wasn't selling dummies for Blackburn Rovers and England. He was a natural successor to Stanley Matthews in the No. 7 shirt, and was equally efficient as a midfield schemer.

MIKE DOYLE, the son of a Stockport policeman, was a schoolboy busily composing a prize-winning letter to the *Manchester Evening News* in which he revealed that his ambition was to become a professional footballer. Manchester City scout Harry Godwin took note, saw him play and then invited him to join the groundstaff at Maine Road.

GEORGE EASTHAM was the pass master at Newcastle and was getting ready for a transfer showdown that was to reveal that footballers were 'soccer slaves'. The dispute was to end in a High Court judgement that the players' retain-and-transfer system was an unlawful restraint of trade. By then, George – the Matchstick Man – would be at Arsenal.

MIKE ENGLAND was 18 and starting to make an impression with Blackburn Rovers after serving his apprenticeship at Ewood Park. He was two years away from his first Welsh cap.

RON FLOWERS was the midfield strong man for Wolves and England as we came into the 'sixties, a decade that was to see the startling decline of Wolves as a major power in English football.

BILL FOULKES, a survivor of the Munich air crash, was into his eighth season with Manchester United, little realising that his greatest successes were yet to come.

JOHNNY GILES was into his third season with Manchester United, having joined them as a right-winger from Irish club Home Farm. His great days as a midfield marshal were ahead of him.

ALAN GILZEAN was a 21-year-old centre-forward with Dundee, having guested with Aldershot while doing his National Service in the Army.

GEORGE GRAHAM was preparing to turn his back on a queue of interested Scottish clubs to start his professional football career with Aston Villa.

JIMMY GREAVES. I was halfway through my third season with Chelsea, and was managing to knock in a few goals. So far I had collected five caps with Walter Winterbottom's England team, the last two in partnership with one Brian Clough. On this New Year's Eve that was to take us into the swinging 'sixties I felt that the world was treating me very kindly. I was married with a daughter and there was another baby on the way, and at 19 I had just bought my first car – a 1937 Opel convertible. It cost me £30, and I was one of the few players on the Chelsea staff with my own motor. I felt like the king of King's Road. Happy days.

RON GREENWOOD was assistant manager to George Swindin at Arsenal. He was soon to take over from Ted Fenton at West Ham United, with Billy Wright succeeding him as manager of the England Under-23 team.

JOHN GREIG was a Hearts supporter and was playing in Edinburgh with Whitburn Juniors. It seemed odds-on that he would join his local Tynecastle Park club, but Hearts would allow Rangers to come in and snatch him off their doorstep. It was to be one of the greatest signings in Rangers' history.

RON HARRIS was in his last year at school at Hackney with his brother, Allan. Both of them would soon join the Chelsea groundstaff. 'Chopper' was just getting his blade sharpened and even kicked me in training matches (only joking, Ron).

COLIN HARVEY was a 15-year-old pupil at Cardinal Allen Grammar School in Liverpool and was dreaming of playing for Everton. He would sign as an amateur at Goodison on his 16th birthday and become an apprentice professional a year later. He was to develop into an artist of a midfield player who would become one of Goodison's great servants.

TONY HATELEY had recently started his career with Notts County where – along with Jeff Astle – he received lessons from Tommy Lawton in how a ball should be headed.

JOHNNY HAYNES was captain of Fulham, future skipper of England and the king of the domestic stage. Within two years he would become English football's first £100-a-week player.

WILLIE HENDERSON had signed for Rangers after distinguishing himself as a schoolboy international while at the Caldercruix School. He was to replace Alex Scott on the right wing for Rangers at the age of 17.

JIMMY HILL was a forward with Fulham but, more significantly, he was the chairman of the Professional Footballers' Association leading the fight for the abolition of the maximum wage. He had a beard on that giant chin of his that distinguished him from Fulham chairman Tommy Trinder, who had an identical jaw. Both were great at jaw-jaw.

JOHN HOLLINS was a schoolboy in Guildford dreaming of following his older brother, Dave, as a professional footballer. He would get his opportunity with Chelsea, joining them as a junior and making his debut at the age of 17.

DON HOWE was a right-back with West Bromwich Albion and after a run of 23 matches in the England defence was about to lose his No. 2 shirt to Jimmy Armfield.

ROGER HUNT had finished his National Service and was joint top scorer in the Second Division with Liverpool team-mate Dave Hickson. In his spare time he drove a truck for his dad's haulage business.

NORMAN HUNTER had just been spotted by a Leeds United scout while playing junior football at Eighton Banks, and when he left school at 15 he was to join the Elland Road groundstaff. Mind yer legs!

GEOFF HURST, the son of a former Oldham and Chelmsford professional, was into his second season as a wing-half with West Ham, and it was not until Ron Greenwood became manager that he switched to a front-running role. He had cricket trials with Essex but had chosen a football career.

PAT JENNINGS was a schoolboy star at Gaelic football, and had yet to play soccer. He would leave school during the following year to work in a timber yard before trying his hand at goalkeeping with his local Newry team. The next stop was to be Watford.

JIMMY JOHNSTONE was learning his right-wing trickery with Blantyre Celtic, and was also working as a welder. He would shortly join the Glasgow Celtic groundstaff.

CLIFF JONES was completing his first year at Tottenham after joining them from Swansea for £35,000, which was then a British record fee for a winger.

HOWARD KENDALL was a 13-year-old schoolboy, yet only four years away from a Wembley Cup final. He would start his career as an apprentice with his local club Preston.

CYRIL KNOWLES, playing for Monkton Colliery where he was a pit worker, was about to be spotted by a Middlesbrough scout. He had already failed a trial with Wolves as a winger, but Middlesbrough would see his potential as a left-back.

BRIAN LABONE was torn between going to university or joining Everton. He chose Goodison, combining his football career with keeping a close eye on the family business of plumbers' and builders' merchants.

DENIS LAW was a wonder boy with Huddersfield, who were to shortly sell him to Manchester City for what would be a British record transfer fee of £55,000. He had undergone an operation to right a squint in his eye, and had thrown away his National Health glasses.

FRANCIS LEE had just signed for Bolton after leaving Horwich Technical College against the advice of his headmaster, who wanted him to stay on and sit his GCE exams.

PETER LORIMER had already earned the nickname 'hot shot' while at school, and after he had gained international honours with Scottish schoolboys he was to have a cluster of top clubs chasing him. He would choose to sign for Leeds, and would make his League debut for them at the age of 15.

EDDIE McCREADIE was a part-time professional with East Stirling in the Scottish Second Division. His international career would take off when Tommy Docherty signed him for Chelsea.

JIMMY McILROY was pulling the strings in midfield for Burnley on their way to the League championship. The decline of Burnley would follow the break up of the McIlroy-Jimmy Adamson partnership that was one of the most stylish and successful in football.

DAVE MACKAY was into his first full season with Tottenham after moving to White Hart Lane from Hearts for a fee of £30,000. He was to become an intoxicating influence on the 'Super Spurs' side of the 'sixties.

FRANK McLINTOCK had celebrated his 20th birthday three days before, and was combining his football at Leicester City with a job as a painter and decorator.

BILLY McNEILL, a soldier's son who had once been to a rugby-playing school in Hereford, was into his second season with Celtic after joining them from Blantyre Victoria.

PAUL MADELEY was a Leeds schoolboy star living within goal-kicking distance of Elland Road. His potential had already been spotted while he was playing for local club Farsley Celtic, and he would soon join Leeds as a centre-half who was to develop into the complete all-rounder.

RODNEY MARSH, the son of a London docker, was about to have the heartbreak of being told he was not wanted by West Ham where he had played as a junior. He would start his apprenticeship across London at Fulham.

BOBBY MOORE was captain of the England youth team and was about to establish himself in the West Ham defence in succession to one of his idols, Malcolm Allison.

STANLEY MATTHEWS, 'Mr Football', was 44 years young and still a regular in the First Division with Blackpool. He would return to Stoke, where he started his career, and play first-team football at the age of 50.

JOE MERCER, old banana legs, was starting his second year in charge at Aston Villa. His greatest years as a manager were to come during the 'sixties at Manchester City in harness with Malcolm Allison.

BOBBY MONCUR was starting his apprenticeship at St James' Park after winning Scotland schoolboy international honours while at home in Perth.

ALAN MULLERY had given up the idea of studying to be a priest to settle on a career in football, and was into his first full season as a professional with Fulham.

TERRY NEILL had been with Arsenal for less than a month, having joined them from Bangor as a 17-year-old apprentice professional.

BILL NICHOLSON was into his second season as manager of Tottenham and was piecing together a team that would electrify the early years of the new decade.

PETER OSGOOD was a schoolboy in Windsor where he would work as a bricklayer before being invited to join the groundstaff at Chelsea.

TERRY PAINE, spotted while playing for his local team Winchester City, was on his way to setting a League appearances record with Southampton.

MARTIN PETERS, the son of an East London lighterman who steered barges on the Thames, was the England Schoolboys captain and was about to join the West Ham groundstaff.

ALF RAMSEY was fitting the final pieces of his Ipswich jigsaw that would produce a championship-winning team and escalate him to the job of England manager.

DON REVIE was winding down his playing career with Leeds United before a switch to management that would make both him and Leeds great achievers of the 'sixties.

BOBBY ROBSON was a midfield player with West Bromwich Albion and England, and was to return to his first club Fulham before starting a career as a manager.

IAN St JOHN was banging in goals as a stylish centre-forward for Motherwell, and Liverpool scouts were beginning to eye 'The Saint'. He was to become such an idol at Anfield that when a Liverpool church poster asked the challenging question, 'What will you do when Jesus comes back?' a fan scrawled the reply, 'Move St John to inside-left'!

BILL SHANKLY had been manager at Liverpool for just 30 days, having joined them from Huddersfield. A revolution was about to start.

PETER SHILTON was a ten-year-old schoolboy who would soon start training with Leicester City and would watch his hero Gordon Banks from the Filbert Street terraces.

BOBBY SMITH was plundering goals for Tottenham and was to be a key man in the 'Super Spurs' side. I was to be lucky to play alongside him for club and country.

TOMMY SMITH was captain of the Liverpool Schools team and was preparing for his last term at Cardinal Godfrey School before joining the Anfield groundstaff.

JOCK STEIN was about to start his managerial career with Dunfermline Athletic and would then move on to Hibernian before turning Celtic into the kings of Europe.

ALEX STEPNEY was into his last year at school and would soon join his local amateur club Tooting and Mitcham before signing for Millwall.

NOBBY STILES, the son of a Manchester undertaker, was on the Old Trafford groundstaff after playing for England schoolboys. He had all his own teeth and hair!

MIKE SUMMERBEE, the son of a former League professional, was 17 two weeks earlier and was starting his career with Swindon after having been discovered playing for his local Cheltenham team.

PETER THOMPSON had been a professional for one month. The star of the England schoolboys team had signed with Preston, who had beaten 16 other clubs for his signature. His glory days would come with Liverpool.

TERRY VENABLES had joined me at Chelsea and had just launched his League career as one of the 'Ted Drake Ducklings'. So far he had not tried to buy the club.

ROY VERNON, spotted playing for the Rhyl Grammar School team, was now a mastermind in the Blackburn Rovers attack, and he would soon attract the attention of Everton.

RAY WILSON was playing in the Second Division with Huddersfield, and had just established himself as England's regular left-back. Chelsea had made four bids for him, and each one had been turned down by manager Bill Shankly before he moved on to Liverpool. Ray was bound for his greatest success with Everton, down the road from Shanks!

RON YEATS had finished his apprenticeship as a slaughterman and was now a tower of strength in the middle of the Dundee United defence. Liverpool were on his trail.

ALEX YOUNG was the silky-smooth leader of the Hearts attack. Everton would soon take him to Goodison, where he would become known as the 'Golden Vision'.

1959-60: ON ANOTHER PLANET

A 1990s footballer finding himself dropped into 1960 would feel as if he had landed on another planet. We even spoke a different language in the soccerland of 1960. There were wing- halves, inside-forwards and wingers, two points for a win and shoulder-charges were allowed against goalkeepers who had never heard of the four-step rule. Words and phrases like striker, overlap, workrate, tackling back, centre-back, man-to-man marking, substitutes and the professional foul had yet to enter our vocabulary.

We played with five forwards, including two wingers who used the full width of the pitch. The most common playing formation was 2-3-5 – two fullbacks, three half-backs and five forwards. The more progressive teams were boldly experimenting with the 4-2-4 line-up that served world champions Brazil so well in the 1958 World Cup in Sweden. On the packed terraces they waved rattles and cheered, and about the most imaginative chant they stretched to was 'two-four-six-eight ... who do we appreciate'. There was not a hooligan in sight and Liverpool's fans had yet to introduce the ee-aye-addio singing sounds that were to transform terraces throughout the land. These were the good old days when we still had threepenny bits and tanner coins, and it cost you just a couple of bob (10p) to stand on the terraces to watch your favourite team, and for an Oxford scholar (a dollar ... five shillings ... 25p) you could sit in comfort in the stand. A programme cost you between twopence and sixpence, and you could expect long queues at the turnstiles because average attendances for the First Division clubs stood at 31,000, with Tottenham and Manchester United both topping 47,000. Floodlit football was just seeing the light of day, and Saturday was the big football day when millions of listeners would tune in to Sports Report on the BBC wireless Light Programme on which Eamonn Andrews would introduce the 5 o'clock results and reports. Television hardly got a look in.

It was being suggested that football was going crazy because, in March, 1960, a British record transfer fee of £55,000 changed hands between Manchester City and Huddersfield Town. In return City got a skinny, 19-year-old Scottish goal hunter called Denis Law. If this had been the 'nineties, £5 million would not have bought him. Yes, he was that good. The 1990s player would have mostly felt the difference between the two worlds in his pocket. The maximum wage that a player could earn in 1960 was £20 a week, regardless of how talented he might be. Thousands still flocked to watch Stanley Matthews perform his dribbling wizardry with Blackpool, but his weekly wage packet was still the same £20 as that paid to, say, young Johnny Byrne, who was on the first rungs of his career with Crystal Palace down in the Fourth Division. But there were rumblings of discontent over what was to become known as the 'soccer slave' system. A smell of revolution mixed with the aroma of embrocation in dressing-rooms up and down the country as the 'sixties dawned, and the face of football was about to be changed beyond recognition. As we entered the football world of the 'sixties the old guard were coming to the end of their reign. Billy Wright, the heart of the Wolves, had recently retired after a record 105 matches for England. Wolves would win the FA Cup at Wembley that May, but it would be the last gasp of a giant that had trampled on the opposition throughout the 'fifties. Manchester United, rivals to Wolves as the kings of the last decade, were rebuilding after the horrific Munich air crash of 1958 that claimed the lives of eight of their 'Busby Babes'.

Exceptional players of the previous 20 years like Tommy Lawton, Tom Finney, Raich Carter, Stan Mortensen, Len Shackleton, Billy Liddell, Jackie Milburn, Wilf Mannion and Nat Lofthouse had recently retired or were about to fire their final shots. There was a new wave of players coming through, and I was lucky to be one of them. We were the wartime babies who had grown up on ration-book food and with bomb sites as our playgrounds. Many of us were born to the accompaniment of falling bombs and into a world that was off its head. We learned our football in the traffic-free streets, with tennis balls and old tin cans at our feet and with our coats on the ground as goalposts. Little did I realise that, as 1960 arrived, I was standing on the doorstep of the most exciting era in the history of British football. The Age of Austerity was over. The land of plenty was about to arrive.

THE LEAGUE CHAMPIONS

In the first season that took us into the 'sixties Burnley were writing poetry on their way to the First Division championship. They played smooth, skilled soccer that was a warming advertisement for all that was best about British football. Their main motivators were midfield partners Jimmy Adamson and Jimmy McIlroy. They formed the axis of the side that, apart from winning the title, were to finish four times in the top five of the First Division and reach the 1962 FA Cup final at Wembley.

Their positive football would have been rewarded with more major honours if they had not reached the peak of their power at the same time as the outstanding Tottenham team of the Blanchflower-White-Mackay era. That Spurs side was just getting into its stride and was to finish third in the season's title race, one point behind Wolves who were a further point away from Burnley. The Turf Moor men came through on the rails to snatch the championship in a thrilling climax.

Harry Potts was the manager of Burnley, inheriting a squad that had been shaped and fashioned by his predecessor, Alan Brown, who was mainly responsible for introducing the success-breeding tactics – particularly the quick, short corners and a mesmerising variety of free-kick scams. Potts added the finishing touches by signing creative

The way we were.

That's me *(left, above)* shooting my way into the 'sixties as a 19-year-old 'inside-forward' with Chelsea. I'm privileged to be sharing this page with two of my all-time favourite footballers – the legendary Alfredo di Stefano *(above)* who, in partnership with Ferenc Puskas, turned Real Madrid into the kings of Europe; and Jimmy McIlroy *(left)*, who masterminded Burnley's 1959-60 League championship triumph.

left-back Alex Elder from the Glentoran club that had earlier discovered the magical McIlroy. This Burnley team was brimming with outstanding individual players, and they were encouraged to play with the emphasis more on skill than sweat and stamina. I loved playing against them because they put a smile on the face of football, and even in defeat I wanted to applaud their artistry. In an era when quite a few teams believed in the big boot, they were a league of gentlemen.

This Burnley team was solid rather than spectacular at the back, with Adam Blacklaw – one of the finest goalkeepers ever to come out of Scotland – having taken over in goal after former England international Colin McDonald suffered a broken leg. John Angus and Alex Elder were a beautifully balanced pair of full-backs, Angus reliable and tough on the right and Elder all elegance and left-foot skill on the left. Tommy Cummings was composed and commanding at the heart of the defence in the tradition of the good old pivotal centre-halves.

It was in midfield where Burnley purred with power and precision like a Rolls-Royce engine. This was where Adamson – the greatest player never to be capped by England – and McIlroy reigned supreme. They were bolstered by the industrious Brian Miller, who doubled as an attacking wing-half and a support defender to Cummings. Adamson, tall and stately, won the ball with determined tackles and then drove the attack forward with purposeful passes, while McIlroy, stocky and almost arrogant, inspired everybody around him with wonderfully imaginative and intelligent positioning and passing. Bobby Seith, soon to be on his way back into Scottish football with Dundee, was a rock-hard anchorman, while right-half Adamson and inside-forward McIlroy concentrated on conducting and orchestrating the attack.

Ray Pointer, quick and adventurous, led the attack with a dash, and fed on the skilled support play of players of the calibre of Trevor Meredith, John Connelly, Jim Robson, Brian Pilkington and, on the run-in to the title, powerful left-winger Gordon Harris. Connelly, an England team-mate of mine, was a lightning-quick outside-right who liked to cut inside at full speed, decisive tactics that brought him 20 goals in this championship season at Turf Moor. He was top marksman, with Pointer (19) and Robson (18) also getting into double figures.

> *'In our championship season manager Harry Potts nearly always gave us the same final instructions before we left the dressing-room: "Play football but, above all, enjoy your game". It was a refreshing attitude and one that would certainly bring an improvement if it were adopted in the modern game. Skill was always our priority. Phrases such as "get stuck in" and "belt the ball" were not in our vocabulary. We had a great sense of achievement because we won the championship by playing football pure and simple.'* – **Jimmy McIlroy**.

THE FA CUP WINNERS

All that glistered on the English soccer stage during the 1950s were the old gold shirts of Wolves as they powered through a startling sequence of success. In nine years from 1952-53 they won the League title three times, including successive championships, finished out of the first three only once and in the 1959-60 season were to miss a hat- trick of First Division titles and the FA Cup and League double by just one point. It was to be the final chapter in their story of supremacy.

Manager Stan Cullis, known as the 'Martinet of Molineux' because of his tough discipline and demanding leadership, had always put a heavy emphasis on fitness and strength. His teams throughout the 'fifties had given an overall impression of muscularity and raw power, but there was also a thread of artistry running through the side and they had provided a procession of players for the England team. Their greatest servant, both for club and country, was Billy Wright, but his retirement in 1959 was the first sign that the team was beginning to creak and the 'sixties were to prove a bridge too far for both Cullis and his club. It was to be one of the sensations of the 'sixties when Cullis was sacked in 1964 after a short period of relative failure. He had driven everybody with an almost savage dedication to duty – driving himself hardest of all. His health suffered because of his unremitting quest for success, and it was while he was unwell that the Wolves directors would perpetrate one of the most heartless sackings in football history. Wolves have never since been able to get near the standards that the Cullis teams met and maintained. Their final march to the tunes of glory under the direction of Cullis came at Wembley when they faced Blackburn Rovers in the FA Cup final.

Wolves and Blackburn were poles apart in their approach to playing the game. The Wolves method was to pump long balls out of defence for their forwards to chase, a crude but successful tactic that was to be revived in the 'eighties by teams like Wimbledon, Sheffield United and Watford. There was sneering criticism of the Wolves method from so-called purists in the game who dismissed it as 'kick and rush'. It was more like a goal rush. In their nine peak-success years they scored 878 goals and topped the century mark in the First Division in four consecutive seasons.

The Cullis theory was a simple one. He argued that one long ball, accurately placed in the path of fast-moving attacking players, could do the work of three or four short passes and in half the time. A feature of the Wolves format was the flying wing play of Norman Deeley and South African Des Horne, who were carrying on the tradition started in the early 'fifties by Johnny Hancocks and Jimmy Mullen. Waiting in the middle to convert the crosses from the flanks were Jim Murray and Barry Stobart, who played as twin centre-forwards.

With the calculating Cullis insisting on quick release, the ball rarely stayed long in midfield. The chief architect of the attacking movements was Peter Broadbent, a master of ball control and precise passing. He was one of the few players allowed the luxury of dwelling on the ball while he looked for the best place to deposit it with passes that were both accurate and incisive.

The all-international half-back combination of Eddie Clamp, Bill Slater and Ron Flowers epitomised the Wolves style of play. Their driving enthusiasm, efficiency and vigorous challenges for the ball could undermine the confidence of the strongest op- position. Slater, a university graduate who had grace to go with his power, had taken over the captaincy from Billy Wright, and his influence on the team was underlined when he was elected Footballer of the Year.

The goalkeeping was in the safe hands of Malcolm Finlayson, the flying Scot who had taken over from long-time Molineux favourite Bert Williams. Finlayson, like Wil- liams before him, had bravery to go with his talent, and could withstand physical chal- lenges from shoulder-charging forwards in an era when goalkeepers had little of the protection that was to be given to them in the 'nineties by 'thou-shalt-not-touch' laws.

Wolves were wall-solid at full-back with George Showell and Gerry Harris as reso- lute partners. They were dependable defenders who were strong in the tackle and well drilled in the art (if art was the right word) of hammering huge clearances deep into opposition territory. These were the days when all teams played two orthodox wingers – so full-backs were detailed to full-time defensive duties and 'overlaps' were exclu- sive to envelopes. Wingers did not relish facing Wolves because they had a tradition for producing full-backs who were prepared almost to lay down their lives rather than let anybody past them.

Wolves had reached the final by beating Newcastle after a replay, Charlton, Luton Town, Leicester City and then, in the semi-final, Aston Villa. Waiting for them in the final was a Blackburn Rovers team that had one of the most creative forward lines in the League: Louis Bimpson, Peter Dobing, Derek Dougan, Bryan Douglas and Ally McLeod (later to make his name as a praised-then-persecuted manager of Scotland). They would have been even more formidable had they not been so short-sighted as to sell brilliant Welsh international forward Roy Vernon that February for £27,000. He could have made all the difference at Wembley.

While Wolves thrived on the long-ball game, Rovers were all about skill and virtuos- ity. Bryan Douglas, a wizard of a winger switched to inside-forward, was the conductor of the attack and the deadly duo of Dobing and Dougan were ruthlessly efficient in put- ting the finishing touch. The half-back line featured the then England captain Ronnie Clayton as an inspirational right-half, with Irish international dynamo Mick McGrath at left-half and big Matt Woods at centre-half. John Bray and Dave Whelan were reliable full-back partners, and goalkeeper Harry Leyland was a safe last line of defence.

Blackburn had got through to the final on the backs of Sunderland after a replay, Black- pool after a replay, Tottenham, Burnley after a replay and then Sheffield Wednesday in the semi-final. It had been a long and winding road to Wembley, but on the way they had beaten five exceptional teams.

Derek Dougan *(above)* shows his goal-plundering power for Blackburn against Arsenal at Highbury in February, 1960. Three months later he posted a transfer request on his way to Wembley with Rovers for the FA Cup final against Wolves. It was Wolves skipper Bill Slater *(below)* who was shouldered around Wembley in triumph after Norman Deeley's two goals had clinched a 3-0 victory.

On paper they had the players to give Wolves all sorts of problems, but on the pitch their victory hopes disappeared when left-back Dave Whelan was carried off with a broken leg just before half-time following a collision with Norman Deeley. It was the fifth time in the last ten finals that a serious injury had spoiled the match. When would they have the sense to allow substitutes? Rovers were no match for a Wolves team that was determined to make up for the disappointment of being pipped for the League championship by Burnley just six days before the final.

A McGrath own goal put Wolves ahead shortly before Whelan was carried off, and two second-half goals from Deeley clinched a comfortable victory. There was a lack of spirit in the Rovers team and we later learned that Derek Dougan had posted a transfer request on the very morning of the match. Doog, who played despite a nagging muscle injury, later described it as the daftest thing he ever did.

As skipper Bill Slater collected the Cup it was impossible to imagine that this was the end of Wolves as a major power in football. They were just one point away from winning the First Division championship for the third successive year, and from becoming the first team this century to achieve the elusive Cup and League double. Yet before the 'sixties were halfway through Cullis would no longer be the master of Molineux and his team would be down in the Second Division.

> *The whole style of our play in my time as manager was geared towards keeping the ball in the opponents' penalty area for as long as possible. We had the players to make our plan work. It was really exhilarating. There were critics of the way we played, but I had not the slightest doubt that the entertainment value of our matches was higher than at any time in my long experience of the game. We gave the spectators goals and excitement and we managed to win all the trophies that mattered. It would be an understatement to say that I was stunned when Wolves sacked me. I had created a yardstick against which they could measure me and criticise me.' – **Stan Cullis**.*

CHAMPIONS OF EUROPE

On 18 May, 1960, all we League professionals were made to suddenly realise that we were light years behind the best teams in the world. We watched open-mouthed as Real Madrid took on Eintracht Frankfurt in the European Cup final at Hampden Park. It was a match in a million that will live on in football legend as one of the classic contests of all time.

The footballing aristocrats of Real had dominated the European Cup since its inception in 1955, and they were bidding to win the trophy for a fifth successive year. Hampden was heaving with 127,621 spectators, many of them Rangers fans who believed they were gathering to see the end of the Real Madrid reign. They were still flabbergasted by the way Eintracht blasted Rangers to defeat on an aggregate of 12-4 in the semi-finals, and they were convinced that any team capable of twice scoring six goals against their Ibrox idols could topple the old masters of Madrid.

Real were a team of soccer mercenaries, drawn from all points of the compass to give them punch and panache. Their formidable defence was shaped around intimidating Uruguayan centre-half Santamaria and Argentinian goalkeeper Dominguez, but it was for their attacking prowess that they were acclaimed. The forward line was under the arrogant command of Alfredo di Stefano, who had come from Colombia via his native Argentina and, at 34, was still one of the world's premier purveyors of the footballing arts. He pulled the strings for an attack that included the whiplash left-foot shooting of the incomparable Hungarian Ferenc Puskas, the pace and dribbling skills of home-grown heroes Luis Del Sol and Paco Gento and the invention of Brazilian winger Canario.

An indication of Real's riches was that they were able to leave another Brazilian, 1958 World Cup star Didi, on the bench. Eurovision was a new enterprise that brought the game 'live' to an armchair audience of millions, and across Europe viewers looked on in awe as Real and Eintracht conjured a match of such balletic beauty that it deserved to be set to music. I watched it in a wooden chalet on the shores of Lake Balaton in Hungary with the England team during an end-of-season tour, and it was one of my stranger telly-watching experiences. A special aerial was fixed so that we could pick up the Austrian television service. The game was banned from the screens in Hungary because Puskas had not been forgiven by the Russian puppet govern-ment for defecting after the Revolution. So we watched the game in secret behind locked doors, and we all agreed we had not seen club football to equal it.

For 19 minutes the two teams sparred like stylish boxers looking for an opening for the knockout punch, and then Richard Kress scored for Eintracht to open the flood-gates – and it was goals from Real that came pouring through.

Di Stefano, gliding across the Hampden turf like a Nureyev on grass, equalised eight minutes later at the end of a five-man passing movement that had the spectators purring. It was Scottish teams who first pioneered the measured, 'along-the-carpet' passing game, and the crowd were treated to a perfect exhibition of this sophisticated style of play. By half-time di Stefano and Puskas had made it 3-1 to Real, the Puskas goal being a thing of wonder when he somehow managed to fire a rising shot into the net from what seemed an impossible angle.

There were 30 minutes in the second half when Real produced football so majestic and so artistic that all of us lucky to be watching thought we had been transported to paradise. By the 70th minute it was Real 6, Eintracht 1 – and the peerless Puskas had lifted his personal tally to four goals, including a penalty. Eintracht were playing much more than a walk-on part and after hitting the woodwork twice got the goal they deserved when centre-forward Erwin Stein scored with a stinging shot in the 72nd minute.

Almost from the restart di Stefano collected Real's seventh goal ... and what a goal. He moved imperiously from a deep-lying position, exchanging passes with colleagues and always demanding the return of the ball until he ended his advance with a deadly accurate shot that beat goalkeeper Loy all ends up. It was Stein – Erwin, not Jock – who had the final word in the ten-goal extravaganza when he intercepted a rare mishit pass by Real defender Vidal and rounded goalkeeper Dominguez before scoring.

The breathless crowd gave both teams an ovation that lasted a full 15 minutes after a magnificent match that had been preserved on film as evidence of how the game of football could be played at the highest level.

I could not let the memory of this match go without special mention of the perfor- mances of di Stefano and Puskas, two giants of the game whose careers bridged the 'fifties and 'sixties. There had probably never been a duo to match them at club level. Capped by his native Argentina and Spain, di Stefano scored more than 500 goals in 11 years with Real Madrid, including 49 in 58 European Cup ties. Surprisingly he never played in a World Cup final series. He travelled with Spain to the 1962 finals in Chile but was injured in a pre-tournament club match. The son of a bus conductor, Alfredo was born in Buenos Aires on 4 July, 1926. He was a worshipped member of the River Plate team in Argentina when he shocked his home fans by signing for the then outlawed Colombian club Los Millionarios in 1949. Three years later he was involved in a transfer tug of war between Barcelona and Real Madrid. Real's victory in the battle for his signature coincided with the start of the greatest period in their his- tory, and there was no doubt that it was Alfredo the Great who generated the success.

As moody off the pitch as he was magnificent on it, father-of-six di Stefano wound down his playing career with Español before becoming a successful manager with Boca Juniors in his homeland. He then returned to Spain as manager-coach of Valencia and later had a spell in charge at Real.

Puskas, with his stunningly powerful left-foot shot and his ability to be a thought and a deed ahead of most defenders, was the most influential player in the magnificent Hungarian team of the 'fifties that went four years and 29 games without a single defeat. The unbeaten run sadly ended in the 1954 World Cup final when Puskas insisted on playing despite an ankle injury which robbed him of much of his fire and flair. After the 1956 Hungarian Uprising, Puskas added to his reputation as one of the greatest players of all time by becoming a front-line master with Real Madrid, for whom he scored not only those four goals in the 1960 European Cup final but also three in the 1962 final.

Born in Budapest in 1926, Puskas became Hungarian captain, and notched 85 goals in 84 internationals, before his decision to defect in 1956. He was top Hungarian League marksman in 1947, 1950 and 1953, and became known as 'The Galloping Major' in the Honved team that consisted of players who had been specially commissioned in the Hungarian Army. It was Puskas who led the 'Magical Magyars' to their historic 6-3 and

Alfredo di Stefano, 'The Master', *(above)* scores the first of his three goals in Real Madrid's spectacular 7-3 victory over Eintracht Frankfurt at Hampden Park in 1960. Ferenc Puskas, 'The Magical Magyar', contributed the other four goals in one of the most memorable matches ever played.

George Eastham *(left)* was just about to start on his passing-out parade with Arsenal after his long-running freedom battle with Newcastle, which led to the shackles coming off all we 'soccer slaves'.

7-1 victories over England in 1953-54, defeats that destroyed the myth that we were still masters of world football. He collected a gold medal in the 1952 Olympics and then had the biggest disappointment of his career in the 1954 World Cup final.

He struck up a devastating partnership with di Stefano for Real and was top Spanish League scorer in 1960,1961,1963 and 1964. He played for Spain in three World Cup final matches in 1962 but was then 36 and slowed to a stroll by a spreading waistline. At the end of his playing career he switched to management and led Panathanaikos of Athens to the 1971 European Cup final.

Puskas and di Stefano were giants of the 'fifties who managed to put their mark on the 'sixties, and they were among the few players who could be put on the same pedestal as Pele.

British clubs had yet to win a major European trophy. Birmingham come close at the end of the 1959-60 season when they reached the Inter-Cities Fairs Cup final in which they met Real's great rivals, Barcelona. After a brave goalless draw in the first leg at St Andrews, Birmingham went down 4-1 in Barcelona.

'I played in many fine matches, but none greater than the 1960 European Cup final. Everything we tried worked to perfection. It was an honour and a privilege to be part of it. Ferenc and I had our names on the scoresheet, but this match was a triumph for everybody on the pitch – including the Eintracht players. I must also pay tribute to the spectators. Most were neutral but they encouraged us to keep raising the standard of our play.' – **Alfredo di Stefano.**

GREAVSIE'S FOOTBALL DIARY
1959-60

My season-by-season diary is intended to give a flavour of the 'sixties, rather than a complete record. While it is highly personalised, I have also tried to record the main events. We have provided a full breakdown of all the winners – and losers – at the end of each chapter.

1959

25 July: The Football League at last wake up to the value of our game. They slap a copyright on the League fixture list. The money-grabbing Pools Promoters agree to pay a minimum £245,000 each year for ten years in return for printing the fixtures on their coupons. Now we are waiting for the League to wake up to the value of their players. Jimmy Hill, jut-jawed, bearded and highly articulate chairman of the Professional Footballers' Association, is starting a campaign to kick out the £20 maximum wage. We are even talking about strike action.

7 August: Billy Wright announces his retirement. He has won a record 105 England caps, including a run of 70 consecutive games, and he has skippered the team in 90 internationals. He has played more than 500 League and Cup matches for Wolves after making his debut at the age of 15 during the first year of the war, was captain of three championship-winning teams and lifted the FA Cup in 1949. Billy was captain in my first three matches for England, and I'll always have a soft spot for him. He has been one of the game's great ambassadors (Little do I know that some 20 years later he will become my executive boss at Central Television. It's a funny old life).

22 August: The start of the season, and Chelsea beat Preston 4-2 at Stamford Bridge. I help myself to a hat-trick. The attendance is 46,000 and we will average 39,500 for our home matches despite an up-and-down season during which we will score 76 goals but concede 91. We call ourselves the 'All the best' team. The only tactical talk we get from our lovely old manager Ted Drake are his words as we prepare to run out on to the pitch: 'All the best, lads'. We are known as 'Drake's Ducklings' with an average age of little more than 22. When we come up against teams like Burnley, Wolves, Tottenham and Manchester United we are boys trying to do mens' work.

23 September: Brian Clough, the non-stop Middlesbrough goal machine, scores all five goals for the Football League in their 5-0 victory over the Irish League in Belfast. It earns him his first England cap. Will it fit his big head, I wonder (just joking, Cloughie). He will also benefit from the £60 appearance fee that England players collect—equal to three weeks' wages. Sunderland already had envious eyes on Clough.

8 October: Tottenham sign John White from Falkirk for a bargain £20,000. It completes one of the greatest midfield trios in club football—Blanchflower, White, Mackay. Here come the 'Super Spurs'!

17 October: England are held to a 1-1 draw by Wales in Cardiff. We should have won, but miss chances in front of goal. I am a culprit, and so is my new side-kick—the one and only Cloughie, who even then is full of strong opinions and bold ideas that will one day make him one of the game's great managers. Ronnie Clayton is the new skipper, and team boss Walter Winterbottom promotes Tony Allen, Trevor Smith, John Connelly and Cloughie's Middlesbrough team-mate Eddie Holliday from the Under-23s. It is one of the youngest England teams of all time, and our inexperience shows. I score our goal, but it is the ones that got away that I remember.

28 October: Oh dear. An unchanged England team go down 3-2 to Sweden, the 1958 World Cup runners-up. It is only England's second home defeat by a foreign side on the sacred Wembley turf. Our goalkeeper Eddie Hopkinson has a bit of a nightmare and gets the bird from the fans. We are little better at the other end of the pitch where Cloughie and I fail to click. There is one hilarious moment when, during a goalmouth scramble, Cloughie finds himself sitting on the ball on the goal-line. 'It was if I was trying to hatch the bloody thing', he says later. Cloughie unfairly carries the can for the defeat and is never selected for England again.

1 December: Bill Shankly moves from Huddersfield Town to take over as manager of Liverpool, who are languishing in the Second Division. He starts by confirming his backroom team—coach Reuben Bennett, first-team trainer Bob Paisley and second-team trainer Joe Fagan. The red revolution is about to start.

19 December: Quite a day up at Preston. I score a hat-trick to put Chelsea 3-0 in the lead, but then we let Preston back in and they are level halfway through the second half. I bang in a fourth, but Preston immediately make it 4-4. My mate Peter Sillett, playing as the full-back partner to his brother, John 'Schnozz' Sillett, shouts: 'Come on, Jim. Stop loafing about. One more will finish them off'. I duly get a fifth goal, and our victory knocks Preston off the top of the table. I celebrate by trading in my £30 1937 Opel convertible for a 1938 Standard '8'. It becomes like a team bus with all the players trying to crowd in after training and matches while we head for the nearest pub for a pint. Lovely days.

30 January: Gerry Baker bangs in ten goals for St Mirren against Glasgow University in the first round of the Scottish Cup. I'm told that when the University goalkeeper went to collect his degree he dropped it.

3 February: Tottenham beat Crewe 13-2 in a fourth round FA Cup replay at White Hart Lane in front of a crowd of 64,365. Spurs are stung by the criticism that is aimed at them for being held to a draw at Crewe. Dave Mackay's competitive spirit is clear for all to see when he is warned by the referee for going in too hard when Spurs are leading 7-1. Les Allen scores five, Bobby Smith four and Cliffie Jones three. It's the taste of things to come from Tottenham.

2 March: A cracker of a match at Ibrox where Scotland and England draw 4-4 in an Under-23 international. I manage a hat-trick and a young Jock from Motherwell called Ian St John bangs in two. It's a forerunner of the Saint and Greavsie show!

9 April: Scotland 1, England 1 at Hampden in front of a crowd of 129,783. Bobby Charlton, our blond-haired winger, scores our goal from the penalty spot and then misses a second penalty. I think that was when Bobby started tearing his hair out. Our star player is 20-year-old centre-forward Joe Baker, Gerry's brother, who was brought up in Scotland and has the broadest Scots accent you'll ever hear in an England dressing-room. There is an almighty row before the kick-off when Spurs refuse to re-lease Bill Brown, Dave Mackay and John White for the Saturday match because they are chasing the League title. Wolves, also in the race for the championship, claim that it is unfair that they have to give up Bill Slater and Ron Flowers for England, and the Football League agree to postpone their League game against West Ham. It leads to a ruling that any club having two or more players called up for international duty can call for a postponement of their League match.

16 April: Cliff Holton, the League's top goalscorer this season with Watford, com-pletes a unique double when he nets a hat-trick against Gateshead. The previous day—Good Friday—he notched three goals against Chester. He is the first player in post-war League football to score hat-tricks on successive days. Hefty Cliff, who started his career with Oxford City as a full-back before joining Arsenal, is remarkably light on his feet and mobile for such a big man. He will finish this season with a haul of 42 League goals, but Watford will just miss promotion from the Fourth Division. Equal second to Holton in the League scoring list is the Ayresome Park Assassin Brian Clough. He and Southampton's Derek Reeves both bang in 39 goals. Cloughie is losing his touch. Last season he scored 43 League goals for Middlesbrough.

2 May: It's the Monday before the FA Cup final, and the League championship will be decided today. Burnley must win against Manchester City at Maine Road to rob Wolves of a hat-trick of title wins and the possibility of the first League and Cup double of the century. Wolves have finished their League programme and are top of the table, a point ahead of Burnley. In an incredible sprint finish, Burnley have come from behind to challenge for the title after clearing a back-log of fixtures. The match at Maine Road is their final game of the season. They win 2-1 to take the championship to Turf Moor.

11 May: England draw 3-3 with Yugoslavia at Wembley. I join Bryan Douglas and Johnny Haynes on the scoresheet. We are losing 3-2 with a minute to go when Joe Baker heads against the bar and Johnny Haynes rams in the rebound. In the final seconds Baker hits the bar with another header, and I just fail to get to the rebound.

15 May: The rain in Spain is mainly on the pitch as England go down 3-0 to a team that keeps its feet better than we do during a non-stop torrential downpour. The master Alfredo di Stefano makes no secret of the fact that he is saving himself for Real Madrid's European Cup final date at Hampden in three days' time, but even at half pace he is a class above everybody else on the pitch. Alfredo has said in a newspaper interview before the match that he will only play for the first half, and will then be substituted. Sir Stanley Rous, the FA secretary, protests and scuppers the plan (this, remember, is in the days before substitutes are allowed). I think Sir Stanley should have bitten his tongue. We would have been relieved to have seen the back of Alfredo the Great.

THE CHAMPIONS OF
1959-60

FIRST DIVISION:
1: Burnley (55 points)
2: Wolverhampton Wanderers (54)
3: Tottenham Hotspur (53)

Championship squad:
Adamson (42 appearances), Angus (41), Blacklaw (41), Connelly (34), Cummings (23), Elder (34), Furnell (1), Harris (2), Lawson (8), Marshall (1), Meredith (7), Miller (42), McIlroy (31), Pilkington (41), Pointer (42), Robson (39), Seith (27), White (6).
Goalscorers: Connelly (20), Pointer (19), Robson (18), Pilkington (9), McIlroy (6), Lawson (3), Meredith (3), Miller (3), White (2), Adamson (1), 1 own goal.

SECOND DIVISION:
1: Aston Villa (59 points)
2: Cardiff City (58)
3: Liverpool (50)

Championship squad:
Adam (21 appearances), Ashe (1), Birch (1), Burrows (1), Crowe (41), Deakin (1), Dixon (4), Dugdale (39), Handley (3), Hitchens (36), Keelan (3), Lynn (42), McEwan (28), McParland (41), Morrall (3), Neal (41), Saward (40), Sewell (2), Sims (39), Tindall (2), Thomson (34), Winton (1), Wylie (38).
Goalscorers: Hitchens (23), McParland (22), Thomson (20), Lynn (7), McEwan (5), Wylie (4), Adam (3), Crowe (2), Dugdale (1), Sewell (1), 1 own goal.

THIRD DIVISION:
1: Southampton (61 points)
2: Norwich City (59)
3: Shrewsbury Town (52)

Championship squad:
Brown (5 appearances), Charles (24), Clifton (8), Conner (45), Davies (46), Godfrey (11), Harrison (3), Holmes (1), Huxford (46), Kennedy (2), Maughan (33), Mulgrew (33), O'Brien (42), Page (45), Paine (46), Reeves (46), Reynolds (11), Scurr (1), Simpson (1), Sydenham (45), Traynor (43).
Goalscorers: Reeves (39), O'Brien (23), Mulgrew (11), Clifton (8), Paine (8), Page (8), Brown (2), Conner (2), Huxford (1), Sydenham (2), 1 own goal.

FOURTH DIVISION:
1: Walsall (65 points)
2: Notts County (60)
3: Torquay United (60)

Championship squad:
Askey (12 appearances), Ball (3), Billingham (27), Christie (33), Davies (36), Dudley (24), Faulkner (43), Foster (1), Guttridge (34), Haddington (46), Hill (2), Hodgkisson (44), Jones (12), McPherson (35), Rawlings (36), Richards (46), Rowe (1), Sharples (12), Taylor (45), Walker (2).
Goalscorers: Richards (24), Faulkner (23), Taylor (21), Davies (12), Hodgkisson (11), Billingham (5), Dudley (3), Askey (2), 1 own goal.

SCOTTISH FIRST DIVISION:

1: Heart of Midlothian (54 points)
2: Kilmarnock (50)
3: Rangers (42)

Championship squad:

Kirk (34 appearances), Thomson (34), Marshall (33), Cumming (32), Smith (29), Blackwood (28), Young (28), Hamilton (27), Milne (25), Bowman (24), Higgins (21), Murray (18), Crawford (18), Bauld (17), McFadzean (5), Brown (1).
Goalscorers: Young (22), Blackwood (12), Murray (12), Crawford (11), Bauld (10), Smith (10), Hamilton (7), Cumming (5), Thomson (4), Higgins (3), McFadzean (2), 4 own goals.

SCOTTISH SECOND DIVISION:

1: St Johnstone (53 points)
2: Dundee United (50)
3: Queen of the South (49)

FA CUP FINAL:

Wolverhampton Wanderers 3 *(McGrath own goal, Deeley 2)*
Finlayson, Showell, Harris, Clamp, Slater, Flowers, Deeley, Stobart, Murray, Broadbent, Horne.
Blackburn Rovers 0
Leyland, Bray, Whelan, Clayton, Woods, McGrath, Bimpson, Dobing, Dougan, Douglas, McLeod.

SCOTTISH FA CUP FINAL:

Rangers 2 *(Millar 2)*
Niven, Caldow, Little, McColl, Paterson, Stevenson, Scott, McMillan, Millar, Baird, Wilson.
Kilmarnock 0
Brown, Richmond, Watson, Beattie, Toner, Kennedy, Stewart, McInally, Kerr, Black, Muir.

SCOTTISH LEAGUE CUP FINAL:

Heart of Midlothian 2 *(Hamilton, Young)*
Marshall, Kirk, Thomson, Bowman, Cumming, Higgins, Smith, Crawford, Young, Blackwood, Hamilton.
Third Lanark 1 *(Gray)*
Brown, Richmond, Watson, Beattie, Toner, Kennedy, Stewart, McInally, Kerr, Black, Muir.

EUROPEAN CUP FINAL:

Played at Hampden Park, Glasgow
Real Madrid 7 *(Di Stefano 3, Puskas 4)*
Dominguez, Marquitos, Pachin, Vidal, Santamaria, Zarraga, Canario, Del Sol, Di Stefano, Puskas, Gento.
Eintracht Frankfurt 3 *(Kress, Stein 2)*
Loy, Lutz, Hoefer, Wellbaecher, Eigenbrodt, Stinka, Kress, Lindner, Stein, Pfaff, Meier.

INTER-CITIES FAIRS CUP FINAL:

First leg:
Birmingham City 0
Schofield, Farmer, Allen, Watts, Smith, Neal, Astall, Gordon, Weston, Orritt, Hooper.
Barcelona 0
Ramallets, Olivella, Gracia, Rodri, Segarra, Gensana, Coll, Kocsis, Martinez, Ribellas, Villaverde.
Second leg:
Barcelona 4 *(Martinez, Czibor 2, Coll)*
Ramallets, Olivella, Gracia, Rodri, Segarra, Verges, Coll, Kubala, Martinez, Ribellas, Czibor.
Birmingham City 1 *(Hooper)*
Schofield, Farmer, Allen, Watts, Smith, Neal, Astall, Gordon, Weston, Murphy, Hooper.
Barcelona win 4-1 on aggregate.

EUROPEAN NATIONS CUP FINAL 1958-60

Played in Paris
Russia 2 *(Metreveli, Ponedelnik)*
Yashin, Tchekeli, Kroutikov, Voinov, Maslenkin, Netto, Metreveli, Ivanov, Ponedelnik, Bubukin, Meshki.

Yugoslavia 1 (Netto own goal)
Vidinic, Durkovic, Jusufi, Zanetic, Miladinovic, Perusic, Sekularac, Jerkovic, Galic, Matus, Kostic.
(after extra time)

TOP FOOTBALL LEAGUE GOALSCORERS:

Cliff Holton (Watford)	42
Brian Clough (Middlesbrough)	39
Derek Reeves (Southampton)	39
Arthur Rowley (Shrewsbury Town)	32
Ralph Hunt (Grimsby Town)	33
Dennis Viollet (Manchester United)	32
Martin King (Colchester United)	30
Dennis Uphill (Watford)	30
Jim Murray (Wolverhampton Wanderers)	29
Jimmy Greaves (Chelsea)	29

TOP SCOTTISH FIRST DIVISION MARKSMAN:
Joe Baker (Hibernian) 42 goals

HIGHEST AVERAGE LEAGUE ATTENDANCE:
Tottenham (47,864)

FOOTBALLER OF THE YEAR:
Bill Slater (Wolverhampton Wanderers)

EUROPEAN FOOTBALLER OF THE YEAR:
Luis Suarez (Barcelona)

WORLD CLUB CHAMPIONSHIP:
Real Madrid beat Penarol 0-0, 5-1

1960-61: BREAKING THE SHACKLES

Five good men and true were mainly responsible for breaking the shackles that bound the 'soccer slaves' of League football as we entered the 'sixties: Newcastle and England inside-left George Eastham, Professional Footballers' Association chairman Jimmy Hill and secretary Cliff Lloyd, Gerald Gardiner QC, and High Court judge Mr Justice Wilberforce.

These were the mould-breakers who would do most to drag the football rulers into the 20th century, kicking and struggling like misers being prised away from their gold coin collection.

It was Eastham, the son of a former professional footballer and himself a pass-master of the soccer arts, who started the ball rolling in 1960. He wanted a transfer from Newcastle, the club he had served well for four years. Manager Charlie Mitten bluntly told him: 'No. We are holding you to your contract'.

George was tied hand and foot by the old 'retain-and-transfer' system that could have been drawn up by a baron to keep his serfs slaving on his land in the Middle Ages. What the contract meant was that a player signing for a club was bound to them for the whole of his career unless the club wished to sell him. The player had no say in the matter. It was a case of: 'Take your £20 a week and do as you're told'. (And in the close-season we were paid just £17 a week to do as we were told).

'All I want,' announced Eastham, 'is the right of every free man ... to work for whom I please and where I please.'

Newcastle did not realise quite what explosives they were setting off by refusing Eastham his transfer request. With the support of a wealthy football follower called Ernie Clay, he went on a one-man strike. Newcastle caved in and sold him to Arsenal for £47,500 in November, 1960. Eastham collected a derisory £20 signing-on fee, and decided to continue his battle against the archaic system – 'as a matter of principle'.

Gerald Gardiner QC was Eastham's mouthpiece in what was to become an historic High Court case – Eastham v Newcastle United. Gardiner told the judge, Mr Justice Wilberforce: 'It would be unthinkable that a watchmaker could sell his skilled watch repairer like a chattel. Footballers are tied like slaves to a system from the Middle Ages'.

Good old Judge Wilberforce agreed, as would any reasonably-minded man. He delivered a 16,000-word judgement which included the one paragraph that really mattered: 'The rules of the Football Association and the regulations of the Football League relating to the retention and transfer of players of professional football, including

The two faces of Jimmy Hill: the negotiator with players' union secretary Cliff Lloyd *(above),* and the goal hunter with Fulham, challenging Luton Town goalkeeper Ron Baynham for the ball *(left).* Jimmy the Jaw, now best known for his comments as a television pundit, made an enormous impact on soccer in the 'sixties, first as the man who did most to kick out the maximum wage and then as an enterprising and inventive manager of Coventry City.

the plaintiff, are not binding upon the plaintiff and are *an unreasonable restraint of trade'*.

Suddenly players were free to negotiate their own terms once their contracts had ended or a transfer had been agreed. The shackles were off. We were no longer slaves.

All of this took three years to come about, and it was 4 July, 1963, when Judge Wilberforce finally gave footballers their greatest victory. While all this was going on Jimmy Hill and Cliff Lloyd used the impetus of the Eastham case to step up the campaign to get rid of the maximum wage. Dear old Jimmy became the man with the golden tongue as he ripped into stubborn League secretary Alan Hardaker and his thick-skinned League Management Committee. 'You can no longer expect footballers to be serfs for six days a week and then an executive on the seventh', he roared.

With the cream of Britain's players looking towards the treasure chests that were being opened for them in Italy, the League at last relented and on 18 January, 1961 – under strike threat from the players – they gave in following arbitration talks with the Ministry of Labour. Suddenly clubs could pay individual players what they were worth, and on 24 April, 1961, Fulham chairman and popular comedian Tommy Trinder delivered his funniest line when he announced: 'We do not want Johnny Haynes to go to Italy, and so we are going to pay him £100 a week'. Johnny was laughing all the way to the bank.

There were, sadly, unpleasant side-issues to the new deal for footballers. Dozens of players suddenly found themselves out of work as clubs that had been carrying staffs of 40 and more professionals chopped their numbers in half. But at least they were no longer getting the crowd-pulling footballers who could really play the game on the cheap. It was also sad to see the new freedom of movement and access to decent money coming too late for the likes of football masters like Tommy Lawton, Nat Lofthouse, Stan Mortensen, Tom Finney, Len Shackleton, Jackie Milburn and so many more who for years had been paid peanuts while packing grounds with First Division crowds regularly over 50,000.

Tommy Trinder had the players roaring with laughter when he made Johnny Haynes Britain's first £100-a-week footballer. But I was too confused to laugh. I had gone and tied myself to a future in Italy. It was a transfer saga that became a mixture of farce and frustration, and I will save the gory details for my diary later in the chapter ... because now it is time for a rousing fanfare as we switch the spotlight on to the 'Super Spurs'...

Few club sides – before or since – have been able to match the magic of the Tottenham team that monopolised the 1960-61 season. They had all the qualities necessary for sustained % success: skill, imagination, industry, driving and intelligent leadership, determination in defence, artistry in attack and a willingness to work for each other. Five world-class players were able to freely express themselves within the framework of a flexible formation. They would touch their peak by becoming the first team this century to capture both the League championship and the FA Cup in the same season.

The team had been put together with expert knowledge and almost loving care by Bill Nicholson, a man who was soon to play a big part in my footballing life. The day Bill Nick took over as manager at White Hart Lane in 1958 Spurs trounced Everton 10-4. It was a standard he was always striving to maintain over the next fifteen years of his reign. A key player in the famous push-and-run Spurs side of the 'fifties, Scarborough-born Nicholson was an outstanding coach and tactician whose total belief in a policy of flair and attack belied his shy, cautious personality away from football. It was his ideas and theories on paper that were put into practice on the pitch, and Tottenham's success was due largely to his meticulous planning and preparation.

Cynics could sneer that Nicholson was a chequebook manager, but Tottenham's money could easily have been squandered in the hands of a less discerning manager. He always spent with care and caution, almost as if the money was coming out of his own pocket. There has rarely, if ever, been a more conscientious and caring manager. He matched even Stan Cullis for dedication to duty, and the reward for all his effort was a dream of a team.

The 'Super Spurs' of 1960-61 were never defence minded, as was revealed by the fact that they conceded 50 League goals on the way to the League title. But they were sufficiently steady at the back to allow heavy concentration on attack. Goalkeeper Bill Brown was one of those rare creatures, a Scottish custodian who could always be relied on to catch the ball. He had excellent reactions and a safe pair of hands which made up for his occasional positioning misjudgement. He had a fine understanding with the towering Norfolk-born centre-half Maurice Norman, a dominating defender whose run of 23 England caps was cruelly halted by a broken leg. In a 3-3-4 formation, Norman was flanked by full backs Peter Baker and Ron Henry, both of whom were disciplined and determined and had unyielding competitive attitudes. Dave Mackay was always quick to take up a defensive position when needed and his tackles were like a clap of thunder. The pros in the game said that anybody who took the full weight of a Mackay challenge went home feeling as if he was still with them. Danny Blanchflower was not noted for his tackling, but he was a shrewd enough positional player to manage to get himself between the opponent in possession and the goal. He defended with the instincts of a sheepdog, cornering the opposition by steering them into cul-de-sacs rather than biting them.

The attacking movements, full of fluency and fire, were masterminded from midfield by three of the greatest players to come together in one club team: Blanchflower, Mackay and John White. Irish international Blanchflower, a hugely inspiring captain, was the brains of the team who had an instinctive feel for the game and the ability to lift the players around him with measured passes and intelligent tactical commands. Mackay, the Scot with an in-built swagger and a he-man's barrel chest, was the heart of the side, always playing with enormous enthusiasm, power and panache. White, an artist of an inside-forward in the best traditions of purist Scottish football, was the eyes of the team, seeing openings that escaped the vision of lesser players and then dismantling defences with precision passes and blind-side runs that earned him the nickname 'The Ghost of White Hart Lane'. This talented trio were essentially buccaneering, forward-propelling players, but they were sufficiently geared to team discipline to help out in defence when necessary.

They motivated a front line in which burly, bulldozing Bobby Smith, a 15-cap England centre-forward and one of my favourite playing partners, mixed subtle skill with awesome strength. He was the main marksman in this double year with 33 League and Cup goals. He was in harness with Les Allen, a clever, under-rated player who was the father of 1980s England international Clive Allen. Les, from the same Dagenham manor as myself, had played alongside me when I first started my career with Chelsea, and Bobby Smith was also a Stamford Bridge old boy. Les contributed an invaluable haul of 23 goals to Tottenham's championship season.

Out on the wings Spurs had Terry Dyson – tiny, quick and taunting, the son of a Yorkshire jockey – and the marvellous Cliff Jones, one of the 'Untouchables' of Welsh international football who could take the tightest defence apart with his fast, diagonal runs. In reserve Spurs had players of the calibre of Welsh terrier Terry Medwin, fearless Frank Saul and cultured wing-halves Tony Marchi and John Smith, all of whom made occasional appearances during this memorable 'double' year.

Spurs scored a record 115 goals on their way to winning the First Division title by a margin of eight points from closest challengers Sheffield Wednesday. They opened the season with 11 successive victories and remained unbeaten for five more games. There were 16 away wins and as many points collected away (33) as at home, where the average attendance was 53,315. Their 66 points equalled the First Division record set by Herbert Chapman's Arsenal in 1930-31.

I played against them twice with Chelsea, and we were beaten 3-2 and then 4-2. They purred along like a Rolls-Royce, with Blanchflower, White and Mackay at the wheel. When they wanted a touch on the accelerator there was Cliff Jones to break the speed limit down either wing; and if they needed a full show of horsepower, Bobby Smith was put into the driving seat. These were the five world-class players around whom Bill Nick built his magnificent team.

In the League, Spurs achieved 11 double home-and-away victories over First Division rivals which matched the record set by Manchester United (1956-57) and Wolves

One of the greatest of all club sides, the Tottenham team that achieved the double in 1960-61 *(above),* back row, left to right, Ron Henry, Maurice Norman, Bill Brown, Bobby Smith, Peter Baker; front, Cliff Jones, John White, Danny Blanchflower, Les Allen, Terry Dyson, Dave Mackay. Missing is Terry Medwin, who shared wing duties with Dyson. Skipper Blanchflower and centre-forward Smith *(left)* form an arch of triumph for Dyson after the FA Cup final victory over Leicester City clinched the double.

(1958-59). They rushed to a collection of 50 points in just 29 games, faster than it had ever been done before in those days of just two points for a win. All five first-choice forwards reached double figures with League goals – Smith (28), Allen (23), Jones (15), White (13) and Dyson (12).

They had the League title wrapped up 19 days before the FA Cup final in which they failed to touch the peak of their power. But they played well enough to get a comfortable 2-0 victory, with goals from Smith and Dyson against a Leicester team handicapped by an injury to right-back Len Chalmers.

> *Everything was right. The balance of the team. The attitude of the players. We managed to find the perfect blend and everybody gave 100 per cent in effort and enthusiasm. I kept pushing an old theory: "When you're not in possession get into position". The man without the ball was important, because he could make things happen by getting into the right place at the right time. '* – **Bill Nicholson**.

A MATCH TO REMEMBER

England team manager Walter Winterbottom pledged at the start of the 1960-61 season that he would make only injury-forced changes to his side throughout the campaign. He wanted to see what could be achieved by fielding a settled side of players not burdened with the worry that a mistake or brief loss of form could cost them their place. Overwhelming evidence that the plan worked was that England won all their five matches, scoring 32 goals and conceding eight. I am happy to go on record and say that this was the finest England team of them all. Yes, superior even to the Alf Ramsey side that was to win the World Cup in 1966, and certainly more gifted than Bobby Robson's side that reached the World Cup semi-finals in 1990.

It was one of the best balanced teams ever to represent England, and our newly introduced 4-2-4 formation allowed for boldness and adventure in attack from a springboard of a disciplined and defiant defence. The new system revolved around the precise passing skill in midfield of skipper Johnny Haynes and his versatile side-kick, one Bobby Robson.

Their dual role was to provide the ball for a four-man firing line that featured the dribbling talent of Bryan Douglas on the right wing and the pace and the power of young blond Bobby Charlton on the left wing. In the middle I was striking up a great under-standing with the human bulldozer Bobby Smith, a productive partnership that we would soon be happy to continue for Tottenham.

In our first four matches together England hammered Northern Ireland 5-2, Luxembourg 9-0, a star-spangled Spanish team 4-2 and Wales 5-1. But according to many people in the game – particularly north of the border – the real test would come at Wembley on 15 April, 1961, from a Scottish side studded with the skills of players of the class of Denis Law, Ian St John and wing wizards John McLeod and Davie Wilson. And England, it was claimed, would not find goals easy to come by against a defence that included three of the finest defenders in British football in Eric Caldow, Billy McNeill and the granite-tough Dave Mackay, who during the season just ending had been a main driving force behind Tottenham's historic League and Cup double triumph. These were the teams for a match that was to become one of the most mem-orable of the decade – unless you are Scottish:

England: Springett, Armfield, McNeil, Robson, Swan, Flowers, Douglas, Greaves, Smith, Haynes, Charlton.

Scotland: Haffey, Shearer, Caldow, Mackay, McNeill, McCann, McLeod, Law, St John, Quinn, Wilson.

Celtic goalkeeper Frank Haffey was like a man in a nightmare as he faced an England attack determined to prove our supremacy over 'the auld enemy'. His positioning was questionable with all three goals carved out by England in the first half. Bobby Robson started the spree in the ninth minute and I nipped in for a couple of goals in the 20th and 29th minutes, putting the finishing touches to moves masterminded by Johnny Haynes. Scotland were filled with false optimism that they could get back into the match when Mackay and Wilson scored to make it 3-2 early in the second half, but they pushed forward suicidally and left themselves wide open to counter attacks.

There were great gaps for Haynes to fill with a procession of paralysing passes, and we sunk the Scots without trace under a storm of five goals in 11 minutes. I com-pleted a hat-trick and was choked when what I considered a perfectly good goal was ruled offside. It would had been lovely to have stuffed ten goals into the Scottish net, but we had to be satisfied with a 9-3 victory. A goal from Bryan Douglas and two each from Bobby Smith and man-of-the-match Johnny Haynes did the damage, with Moth-erwell inside- left Quinn briefly interrupting the torture with a third goal for Scotland. We carried Johnny Haynes off shoulder-high as we celebrated our finest victory, while inconsolable goalkeeper Frank Haffey – cruelly dubbed 'Slap-Haffey' by the headline writers – slumped off the Wembley pitch in tears, although we later heard that this extrovert character was cracking jokes in the dressing-room.

My abiding memory is of Dave Mackay charging murderously at any Englishman in possession in the closing stages. My Scottish mates in the game like Dave, Denis Law and, of course, The Saint, were to carry the scars of this demoralising defeat for years.

Goalkeeper Frank Haffey *(above)* looks back in agony as I complete a hat-trick against Scotland at Wembley in 1961, and *(left)* Peter Swan and Jimmy Armfield give skipper Johnny Haynes a hero's lift after England had gone one over the eight against the Scots. Sadly for Swan, his career was to come to a sensational end in 1965 when he was jailed for his involvement in a football betting scandal.

More than anybody, we owed the victory to the contribution of skipper Haynes, whom I rate the finest of all England's midfield generals. They should put a plaque on the wall down at Fulham's Craven Cottage with the inscription: 'Johnny Haynes passed this way, 1952-1970'. For all those 18 years Haynes was the pass master of English football. His accuracy at distances of up to 70 yards was unmatched. He could take a defence apart with one stunning cross-field pass, usually struck with his right foot. Johnny was the midfield general for England in 56 internationals, 22 of them as captain. He would have collected many more caps but for a car smash in the summer of 1962 that put him out of action for a year.

Just a week after Haynes steered England to this crushing win over Scotland, Tommy Trinder made him Britain's first £100-a-week footballer. This was his bold response to an attempt by Inter-Milan to poach him. He was also selected as the new 'Brylcreem Boy' of sport, taking over from cricket idol Denis Compton. Suddenly the money was rolling in for Johnny, and it couldn't happen to a nicer bloke. He had a public image of being a big-head. This was because he was such a perfectionist on the pitch that he had no patience with players who could not meet his sky-scraping standards. But off the pitch he was a lovely bloke, and a marvellous advertisement for football.

Born in Kentish Town on 17 October, 1934, Johnny was a schoolboy international who helped England beat a Scotland team including Dave Mackay 8-2 at Wembley in 1950. He was to have 17 days as Fulham player-manager in 1968, but gave up the job because he reckoned it was turning his Brylcreemed hair grey before its time. He would hold his passing out parade with Durban City before returning to Britain to concentrate on a business career. And where would he base himself? In Scotland!

England stretched their unbeaten run to eight matches with an 8-0 victory against Mexico, a 1-1 draw in Portugal and then a 3-2 win in Italy, before going down 3-1 against Austria in Vienna. We had scored 45 goals and conceded 14 in nine games.

'There have been few – if any – better England teams than the one I was privileged to lead in that 9-3 win over Scotland. the Scottish press and selectors made poor Frank Haffey the scapegoat but I am convinced we would have run away with the match regardless of who was in goal that day. If we could have held our peak for another year we would have made a strong challenge for the World Cup in chile, but we had gone off the boil by then.'– **Johnny Haynes**.

CHAMPIONS OF EUROPE

This is was the year that saw the end of Real Madrid's total domination of the European Cup, and the death blow came on their own soil where bitter rivals Barcelona won 4-3 on aggregate in a first round tie. It was Real's first defeat in the tournament since it was first launched more than five years earlier. Barcelona were favourites to keep the championship in Spain and powered through to the final with victories over Spartak Kralus and SV Hamburg, the team that dismissed Burnley in the quarter-finals.

Waiting to meet Barcelona for the European Cup in Berne on 31 March, 1961, were Portuguese champions Benfica, who had rattled in 24 goals in eight matches on their way into the final. Benfica were a powerhouse of a team, with Germano a rock at centre-half, Coluna from Mozambique a dynamo in midfield and Aguas, a panther-like centre-forward who had scored an average of a goal a game over a stretch of more than 500 matches. At the back was one of the greatest of all Continental goalkeepers, Costa Pereira. Their manager and mastermind was a Hungarian tactical genius, Bela Guttman.

But Benfica were not expected to be able to deal with the all-round quality of Barcelona, whose 'Famous Five' forwards – Kubala, Everisto, Kocsis, Suarez and Czibor– were reckoned to be on a par with the Real attackers who had clocked up seven goals in the previous year's European Cup final classic. Three Hungarians, a Spaniard – Luis Suarez – and a Brazilian made up an explosive cocktail of an attacking force.

It looked an odds-on victory for Barcelona when the 1960 European Footballer of the Year Suarez floated over a centre that Hungarian master Kocsis met with his head to steer the ball into the net. But ten minutes later Barcelona's confidence was badly shaken when goalkeeper Ramallets had a sudden rush of blood to the head. For some reason he came dashing yards off his line to leave an inviting hole for Aguas to shoot an equalising goal. Worse was to come in the very next Benfica attack. This time Ramallets, highly regarded as Spain's No. 1 goalkeeper, mispunched a harmless-looking cross that he should have caught. The ball screwed away and crossed the goal-line to gift a second goal to Benfica. Ramallets later revealed that he had been blinded by the setting sun, and was unable to see the ball properly when he had tried to punch it clear.

Ten minutes into the second half Coluna seemed to have cemented Benfica's victory when his long-range shot threaded through a forest of legs, caught poor Ramallets unsighted and thumped into the net. But Barcelona battled back with some of the finest football ever witnessed, as good as that exhibited by Real Madrid at Hampden during the previous year. Pereira was forced to make a series of stunning saves, and no fewer than five times Benfica were saved by the woodwork. Czibor, the jet-paced Hungarian left-winger, made it 3-2 with a rocket shot that at last hit the target, but Benfica held out for victory.

*'The footballing gods were with us when Barcelona made their spirited fight-back in the last half hour, but I thought that we deserved to win because of our performance in the first hour. We now want to prove ourselves worthy European champions, and will try to meet the standards set by the outstanding Real Madrid team of the last five years. ' – **Bela Guttman**.*

THE EUROPEAN CUP-WINNERS' CUP

A new tournament was launched which was to become almost as prestigious as the European Cup, if a little clumsily titled: the European Cup-Winners' Cup. It got off to a low-key start, with only ten teams entering. Rangers were Scotland's entry and Wolves carried the England banner.

Wolves got a bye in the first round, while Rangers saw off Hungarian Cup-holders Ferencvaros 6-3 on aggregate. In the quarter-final Wolves – the club that boldly pioneered competitive European club matches in the 'fifties – crushed FK Austria 5-0 at Molineux after losing the first leg 2-0. Rangers destroyed Borussia Moenchengladbach 3-0 and 8-0 to get some sort of revenge for their 12-4 hammering by Eintracht Frankfurt in the previous year's European Cup semi-final.

Rangers and Wolves were drawn to meet each other in the semi-final, and Rangers won the first leg at Ibrox 2-0 and then held on for a 1-1 draw at Molineux to clinch a place in the final. The Rangers team revolved around the wonderfully skilled 'Slim' Jim Baxter, who was already bossing the midfield in his first season after a transfer from Raith Rovers. Baxter's delicate skills were protected by the tackling power of a squad of exceptional players gathered around him, including Eric Caldow, Bobby Shearer and Harold Davis. Flying wingers Alex Scott and Davie Wilson and twin centre-forwards Ralph Brand and Jimmy Millar all fed off the procession of passes skimming from Baxter, who could use his left foot like a chipping wedge-iron.

Rangers captured the Scottish First Division title and the Scottish League Cup, but their bid for a hat-trick in the European Cup-Winners' Cup fell at the final hurdle against Fiorentina. Watched by a crowd of 80,000, they lost the first leg on 17 May at Ibrox – going down to a goal in each half from the industrious Milan, who cashed in on the artistic approach work of Swedish international right-winger Kurt Hamrin. In the second leg in Italy on 27 May Hamrin ran the show again, and steered Fiorentina to victory by an aggregate of 4-1.

'The player who impressed us most in the Rangers team was the No. 6 - Baxter. We knew nothing about him before the final, but he put on such an outstanding display in Glasgow that we knew we had to watch him very carefully in the return leg. We put a marker on him when we played in Italy, and this meant that Rangers were not nearly as effective. I believe Baxter is the type of player who would do very well in Italian football. He has so much skill and imagination. '– **Kurt Hamrin**.

GREAVSIE'S FOOTBALL DIARY
1960-61

1960

20 August: The kick-off to what is to be one of the most eventful seasons of all time. Chelsea lose 4-2 against Aston Villa at Villa Park. This will be the story throughout the season. As quick as we score goals at one end our defence lets them in at the back. I manage my best-ever League goals haul of 41 in a Chelsea total of 98. That's the good news. The bad news is that we concede 100 goals! Tottenham launch their 'double' year with a 2-0 victory over Everton at White Hart Lane. Down in the Fourth Division Peterborough are at last allowed to make their entry into the League after kicking at the door for 21 years. They beat Wrexham 3-0 and Terry Bly, their new signing from Norwich City, scores the first of 52 goals as his contribution to Peterborough's record haul of 134 goals on their way to the Fourth Division title.

10 September: Bolton beat Blackpool 1-0 at Bloomfield Road in the first Football League match screened 'live' on television. It's a lousy game and the low crowd that it draws convinces many clubs that this ITV Friday night experiment is a bad thing for the game and they refuse to appear in front of the cameras. In my opinion this television football will never catch on. Who wants to listen to so-called experts spouting their opinions?

26 September: The Football League Cup is launched with something less than full enthusiasm. It is the idea of League secretary Alan Hardaker, and many clubs see it as one competition too many. Wolves, Tottenham, West Brom, Arsenal and Sheffield Wednesday all refuse to compete. Other major clubs field weakened teams rather than risk injuries to star players.

8 October: Bobby Smith makes his England debut alongside me against Northern Ireland at Windsor Park, Belfast, and he scores with only his second kick of the game after Johnny Haynes rolls a free-kick into his path. We win 5-2 and one of my two goals is a walk-in job just seconds after Mick McNeill has cleared the ball off our goal-line at the other end.

19 October: We win the first of our six qualifying matches for the 1962 World Cup with a 9-0 canter in Luxembourg. Bobby Charlton and I each grab a hat-trick, Bobby Smith scores twice and skipper Johnny Haynes scores the goal of the game with a scorching shot. There is a barber's shop next door to our hotel and when we see a large poster of 'Brylcreem Boy' Haynesie in the window we take great delight in taking him inside and showing him off to the barber. While Johnny is signing autographs one of the lads blacks in a couple of his teeth on the poster with a pen. I thought it was a great improvement. Boys will be boys.

26 October: We beat Spain 4-2 in a rain-storm at Wembley. It is as good a performance as an England team has produced in my time with them. The Spaniards have come determined to win and include all their top guns like di Stefano, Luis Suarez, Del Sol, Gracia and the genius of a winger, Gento. Bobby Smith conjures a spectacular goal with a magnificent chip over the head of goalkeeper Ramallets.

5 November: A funny thing happens to me after we beat Newcastle 4-2 at Stamford Bridge. I am nobbled by a Newcastle director, who tells me that if I could find a way to get on the transfer list they would buy me. He says I will be given £1,000 in my hand plus a £200-a-month car-salesman's job that would require no more than two hours of my time a week. Sounds too much like hard work to me! Actually, he has caught me when I am feeling very fidgety about my future at Chelsea. The club seems to lack ambition, and it's frustrating to be scoring so many goals with nothing to show for it. I have told manager Ted Drake that I would like a move, and he has said that he will discuss it with the board. What I am keeping to myself is that I have been approached on the old hush- hush by an Italian agent representing AC Milan. He is talking telephone numbers that would mean I could buy a car salesroom rather than work in it.

23 November: Wales are the next visitors to Wembley, and we send them packing with a 5-1 defeat. This brings our tally for the first four international matches of the season to 23 goals. I score two goals, and I reckon it will put a few million lire on my transfer fee. Only I know that an AC Milan scout is watching me from the Wembley stand.

3 December: Chelsea hammer West Brom – including my England buddies Don Howe and Bobby Robson – by 7-1, and I manage to bang in five of them. One of the goals takes my League collection to 100, and at 20 I am the youngest player to have reached the target. I have not helped my case for a transfer because Chelsea fans now start petitioning the club for me to stay.

15 December: At a tense meeting of the Professional Footballers' Association in London we players agree to take strike action, and we give the Football League chiefs one month to reach agreement over pay and conditions of contract. Otherwise the ball will stop rolling.

18 January: The League give in and agree to kick out the £20 maximum wage. Our strike threat is called off at the last minute. Suddenly the sky's the limit for professional footballers. I can't take my eyes off the blue skies over Italy, and I secretly put my signature to an option contract. Silly boy. I will live to regret it.

31 January: Alan Mullery sets a record he would rather forget – the fastest own goal in League history. Playing for Fulham against Sheffield Wednesday at Craven Cottage, Mullers sends a 20-yard back pass into his own net after just 30 seconds. Sheffield Wednesday become the first team in League history to score a goal without a single one of their players touching the ball. Things do not get better. Fulham finally lose 6-1.

10 February: Tommy Docherty joins Chelsea as player-coach. He brings much-needed professionalism to the club, but it is too late for me. The Doc has more jokes than a Glasgow music hall comedian. He tells one of our full-backs: 'I've seen milk turn faster'.

17 March: Don Revie is appointed manager of Leeds United. It is the start of what will be a stunning success story at Elland Road.

6 April: The secret is out. Chelsea and AC Milan announce that they have come to an agreement for my transfer once the Italians lift their temporary ban on imported players at the end of this month.

10 April: Ron Greenwood, Arsenal coach and England Under-23 team manager, succeeds Ted Fenton as manager of West Ham United. Good times are on their way for the Hammers.

15 April: Our 9-3 slaughter of the Scots at Wembley. It's the only time I've known The Saint lost for words. Excuse me crowing, but believe me we really suffer when we are on the wrong end of a defeat against the Jocks. The Scottish press manage to put nearly all the blame for the defeat on goalkeeper Frank Haffey. He did have a nightmare, but the mood we were in they would have got stuffed no matter who was in goal. Haffey is a likeable, happy-go-lucky guy, and refuses to treat the defeat too seriously. 'It's not the first or last time that I'll have one over the eight', says the man who will eventually make his way Down Under where he will become a nightclub entertainer. Frank Haffey. What a character.

17 April: 'Super Spurs' clinch the First Division championship with a 2-1 victory over Sheffield Wednesday at White Hart Lane. It's a team that I would love to play for ... but I'm now legally bound to join Milan.

19 April: Harry Catterick starts his new job as manager of Everton after his predecessor, Johnny Carey, is sacked while sharing a taxi with the club chairman John Moores. From

It's hello from him, and goodbye from me! Tommy Docherty *(above)* wins the ball for Chelsea in front of young goalkeeper Peter Bonetti against Sheffield Wednesday at Stamford Bridge in 1961. The Doc had just joined Chelsea as player-coach as I was preparing to wave farewell to English football *(left)* to start my Italian adventure.

this day on whenever an Everton manager is struggling you will hear somebody on the terraces shout: 'Call him a cab!'

24 April: Johnny Haynes kicks out approaches from Inter-Milan when Fulham make him Britain's first £100-a-week footballer. Lucky old Johnny.

29 April: My last match for Chelsea. The fans carry me off shoulder-high after I score all four goals in a 4-3 victory over Nottingham Forest. I am made captain and I clinch victory with a last-minute penalty. Immediately after the game I get involved in an argument with the Chelsea directors, who are insisting I go with the club to Israel for a friendly match. I have a few million other things on my mind and I refuse. The board respond by suspending me for 14 days. It means that I miss England's 8-0 victory against Mexico at Wembley. What a sad, stupid way to end my career with Chelsea.

1 May: I fly to Milan to look over my new club. The AC Milan fans give me an incredible hero's welcome, and I have not kicked a ball yet. I am still hoping to find a way out of the corner into which I have pushed myself, particularly as Chelsea chairman Joe Mears tells the newspapers that if Milan failed to take up their option he would guarantee me a wage that tops that of any other player in the League. Why couldn't Chelsea have made all this clear to me weeks ago?

6 May: Tottenham beat Leicester City 2-0 in the FA Cup final at Wembley to become the first team since 1897 to complete the League and Cup double. During their marvellous season they attract more than two and a half million fans.

21 May: We hold Portugal to a 1-1 draw in Lisbon in a World Cup qualifying match thanks to a late equaliser by good old reliable Ron Flowers. The temperature inside the stadium is up in the 90s and we are pleased with our performance, particularly as Portugal field eight members of the powerful Benfica team that will win the European Cup in ten days' time.

24 May: Back in Italy, this time in Rome for an international match against an Italian team including one of the world's greatest players: Omar Sivori. He sends the 90,000 Italian fans potty when he scores to equalise an early goal by Gerry Hitchens, the Aston Villa centre-forward playing in place of Bobby Smith. Sampdoria centre-forward Brighenti puts Italy 2-1 up, and with 20 minutes to go we are struggling. Then Hitchens notches his second goal after I manage to create an opening for him. Gerry is making such a great impression that Inter-Milan will hurry to clinch a deal for him after the match. Five minutes from the end Johnny Haynes slices the Italian defence open with a superb pass that presents me with the easy job of slotting in a winner that is one of the most satisfying goals I have ever scored. I have made up my mind not to join AC Milan, and Jimmy Hill has come over from England to help argue my case. But my late winner makes the Milan club even more determined to sign me, and make me a final offer that I can't refuse. Remember, I am only just 21 and it is easy to get confused in what is suddenly a world of high finance.

1 June: I am in Alassio to at last sign a personal contract with AC Milan. The promise is that I will earn what is a small fortune of £40,000 over a period of three years and I will receive a £15,000 down payment. In the 1960s that is a lot of bread. What they don't tell me about is a fining system that is going to make it seem as if I have a very big hole in my pocket.

6 June: Here we go with AC Milan. I make my first appearance against Botafogo, and I mark my debut with a goal in a 2-2 draw. I get a tremendous welcome from the 50,000 fans in the magnificent San Siro Stadium. It's a great start to my Italian adventure, but there are nightmares on the way.

THE CHAMPIONS OF
1960-61

FIRST DIVISION:
1: Tottenham Hotspur (66 points)
2: Sheffield Wednesday (58)
3: Wolverhampton Wanderers (57)

Championship squad:
Allen (42 appearances), Baker (41), Barton (1), Blanchflower (42), Brown (41), Dyson (40), Henry (42), Hollowbread (1), Jones (29), Mackay (37), Marchi (6), Medwin (14), Norman (41), Saul (6), John Smith (1), Bobby Smith (36), White (42).
Goalscorers: Bobby Smith (28), Allen (23), Jones (15), White (13), Dyson (12), Blanchflower (6), Medwin (5), Mackay (4), Norman (4), Saul (3), Baker (1), 1 own goal.

SECOND DIVISION:
1: Ipswich Town (59 points)
2: Sheffield United (58)
3: Liverpool (52)

Championship squad:
Bailey (38 appearances), Baxter (19), Carberry (42), Compton (3), Crawford (42), Curtis (5), Elsworthy (39), Hall (4), Laurel (3), Leadbetter (42), Malcolm (41), Millward (19), Nelson (39), Owen (8), Phillips (42), Pickett (24), Rees (16), Siddall (3), Stephenson (33).
Goalscorers: Crawford (40), Phillips (30), Stephenson (9), Millward (6), Rees (4), Elsworthy (3), Leadbetter (3), Curtis (3), Owen (1), 1 own goal.

THIRD DIVISION:
1: Bury (68 points)
2: Walsall (62)
3: Queen's Park Rangers (60)

Championship squad:
Adams (43 appearances), Atherton (46), Bartley (4), Bunner (7), Bradbury (6), Conroy (46), Calder (46), Gallagher (7), Heath (3), Holden (36), Hubbard (44), Jackson (45), McGrath (22), McInnes (1), Moulden (2), Robertson (39), Stokoe (7), Turner (46), Watson (46).
Goalscorers: Jackson (24), Watson (23), Calder (20), Hubbard (17), Holden (15), Turner (4), Atherton (2), Bartley (1), Bradbury (1), 1 own goal.

FOURTH DIVISION:
1: Peterborough United (66points)
2: Crystal Palace (64)
3: Northampton Town (60)

Championship squad:
Banham (12 appearances), Bly (46), Dunne (1), Emery (46), Graham (1), Hails (46), Hogg (2), McNamee (44), Norris (5), Rayner (43), Rigby (40), Ripley (39), Sansby (1), Sheavills (1), Smith (45), Stafford (13), Taylor (1), Walker (43), Walls (46), Whittaker (31).
Goalscorers: Bly (52), Hails (22), Smith (17), McNamee (16), Emery (15), Ripley (5), Dunne (1), Rayner (1), 5 own goals.

SCOTTISH FIRST DIVISION:
1: Rangers (51 points)
2: Kilmarnock (50)
3: Third Lanark (42)

Championship squad:
Wilson (34 appearances), Brand (34), Shearer (33), Caldow (33), Scott (33), Davis (31), Paterson (30), McMillan (28), Baxter (27), Niven (22), Millar (21), Ritchie (12), Stevenson (8), McLean (6), Baillie (5), Murray (5), Henderson (3), Penman (3), Provan (2), McKinnon (2), Hume (2).
Goalscorers: Brand (24), Wilson (19), Scott (12), McMillan (9), Millar (8), Murray (5), McLean (3), Caldow (2), Davis (2), Baxter (1), 3 own goals.

SCOTTISH SECOND DIVISION:
1: Stirling Albion (55 points)
2: Falkirk (54)
3: Stenhousemuir (50)

FA CUP FINAL:
Tottenham Hotspur 2 (Smith, Dyson)
Brown, Baker, Henry, Blanchflower, Norman, Mackay, Jones, White, Smith, Allen, Dyson.
Leicester City 0
Banks, Chalmers, Norman, McLintock, King, Appleton, Riley, Walsh, McIlmoyle, Keyworth, Cheesebrough.

LEAGUE CUP FINAL:
First leg:
Rotherham United 2 (Webster, Kirkman)
Ironside, Perry, Morgan, Lambert, Madden, Waterhouse, Webster, Weston, Houghton, Kirkman, Bambridge.
Aston Villa 0
Sims, Lynn, Lee, Crowe, Dugdale, Deakin, McEwan, Thomson, Brown, Wylie, McParland.

Second leg:
Aston Villa 3 (O'Neill, Burrows, McParland)
Sidebottom, Neal, Lee, Crowe, Dugdale, Deakin, McEwan, Thomson, O'Neill, Burrows, McParland.
Rotherham United 0
Ironside, Perry, Morgan, Lambert, Madden, Waterhouse, Webster, Weston, Houghton, Kirkman, Bambridge.
Aston Villa win 3-2 on aggregate.

SCOTTISH FA CUP FINAL:
Dunfermline Athletic 2 (Thomson, Dickson)
Connaghan, Fraser, Cunningham, Mailer, Miller, Sweeney, Peebles, Smith, Thomson, Dickson, Melrose
Celtic 0
Haffey, MacKay, O'Neill, Creand, O'Neill, Clark, Gallagher, Fernie, Hughes, Chalmers, Byrne
Replay after 0-0 draw

SCOTTISH LEAGUE CUP FINAL:
Rangers 2 (Brand, Scott)
Niven, Shearer, Caldow, Davis, Paterson, Baxter, Scott, McMillan, Millar, Brand, Wilson
Kilmarnock 0
J. Brown, Richmond, Watson, Beattie, Toner, Kennedy, H. Brown, McInally, Kerr, Black, Muir

EUROPEAN CUP FINAL:
Played in Berne, Switzerland
Benfica 3 (Aguas, Ramallets own goal, Coluna)
Costa Pereira, Joao, Angelo, Netto, Germano, Cruz, Augusto, Santana, Aguas, Coluna, Cavem.
Barcelona 2 (Kocsis, Czibor)
Ramallets, Foncho, Gracia, Verges, Garay, Gensana, Kubala, Kocsis, Evaristo, Suarez, Czibor

EUROPEAN CUP-WINNERS' CUP FINAL

First leg:

Rangers 0

Ritchie, Shearer, Caldow, Davis, Paterson, Baxter, Wilson, McMillan, Millar, Brand, Hume.

Fiorentina 2 *(Milan 2)*

Albertosi, Robotti, Castelletti, Gonfiantini, Orzan, Rimbaldo, Hamrin, Micheli, Da Costa, Milan, Petris.

Second leg:

Fiorentina 2 *(Milan, Hamrin)*

Albertosi, Robotti, Castelletti, Gonfiantini, Orzan, Rimbaldo, Hamrin, Micheli, Da Costa, Milan, Petris.

Rangers 1 *(Scott)*

Ritchie, Shearer, Caldow, Davis, Paterson, Baxter, Wilson, McMillan, Millar, Brand, Scott.

Fiorentina win 4-1 on aggregate.

INTER-CITIES FAIRS CUP FINAL:

First leg:

Birmingham City 2 *(Hellawell, Orritt)*

Schofield, Farmer, Sissons, Hennessey, Foster, Beard, Hellawell, Bloomfield, Harris, Orritt, Auld.

A S Roma 2 *(Manfredini 2)*

Cudicini, Fontana, Corsini, Guiliana, Losi, Carpanesi, Orlando, Da Costa, Manfredini, Angelillo, Menichelli.

Second leg:

A S Roma 2 *(Farmer own goal, Pestrin)*

Cudicini, Fontana, Corsini, Pestrin, Losi, Carpanesi, Orlando, Lojacono, Manfredini, Angelillo, Menichelli.

Birmingham City 0

Schofield, Farmer, Sissons, Hennessey, Smith, Beard, Hellawell, Bloomfield, Harris, Orritt, Singer.

A S Roma win 4-2 on aggregate.

Top Football League goalscorers:

Terry Bly (Peterborough United)	52
Jimmy Greaves (Chelsea)	41
Ray Crawford (Ipswich Town)	40
Tony Richards (Walsall)	36
George Hudson (Accrington Stanley)	35
Brian Clough (Middlesbrough)	34
Peter Burridge (Millwall)	34
Colin Taylor (Walsall)	33
Brian Bedford (Queen's Park Rangers)	33
Cliff Holton (Watford)	32
Jimmy Wheeler (Reading)	31
Ted Phillips (Ipswich Town)	30
Johnny Byrne (Crystal Palace)	30

Top Scottish First Division marksmen:
Alex Harley (Third Lanark) 34 goals
Alex Kerr (Kilmarnock) 34 goals

Highest average League attendance:
Tottenham Hotspur(53,315)

Footballer of the Year:
Danny Blanchflower (Tottenham Hotspur)

European Footballer of the Year:
Omar Sivori (Juventus)

World Club Championship:
Penarol beat Benfica 0-1, 5-0, 2-1

1961-62: SPAGHETTI JUNCTION

They were just starting work on the maze of motorways called Spaghetti Junction in Birmingham when I was about to disappear with a flash and a bang up my own Spaghetti Junction in Milan. This was a maze of my own making. It took me a matter of days to realise I had made a mistake in coming to Italy, and four months before I was finally able to tunnel my way out. It was time for a little honesty: I had got involved with Milan solely for mercenary reasons. Money was the only motive for my being there. I wanted to play football in Italy like I wanted a hole in the head. Suddenly back home in dear old Blighty I could earn nearly as much as in Milan where the game was in the choking clutches of the drug of defensive football.

I felt stifled on the pitch where I was followed everywhere by at least two defenders, and even more stifled off the pitch where my movements were restricted by ridiculous disciplinary measures that reduced the AC Milan footballers to the level of prisoners on parole. I like to be a free spirit, and all the restrictions made me rebel and do the opposite to what I was told. Many years later – when the likes of Gazza and David Platt were making the headlines in Italy – I was able to look back rationally on this frustrating period in my life and see that I behaved like an immature, spoilt brat. But in the world of the 'sixties there was a new mood of freedom in the air in British football, and I wanted to be part of it rather than a prisoner in Italy, where their game was polluted with fear and nothing like as adventurous as it would become some 30 years later.

I did my best on the pitch, despite several of my team-mates not wanting to give me the ball because of all the publicity surrounding me. In 14 matches I scored nine goals, which by Italian standards was a real harvest. But I was desperately homesick, and I made no secret of the fact that all I wanted to do was get back to London as quickly as possible. Milan seemed to think that the way to get me to change my mind was to keep hitting me in the pocket, where it hurt. I was fined so many times that my weekly wage was sometimes even lower than when I had been playing for Chelsea.

Gerry Hitchens settled down much quicker to the Italian way of doing things with Inter- Milan, and Denis Law and Joe Baker had each other for company on and off the pitch at Torino. John Charles, our greatest export to Italy and an idol with Juventus, told me in that deep bass voice of his: 'When in Rome do as the Romans do, boyo. It's the only way'.

But I was in Milan, and I didn't like the way they did things. The Italian public could not have been kinder or warmer towards me. It was just that AC Milan began to treat me like some sort of outcast. I was finally put out of my misery when Milan agreed to let me go and Chelsea and Tottenham were the two clubs prepared to meet their price. They came to a private agreement not to get involved in an auction, and when I made it clear to both clubs that I would rather join Spurs, Chelsea sportingly dropped out of the bidding. To save me carrying the burden of being Britain's first £100,000 footballer, Bill Nicholson bought me for the odd fee of £99,999.

For me, a transfer to Spurs was like being given a passport to paradise. I was so keen to join what I considered the greatest team in Europe that I agreed to a wage £65 less than the £120 a week Chelsea dangled in front of me. So much for all that bunkum about my having been a greedy money-grabber. I came home from Italy virtually penniless. Much of my £4,000 signing-on fee had been eaten up by legal fees and air fares.

The 1961 -62 season was more than a third of the way through by the time I made my debut with Tottenham ... and the championship was on its way to a corner of England previously untouched by football mania. Waking everybody up in sleepy Suffolk was a man I used to watch play for Spurs when I had been a kid. His name: Alf Ramsey.

THE LEAGUE CHAMPIONS

If there is such a thing as a miracle in football, then this was exactly what Alf Ramsey was performing at Ipswich. He had I taken a hard-up, unfashionable club staffed by an I assortment of veterans, rejects and raw, promising youngsters and was transforming them into champions.

Ipswich had been dozing in the old Third Division South when Ramsey became manager in August, 1955, after a distinguished playing career. Within seven years, and in successive seasons, he had guided them to the Second Division and First Division championships. It was an extraordinary feat. The players did the business where it mattered on the pitch, but it was Ramsey's planning and organisation that turned them into such a formidable force. The same soccer brain power was to win the World Cup for England in 1966.

I was to get to know Alf Ramsey better than most, and I can reveal that there were two Alfs. In public, he was cold, calculating, cautious and had a shyness that was often mistaken for arrogance. In private, he was warm and caring with a close rapport with his players. As a right-back with Southampton, Spurs and England he had earned the nickname 'The General' because of his obsession with tactical manoeuvres. He read a game as well, perhaps better, than anybody in British football and had total recall of any game and player that he had ever seen. His greatest gift was his ability to motivate players who respected his knowledge and his sincerity. There was nothing false about Alf when he was involved with footballers and his demands for 100 per cent effort and determination were always met. At Ipswich he had them playing out of their skin.

An enormous plus for Alf was that he had the full, enthusiastic and at times eccentric support of Ipswich chairman John Cobbold, a lovely warm-hearted character who could have walked right out of the pages of a PG Wodehouse novel. Alf could do no wrong in his chairman's eyes, and his sometimes prickly manner was countered by 'Mister John', whose approach to football and to life was epitomised by this quote: 'The only crisis we had ever had in this club was when the white wine served in the boardroom was not sufficiently chilled'.

As you would expect of a man who had been an exceptional right-back, Alf built his Ipswich team on the foundation of a strong defence. The essential members of the rearguard were Roy Bailey, an agile goalkeeper signed from Crystal Palace in 1956 (his son, Gary, would later become a respected goalkeeper with Manchester United), fullback partners Lawrie Carberry and John Compton, and half-backs Bill Baxter, Andy Nelson and John Elsworthy, a well-balanced trio under the command of skipper Nelson, whose game blossomed and flourished after he joined Ipswich from West Ham.

In what was a forerunner of his revolutionary 4-3-3 England tactics, Alf switched leftwinger Jimmy Leadbetter to a withdrawn midfield role. Leadbetter, who looked scrawny and underfed but was surprisingly strong and energetic, paralysed defences with cunning running from a position alongside constructive central midfield marshal Doug Moran. Many teams just did not rumble what Leadbetter was up to. They tried to treat him like a conventional outside-left, and defenders were drawn yards out of position as they tried to track his movements off the ball.

Roy 'Little Rocket' Stephenson played an orthodox role on the right wing, concentrating on providing a service for powerful twin strikers Ray Crawford and Ted Phillips, a tandem team that destroyed defences with a mixture of subtle skills and raw strength. Phillips packed one of the hardest shots in the League, while Crawford was a master of positional play and was stunningly accurate with his finishing.

It had been Phillips who had blasted Ipswich to the Third Division South championship in 1957 with a haul of 46 League and Cup goals. After three years of consolidation Ipswich had won the Second Division championship by a point from Sheffield United in 1960-61, the deadly duo of Phillips and Crawford having scored 70 goals between them. Now, in the eventful season of 1961-62, they had struck again – Crawford with 33 goals and Phillips with 28.

Ipswich won the League championship with three points to spare over Burnley, with the Tottenham team that I had joined back in third place. History was repeating itself for Alf, who was a vital member of the famous Spurs push-and-run team that had won the Second and First Division championships in successive seasons at the start of the 'fifties.

> '*Alf Ramsey was a remarkable organiser, and he won the respect of all his players. The balance of the team was exactly right, and we did not have any selfish players. The team effort came first with all of us. It was a pleasure and a privilege to captain such an outstanding side.*' – **Andy Nelson**.

THE FA CUP WINNERS

My reward for having the good sense to join Tottenham came at Wembley on 5 May, 1962, when I was proud to be a member of the 'Super Spurs' side that beat Burnley 3-1 to win the FA Cup. For nine of our players – all except winger Terry Medwin and me – it was a repeat triumph following the previous season's double-clinching victory over Leicester City.

We got off to a dream start against an exceptional Burnley side that had pipped us to the runners-up place in the League title race by one point. The game was barely three minutes old when our goalkeeper Bill Brown belted a clearance upfield to Bobby Smith, who nodded it down into my path. I was going at full pace and briefly over-ran the ball. As I waited for the ball to come back to me I skidded almost to a halt, which had the effect of throwing the five back-pedalling Burnley defenders immediately ahead of me off balance. I spotted an unguarded path to the net and I steered the ball all the way along the ground past each of them and into the corner just wide of the fingers of goalkeeper Adam Blacklaw. What made the goal so special for me was that in the dressing-room before the game started I had pledged to score within the first five minutes. It was not like me to make such a rash promise, but I had just wanted to give myself extra motivation for what was one of the most important matches of my career.

Burnley showed remarkable character after the body-blow of this early goal, and they smoothly pulled themselves back into the game and created an equaliser early in the second half. Ray Pointer swept the ball out to Gordon Harris on the left wing, and his instant centre was squeezed past goalkeeper Bill Brown by Jim Robson for what was the 100th goal to be scored in an FA Cup final at Wembley.

As often happens with a team that battles back to equalise, Burnley relaxed and lost concentration. It was fatal, and within a minute we were back in the lead. Bobby Smith spun to meet and control John White's centre, before firing a blistering shot on the turn into the Burnley net from 15 yards. It was a cracker of a goal, and proved yet again that

Big Maurice Norman and I have our hands full with the silverware *(above)* as we join Tottenham's lap of honour after the 1962 FA Cup final victory over Burnley... and I have my hands full again as I pop the cork in the Wembley dressing-room, with Cliffie Jones lending a hand. In those days I could no doubt have emptied the bottle on my own!

Bobby's game was about much more than just muscle.

Once again Burnley picked themselves up and came back with a burst of productive football. Robson had a 'goal' ruled off-side, Harris drilled a shot straight at Bill Brown and then Robson was just inches off target with a powerful header.

We clinched victory with ten minutes to go when Tommy Cummings handled a Terry Medwin shot on the goal-line. As skipper Danny Blanchflower was preparing to place the ball for the spot-kick his Northern Ireland team-mate and good friend Jimmy McIlroy said to him: 'Bet you miss'.

Danny did not say a word. He placed the ball and sent Blacklaw the wrong way as he stroked the penalty home. As he ran past McIlroy, he said: 'Bet I don't!'

The victory earned us a place in the European Cup-Winners' Cup and made up for our disappointment in just failing to get a place in that season's European Cup final. We had gone out in the semi-final a month earlier after one of the greatest series of matches in which I had ever been involved.

CHAMPIONS OF EUROPE

Ferenc Puskas scored a first-half hat-trick for Real Madrid in the European Cup final in Amsterdam on 2 May – but finished on the losing side. The winners were defending champions Benfica, who now had a black ace in their pack by the name of Eusebio. He plundered two goals to help lift Benfica to a 5-3 victory over the old masters of Madrid, who were trying to regain lost glories on rapidly ageing legs.

Eusebio was a virtual unknown when I first played against him for Spurs in the two-leg European Cup semi-final saga with Benfica. Born Eusebio Ferreira da Silva, in Mozambique in 1942, he had been snapped up from SC Lourenco Marques by Benfica – following a legal battle with neighbours Sporting Lisbon – in May of the previous year. In one of his earliest matches for Benfica he had come on as a substitute against the Brazilian team, Santos, that included the great Pele. The 19-year-old Eusebio proved he was not overawed by scoring a hat-trick. After only 25 matches he had been selected for the Portugal international team. Wearing the No. 10 shirt, he was always being compared with Pele. He did not quite have Pele's presence on the pitch, but his shooting power was as impressive as anything I had ever witnessed.

Nicknamed 'The Black Panther', he moved through defences at sprint speed and he had a violent right-foot shot that was to put him top of the Portuguese League scoring list seven times before a knee injury handicapped him. There had rarely been such a fast rise to the top, and he was to have the honour of being elected European Footballer of the Year in 1965.

We managed to shut him out in the two legs of the semi-final, but Benfica still had enough fire power to beat us 3-1 in Lisbon. It meant we had a mountain to climb in the return leg at White Hart Lane. I have never known an atmosphere like the one generated by our capacity crowd of 65,000 fans as they roared us on with their 'Glory Glory' chants. We won 2-1 after a titanic struggle, during which I had what I will always swear was a perfectly good goal ruled off-side. It was a heartbreaking way to go out, particularly after our victories in the earlier rounds against Gornik, Feyenoord and Dukla Prague.

The astonishing veteran Puskas scored all his three goals in the final in the first half and Real led 3-2 at half-time. But the Spaniards, with right-back Casada a limping passenger on the wing, were overwhelmed in the second half, and after Coluna had equalised Eusebio took over the stage. He was fouled on his way to goal in the 64th minute. He picked himself up and hammered the penalty into the net. Real were throwing everybody forward in a bid to save the game when Eusebio finished them off with a scorching right-foot shot that produced a goal worthy of a European Cup final.

'It was an honour for me to be on the same pitch as legendary players like Puskas and di Stefano. I can hardly believe this was all happening. It seems like only yesterday that I was a young boy in Mozambique kicking the ball around with my bare feet. Our hardest matches in the Cup were against Tottenham. They were a magnificent team.' – **Eusebio**.

THE EUROPEAN CUP-WINNERS CUP

As 1960 FA Cup-holders Spurs were competing in the European Cup, runners-up Leicester City carried England's challenge in to the Cup-Winners' Cup competition. They had comfortably dismissed Glenavon in the first round, and then had given a good account of themselves against eventual Cup winners Atletico Madrid. They had held the Spaniards to a 1-1 draw in the first leg at Filbert Street before going down 2-0 in Madrid.

Dunfermline had battled through to the quarter-finals, where they were thumped 7-1 on aggregate by Ujpest Doza who in turn had gone down in the semi-finals to Cup-holders Fiorentina.

It took four months to decide the final. Atletico Madrid and Fiorentina drew 1-1 after extra-time at Hampden Park, Peiro scoring for Atletico and Hamrin for the Italians.

The replay was delayed until September of the following season, and this time Atletico made no mistake with a convincing 3-0 victory in Stuttgart, the goals coming from Jones and Mendonca in the first half and Peiro after the interval.

We at Tottenham took a special interest in the replay because we would be campaigning for the Cup-Winners' Cup and it was obvious that the Spaniards would be among our chief rivals.

The Fairs Cup final was an all-Spanish affair between Valencia and Barcelona. Valencia had hammered Nottingham Forest B.C. (Before Clough) 7-1 on aggregate in the first round, and Barcelona had squeezed past Sheffield Wednesday in the quarterfinals. In the two-leg final, Valencia swarmed over Barcelona on their home ground to win 6-2 and were content with a 1-1 draw in the return match.

As soon as the European season was over we all departed for South America and the World Cup finals in Chile. I was to wish I had stayed at home...

THE 1962 WORLD CUP FINAL

How do you replace Pele, the greatest footballer on earth? That was the question Brazil had to answer after the jewel in their crown had limped off with a pulled muscle during the early stages of the 1962 World Cup finals. Their answer had been to promote Pele's 22-year-old understudy Amarildo, and he had functioned with such stunning style and skill that by the time the final shots of the tournament were fired he was being hailed as 'The White Pele'.

Amarildo had immediately revealed his class by scoring two goals in his World Cup debut against Spain. Like Pele, he was able to confuse and delude defenders by clever changes of pace, and he shot hard and accurately with either foot and passed the ball with exactly the right weight of contact. Brazil seem to grow these sort of natural players on trees.

But for me, the man who overshadowed even Amarildo as the player of the tournament was Manoel Francisco dos Santos – better known by his nickname Garrincha, meaning 'Little Bird'. There has never been a footballer quite like this incredible character.

Born in the mountain village of Pau Grande in 1933, he had been a cripple at birth. An operation had left one leg shorter than the other and both legs were so bowed you could have run a pig through them without him knowing. But when there was a ball at his feet he could be the most bewitching, bewildering and stunning winger who ever pulled a defence apart. He was such an individualist that even Brazilian coaches, with their preaching of freedom of expression, were petrified of his independent spirit. It was, for instance, only after a deputation of his team-mates had pleaded on his behalf that he had been included in the 1958 World Cup finals, when he and Pele made their debuts

Pele *(above)* was the undoubted king of world football in the 'sixties despite injuries preventing him from making an impact in the 1962 and 1966 World Cup finals. This overhead kick against Scotland, with Billy Bremner (left) in close attendance, typifies his approach to the game. He was always trying to do the impossible, and often succeeded. One of the main rivals for Pele's crown was Mozambique-born Eusebio *(left),* whose thunderbolt shooting lifted Benfica to two European championships and made Portugal serious challengers for the World Cup.

together and immediately transformed Brazil into an unbeatable side.

Garrincha's contribution to the World Cup victories of 1958 and 1962 was, in my opinion, greater than anybody's. Four years later he was to try to motivate the Brazilians again in the 1966 finals in England, but a cartilage operation and injuries collected in a car smash were to rob him of much of his unique magic.

He was to win 68 caps while playing for Botafogo, Corinthians and Flamengo, but his glittering career was tarnished by a series of domestic scandals after he left his wife and seven daughters to marry a vivacious nightclub singer.

There has rarely been anybody to match his skill and invention on the pitch, which he always turned into a stage. I was in the England team that Garrincha destroyed with his amazing artistry in the 1962 World Cup quarter-finals. It was a miserable World Cup for England. For many of us, it was one competition too many after an overworked season at home and we were weary and homesick before a ball was kicked in the finals. We lost 2-1 to Hungary, produced our best performance with an impressive 3-1 win over Argentina and then qualified for the quarter-final clash with Brazil by drawing 0-0 with Bulgaria in one of the dullest matches ever played in the World Cup. Throughout the opening rounds we were stuck out at a copper-mining village halfway up a mountain and in spartan living quarters miles from any sort of sophisticated life. By the time the Brazil match came around we were going out of our minds with boredom. These were not excuses, because even on our best day I doubt if we could had lived with Brazil, who were put on their way to a 3-1 victory with three mesmerising moments from the little genius, Garrincha. He scored with a thumping header, created a goal for Vava with a viciously swerving free-kick, and then unleashed a 20-yard shot that spun into the net like a Jim Laker off-break.

There was a bizarre incident during the game that I will always remember as a personal link with Garrincha. A stray dog invaded the pitch during the first half, and it led a posse of players and ball boys a merry dance before I got down on all fours to capture it. The intruder seemed very relieved when I carried him to the touchline. Too relieved, in fact. He rewarded me by sending a yellow stream running down my England shirt and shorts. I ponged so much that at half-time I had to change all my gear.

Garrincha, an animal-loving country boy who among other things kept 80 birds in his village home, fell in love with the stray and evidently saw the pooch as a lucky omen, because he took command of the match after it had trespassed on the pitch. He adopted the dog, named it Jimmy Greaves and took it home to Brazil with him!

That's a true shaggy dog story.

Anyway, there were no lucky omens for England and we tamely surrendered to Brazil, who then accounted for host country Chile in a bad-tempered semi-final during which Garrincha was sent off. Only after protests from the Brazilian government was he allowed to participate in the final.

Waiting to challenge Garrincha, Amarildo and their gifted team-mates in the final were Czechoslovakia, a strong, unyielding side that based their success on a physically intimidating defence and fleet-footed forwards who were continually on the look out for the opportunity to launch rapier-quick counter attacks.

Brazil, defending the world title they had captured with memorable flair in Sweden, knew they could not lightly dismiss the Europeans. Countering Brazil's fluid 4-2-4 system with a cautious 3-3-4 formation, the Czechs had managed to smother the South Americans in a goalless first round match during which Pele had collected his injury.

Now the world watched to see if Czechoslovakia could repeat the contain-and-counter tactics against Brazil in the final in Santiago. These were the teams waiting to do battle for the greatest prize in football:

Brazil: Gylmar, Djalma Santos, Mauro, Zozimo, Nilton Santos, Zito, Didi, Garrincha, Vava, Amarildo, Zagalo.

Czechoslovakia: Schroif, Tichy, Novak, Pluskal, Popluhar, Masopust, Pospichal, Scherer, Kvasniak, Kadraba, Jelinek.

As in the 1958 final, Brazil were stunned by an early goal. Josef Masopust ghosted through the unsuspecting Brazilian defence in the 15th minute to get on the end of a precise pass from Adolf Scherer and he struck a firm shot, left-footed, past goalkeeper Gylmar. Brazil kept their heads and quickly gained control with their inimitable samba- rhythm football, which was choreographed by Botafogo club-mates Didi, Zagalo, the amazing Amarildo and the extraordinarily inventive Garrincha.

Within minutes Brazil – driven on by inspiring skipper Ramos Mauro – drew level thanks to a superb solo goal by Amarildo. He worked his way down to the by-line and feinted as if to pass into the centre before sending a shot curling round goalkeeper Wilhelm Schroif.

For nearly an hour the game was evenly balanced, Czechoslovakia battling with grit and determination against a side of superior skills. The Czechs, with European Footballer of the Year Masopust causing problems with his probing runs from midfield, were just beginning to get the confidence to be more adventurous when Brazil unleashed a killer blow. Zito made a rare strike forward into the opposition half in the 69th minute, exchanged passes with Amarildo and got goal-side of the massive, balding figure of centre-back Jan Popluhar to head a swinging cross into the net.

Suddenly all doubts about Brazil's ability to retain the World Cup disappeared, and they started to move with the majesty of true champions. Schroif, one of the safest goalkeepers in European football, by then feeling as exposed as a nudist in a hailstorm, 12 minutes from the final whistle dropped a teasing lob from Djalma Santos and the electric-reflexed centre-forward Vava swept the loose ball into the net before any other Czech defender could move a muscle. It was his third goal in two finals.

As the Brazilians celebrated their victory in the dressing-room a fully-clothed Pele leapt into the bath to congratulate his deputy Amarildo.

> 'This was the proudest day of my life. The performance of our team in the 1958 World Cup was a difficult act to follow, but we achieved our one and only aim of retaining the trophy. We were handicapped by the injury to Pele, but Amarildo was almost in Pete's class. There can be no higher praise. Pele encouraged us every step of the way following his injury and remained an invaluable member of the squad.' – **Ramos Mauro.**

GREAVSIE'S FOOTBALL DIARY
1961-62

1961

13 June: Torino clinch the £100,000 transfer of Denis Lawfrom Manchester City. He joins his pal Joe Baker, who was bought from Hibernian for £73,000 last month. They will play in the same Turin stadium as John Charles, who was the king of Juventus.

20 June: Gerry Hitchens joins me in Milan from Aston Villa for £80,000. He will play his home matches in the same San Siro Stadium as me, but with Internazionale, the bitter rivals of AC Milan. The Italian domestic season was scheduled to kick off in August, and I get permission to return home to England for the birth of the baby who was to be our second daughter, Mitzi.

14 July: Brian Clough joins Sunderland from Middlesbrough for £45,000. His remarkable scoring record for his home-town club was 197 goals in 213 League matches.

22 July: Bill Shankly pays out £30,000 for giant Dundee centre-half Ron Yeats, around whom he will build Liverpool's championship defence. Shanks invites the press to Anfield to 'take a walk round our new defender. He's a colossus'.

7 August: I arrive back in Milan the day after Mitzi's birth. She has exercised a woman's prerogative by being two weeks late and I cabled AC Milan to tell them I would be staying with my wife, Irene, until the birth. They had expected me back on 16 July and show a great sense of understanding by threatening to fine me £50 for every day I fail to make an appearance. It was my first indication that they will hit players in the pocket at the slightest excuse. As soon as I return I am locked away with the rest of the AC Milan players in a training camp at Galaratte, about 40 miles outside Milan. I have already got that feeling of being a prisoner.

8 September: My relationship with AC Milan sinks to a new low when they fine me the equivalent of £500 'for breaking city limits' after I took Irene on a sight-seeing trip to Venice. The next day I earn a £300 bonus by scoring the winning goal against our great rivals Inter-Milan.

22 September: AC Milan coach Nereo Rocco has been having a go at me through an interpreter for not helping out in defence. I decide to show him that I can tackle when necessary and I produce my version of a Dave Mackay challenge to take the ball off a Genoa player. He responds by spitting in my face, and I kick out at him in disgust. The referee awards Genoa a free-kick from which they score the winning goal. Rocco goes berserk over my retaliation, and punishes me the only way he seems to know how – with a fine.

18 October: Stanley Matthews, 48 years young, moves from Blackpool back to Stoke City, the club where he started his League career 30 years ago.

20 November: After six weeks of tortuous negotiations I am at last on my way home. Tottenham have agreed to buy me for £99,999. So I have become a nice little earner for the Italians, who paid £80,000 for me just five months ago. As I head out of Milan in a left-hand drive Jaguar that I bought with part of my signing-on fee my old sparring partner Rocco tells the press: 'I am not sorry to see the back of him. He is a fine player, but he did not have his heart here'. I'll go along with that. I drive out of Milan at five miles per hour through the thickest fog I have ever known. Arrividerci Milano! When I drive through customs at Dover I have to pay £500 import duty on the car. Welcome home!

29 November: Jimmy Hill, who has been forced to retire from playing by a knee in-jury, becomes manager of Coventry City. He is succeded as PFA chairman by Tommy Cummings.

9 December: My registration as a Football League player has been delayed while the League Management Committee investigate the deal. They have been looking for dirt under the carpet that does not exist. I make my first appearance in a Spurs shirt in a reserve match at Plymouth Argyle and a record reserve attendance of 13,000 turns out at Home Park. It is a marvellous welcome back into English football.

16 December: I have been cleared to play for Tottenham, and make my League debut against Blackpool at White Hart Lane. I could not have asked for a better start to my Spurs career, and score a hat-trick that includes one of my better goals. Dave Mackay takes one of his long throw-ins, Terry Medwin flicks the ball on and I send the ball on the volley into the net with a scissors kick. It's the start of a long love affair between me and the Spurs supporters, and my team-mates – who were worried about my spoilt-brat image – immediately accept me.

1961

2 January: Tommy Docherty is named as the new manager of Chelsea in succession to Ted Drake. His first signing is Swansea's Welsh international inside-forward Graham Moore.

19 February: Denis Follows takes over as secretary of the Football Association as successor to Sir Stanley Rous, who is now football's top banana as president of FIFA. There is a strong feeling in football that the Lancaster Gate job should have gone to Walter Winterbottom, but he is too imaginative for the old fogies who run our football.

28 February: I pull on an England shirt for the first time in nine months and score a couple of goals for England Under-23s as we beat the Scots 4-2 at Aberdeen. I get my first close-up look at a Dundee forward called Alan Gilzean, who looks a top-class player to me. He is to shoot Dundee to the Scottish First Division title with 24 goals.

8 March: Two major transfer deals today. Johnny Byrne joins West Ham from Crystal Palace in a player-exchange plus cash deal valued at £65,000, and veteran Everton field marshal Bobby Collins signs for Leeds for a bargain £25,000.

16 March: Billy Wright is appointed manager of Arsenal in succession to George Swindin.

21 March: Spurs are beaten 3-1 in the first leg of the European Cup semi-final by Benfica in Lisbon. We pay for going into the match with an uncharacteristic negative attitude. Tony Marchi comes in as an extra defender, when we would have been better off playing our natural attacking game. A Bobby Smith goal keeps alive faint hopes of survival.

30 March: At least we are certain of one final. We sink Manchester United 3-1 in the FA Cup semi-final at Hillsborough.

5 April: We fall to Benfica in the European Cup, despite beating them 2-1 in the second leg at White Hart Lane. Benfica's cagey old manager Bela Guttmann puts pressure on the referee before a ball is kicked by saying that he fears the game could become 'a bloodbath' because of the power of our tackling. It is an emotive phrase that is seized on by the media, and the referee over-reacts and clamps down on Tottenham from the opening minutes. I score a perfectly good goal early in the first half that is ruled off-side, and we hit the Benfica woodwork three times. It was just not meant to be our night.

14 April: England are beaten 2-0 by Scotland at Hampden Park, our first defeat in Glasgow for 25 years. Ouch. We are 1-0 down to a Davie Wilson goal when Johnny Haynes crashes a shot against the underside of the bar. The ball looks to have crossed the line as it comes down, but the referee waves away our protests. Centre-half Peter Swan handles the ball in the closing moments, and Eric Caldow clinches victory from the penalty spot. The 132,441 fans go home happy.

Two of the great centre-forwards of the early 'sixties: Ray Crawford *(above)* challenging Luton goalkeeper Ron Baynham with the sort of determination that powered Ipswich to the League championship in 1961-62, and Tottenham's beefy Bobby Smith *(left),* who is letting Burnley goalkeeper Adam Blacklaw know that he is around. Bobby was a marvellous side kick of mine for both club and country, and I owed a lot of my goals to his mighty foundation work.

5 May: Victory for Spurs in the FA Cup final against Burnley, whose elegant midfield master Jimmy Adamson has the consolation of being elected Footballer of the Year. Ipswich win the League tite, and Roger Hunt's 41 goals shoot Liverpool to the Second Division championship.

9 May: Gerry Hitchens scores a cracking goal as England beat Switzerland 3-1 at Wembley. It clinches his place in the World Cup party at the expense of unlucky Bobby Smith.

20 May: In a warm-up match on the way to Chile I collect a first-half hat-trick against Peru in Lima. Young Bobby Moore gives a composed performance in his debut, and he will knock Bobby Robson out of the England team for the World Cup. We beat Peru 4-1 in a temperature of 100 degrees.

31 May: A dismal start to our World Cup campaign on a rain-soaked pitch. Hungary beat us 2-1 with a late goal from the gifted Florian Albert. Tichy gives the Hungarians a halftime lead which is cancelled out by a Ron Flowers penalty.

2 June: Another Ron Flowers penalty puts us on the way to a comfortable victory over Argentina, with Bobby Charlton and I making it 3-1. Rattin looks an exceptional player.

7 June: The worst game of football in which I have ever played. We are held to a goalless draw by a Bulgarian team that never has fewer than nine players in defence.

10 June: 'Bye, 'bye World Cup. Brazil beat us 3-1 in the quarter-finals. We give the champions a hard time in the first-half, and Gerry Hitchens equalises a headed goal from Garrincha. But we are sunk by two goals within five minutes in the second half. Oh well, back to the drawing board.

THE CHAMPIONS OF
1961-62

FIRST DIVISION:
1: Ipswich Town (56 points)
2: Burnley (53)
3: Tottenham Hotspur (52)

Championship squad:
Bailey (37 appearances), Baxter (40), Carberry (42), Compton (39), Crawford (41), Curtis (4), Elsworthy (41), Hall (5), Leadbetter (41), Malcolm (3), Moran (42), Nelson (42), Owen (1), Phillips (40), Pickett (3), Stephenson (41).
Goalscorers: Crawford (33), Phillips (28), Moran (14), Leadbetter (8), Stephenson (7), Elsworthy (2), 1 own goal.

SECOND DIVISION:
1: Liverpool (62 points)
2: Leyton Orient (54)
3: Sunderland (53)

Championship squad:
A'Court (42 appearances), Arrowsmith (1), Byrne (42), Callaghan (23), Furnell (13), Hunt (41), Leishman (41), Lewis (21), Melia (42), Milne (42), Molyneux (3), Moran (16), Slater (29), St John (40), Wheeler (1), White (24), Yeats (41).
Goalscorers: Hunt (41), St John (18), Melia (14), Lewis (10), A'Court (8), Milne (2), Byrne (1), Callaghan (1), Leishman (1), Moran (1), 2 own goals.

THIRD DIVISION:
1: Portsmouth (65 points)
2: Grimsby Town (62)
3: Bournemouth (59)

Championship squad:
Barton (25 appearances), Beattie (43), Blackburn (20), Brown (44), J. Campbell (9), R. Campbell (2), Chapman (4), Cutler (20), Dickinson (46), Dodson (21), Gordon (44), Gunter (20), Harris (14), Middleton (17), Priscott (5), Rutter (36), Saunders (42), Shearing (3), Snowdon (42), Smith (4), White (6), Wilson (39).
Goalscorers: Saunders (24), Gordon (12), Dodson (10), Barton (9), Blackburn (5), Middleton (5), Brown (3), Cutler (3), Harris (3), J. Campbell (2), Chapman (2), White (1).

FOURTH DIVISION:
1: Millwall (56 points)
2: Colchester United (55)
3: Wrexham (53)

Championship squad:
A. Anderson (43 appearances), D. Anderson (2), P. Brady (42), R. Brady (44), Broadfoot (44), Burridge (42), Cripps (3), Davies (44), Garrett (12), Gilchrist (32), Harper (12), Jones (44), McQuade (23), Obeney (39), Reader (1), Spears (3), Stocks (2), Terry (17), Townend (15), C. Wilson (5), T, Wilson (1), Wright (15).
Goalscorers: Burridge (22), Jones (22), Terry (13),Townend (8), Broadfoot (8), Obeney (5), McQuade (4), C. Wilson (1), 3 own goals.

SCOTTISH FIRST DIVISION:
1: Dundee (54 points)
2: Rangers (51)
3: Celtic (46)

Championship squad:
Liney (34 appearances), Hailton (34), Seith (34), Cousin (34), Ure (34), Robertson (33), Penman (32), Cox (31), Gilzean (29), Wishart (29), Brown (9), Waddell (4), McGeachie (3), Stuart (2).
Goalscorers: Gilzean (24), Penman (18), Cousin (15), Smith (7), Wishart (6), Robertson (6), Seith (2), Waddell (1), 2 own goals.

SCOTTISH SECOND DIVISION:
1: Clyde (54 points)
2: Queen of the South (53)
3: Morton (44)

FA CUP FINAL:
Tottenham Hotspur 3 (Greaves, Smith, Blanchflower pen.)
Brown, Baker, Henry, Blanchflower, Norman, Mackay, Medwin, White, Smith, Greaves, Jones.
Burnley 1 (Robson)
Blacklaw, Angus, Elder, Adamson, Cummings, Miller, Connelly, McIlroy, Pointer, Robson, Harris.

LEAGUE CUP FINAL:
First leg:
Rochdale 0
Burgin; Milburn, Winton; Bodell, Aspden, Thompson; Wragg (Whyke), Hepton (Richardson), Bimpson, Cairns, Whitaker.
Norwich City 3 (Lythgoe 2, Punton)
Kennon, McCrohan, Ashman; Burton, Butler, Mullett; Mannion, Lythgoe, Scott, Hill, Punton.
Second leg:
Norwich City 1 (Hill)
Kennon, McCrohan, Ashman; Burton, Butler, Mullett; Mannion, Lythgoe, Scott, Hill, Punton.

Rochdale 0
Burgin; Milburn, Winton; Bodell, Aspden, Thompson; Wragg (Whyke), Hepton (Richardson), Bimpson, Cairns, Whitaker.
Norwich win 4-0 on aggregate.

SCOTTISH FA CUP FINAL:
Rangers 2 (Brand, Wilson)
Ritchie; Shearer, Caldow; Davis, McKinnon, Baxter; Henderson, McMillan, Millar, Brand, Wilson.
St Mirren 0
Williamson; Campbell, Wilson; Stewart, Clunie, McLean; Henderson, Bryceland, Kerrigan, Fernie, Beck.

SCOTTISH LEAGUE CUP FINAL:
Rangers 3 (Millar, Brand, McMillan)
Ritchie; Shearer, Caldow; Davis, Baillie, Baxter; Scott, McMillan, Millar, Brand, Wilson.
Hearts 1 (Davidson)
Cruikshank; Kirk, Holt; Cumming, Polland, Higgins; Ferguson, Davidson, Bauld, Blackwood, Hamilton.
Replay after 1-1 draw.

EUROPEAN CUP FINAL:
Played in Amsterdam
Benfica 5 (Aguas, Cavem, Coluna, Eusebio 2)
Costa Pereira; Joao, Angelo; Cavem, Germano, Cruz; Augusto, Eusebio, Aguas, Coluna, Simoes.
Real Madrid 3 (Puskas 3)
Araquistain; Casado, Miera, Felo, Santamaria, Pachin, Tejada, Del Sol, Di Stefano, Puskas, Gento.

EUROPEAN CUP-WINNERS' CUP FINAL:
Played at Hampden Park, Glasgow
Atletico Madrid 1 (Peiro)
Madinabeytia; Rivella, Calleja, Ramirez, Griffa, Glaria; Jones, Adelardo, Mendonca, Peiro, Collar

Fiorentina 1 *(Hamrin)*
Albertosi; Robotti, Castelletti, Malatrasi, Orzan, Marchesi, Hamrin, Ferretti, Milan, Dell'Angelo, Petris
Replayed in Stuttgart
Atletico Madrid 3 *(Jones, Mendonca, Peiro)*
Madinabeytia; Rivella, Calleja, Ramirez, Griffa, Glaria; Jones, Adelardo, Mendonca, Peiro, Collar
Fiorentina 0
Albertosi; Robotti, Castelletti, Malatrasi, Orzan, Marchesi, Hamrin, Ferretti, Milan, Dell'Angelo, Petris

EUROPEAN FAIRS CUP FINAL:
First leg
Valencia 6 *(Guillot 3, Waldo 2, Ribebe)*
Zamora, Verdu, Chicao, Piquer, Mestre, Sastre, Ficha, Ribebe, Waldo, Guillot, Coll.
Barcelona 2 *(Kocsis 2)*
Ramallets, Foncho, Gracia, Verges, Gensana, Garay, Kubala, Kocsis, Evaristo, Suarez, Czibor.
Second leg
Barcelona 1 *(Kocsis)*
Ramallets; Foncho, Gracia, Verges, Gensana, Garay, Kubala, Kocsis, Evaristo, Suarez, Czibor.
Valencia 1 *(Guillot)*
Zamora; Verdu, Chicao, Piquer, Mestre, Sastre, Ficha, Urtiaga, Waldo, Guillot, Coll.
Valencia win 7-3 on aggregate.

Top Football League goalscorers:

Roger Hunt (Liverpool),	41
Bobby Hunt (Colchester United)	37
Cliff Holton (Northampton Town)	36
David Layne (Bradford City)	34
Ron Rafferty (Grimsby Town)	34
Brian Bedford (Queen's Park Rangers)	33
Ray Crawford (Ipswich Town)	33
Derek Kevan (West Bromwich Albion)	33
Martyn King (Colchester United)	31
Barrie Thomas (Scunthorpe United)	31
Ray Charnley (Blackpool)	30
Frank Lord (Crewe Alexandra)	30

Top Scottish First Division marksman
Alan Gilzean (Dundee) 24 goals

Highest average League attendance:
Tottenham Hotspur (45,538)

Footballer of the Year:
Jimmy Adamson (Burnley)

European Footballer of the Year:
Josef Masopust (Dukla Prague)

World Club Championship:
Santos beat Benfica 3-2, 5-2

1962-63: ENTER ALF RAMSEY

Two events in the summer of 1962 were about to change the face of English football beyond recognition. On 1 August, Walter Winterbottom announced that he was resigning from the England team manager's job that he had held since the war. On 23 August Johnny Haynes, the England and Fulham skipper around whom Winterbottom had built his team, was dragged from a wrecked car with knee and leg injuries that were to end his distinguished international career.

Winterbottom, disappointed at being overlooked for the job of FA secretary, was to become the chief administrator of the Central Council of Physical Recreation. Walter was an intellectual football theorist whose tactical ideas often went zooming over my head, but I had enormous respect for him both as a man and as a manager, and it was beyond my understanding how the Football Association could have let him slip away from a game to which he had given so much.

The loss of Johnny Haynes to the England team was an even bigger blow. In my view, Johnny was the greatest passer of the ball I have ever played with or against. We had always been on the same wavelength since our first matches together as England Under-23 internationals, and we always knew where to be on the pitch to get the most out of each other. There had rarely been such a dominant figure in the England team. Nearly every forward move was masterminded by Haynes, who could unlock a safe door with that right foot of his. It would take him months to overcome his injuries, by which time England would be on a new course and under new management. The man chosen to succeed Winterbottom was Alf Ramsey, fresh from steering Ipswich Town to the Second and First Division titles in successive years.

The 'Ramsey Revolution' that was to shake English football to its foundations started on a nightmare note. His first match as England manager was a European Nations Cup tie against France in Paris on 21 November, 1962, and we were well and truly stuffed by 5-2. The usually reliable Ron Springett in our goal had the sort of game he would not wish on his worst enemy, and three of the French goals had to be put down to goalkeeper error. It would lead to Ron being replaced as England's first-choice 'keeper by Gordon Banks. Alf must have wondered if he should have stayed in sleepy Suffolk when his suitcase was lost in transit.

There was worse to follow on the pitch in Ramsey's second match. We were beaten 2-1 by Scotland at Wembley, and for Alf coming second to the Scots was like having to drink poison. It was the first match played at the 'new' Wembley with a £500,000 roof running right round the stadium like a giant lip. As we walked out on to the pitch alongside

Not so much the last supper *(above)*, more like the first. It's one of Alf Ramsey's earliest meetings with the England squad after he had taken over from Walter Winterbottom as manager. He is sitting at the head of the table with his faithful trainer Harold Shepherdson on his left, and I'm next to Shep. That's Maurice Norman (front, left) talking across the table to Tottenham team-mate Ron Henry. This gathering was before Ramsey's first match against France. We lost 5-2, which gave Alf real food for thought. Alf *(left)* was known as 'The General' in his playing days with Tottenham, and he planned every match as meticulously as if he was plotting a military campaign. His impact on football in the 'sixties could be measured on the Richter scale.

our Scottish opponents we were greeted by what sounded like the Hampden Roar. There were so many Scots crowded into the ground that I said to our new goalkeeper, Gordon Banks: 'I knew they'd rebuilt Wembley, but I didn't know that it had been shifted up to bloody Glasgow!'

Within five minutes of the kick-off both teams were down to ten men. Our centre-forward Bobby Smith and Scottish skipper Eric Caldow collided like runaway express trains when chasing a loose ball and both were carried off on stretchers. The unfortunate Caldow had a triple fracture of the leg. By the time Smithie limped back into the game with a bruised knee heavily bandaged we were two goals down and struggling.

The first goal was a gift to Scotland from our skipper Jimmy Armfield. He commited the cardinal sin of passing across the face of our defence. Slim Jim Baxter could not believe his luck as the ball rolled into his path, and he coldly drilled the ball out of the reach of the oncoming Banks and into the net.

Baxter was strolling arrogantly around Wembley as if he owned the place, and we were giving him far too much room in which to operate. There was a lack of understanding and command in our defence and in a moment of desperation Ron Flowers bundled Willie Henderson off the ball to concede a penalty. Baxter sent Banksie the wrong way as he slotted home the perfect spot-kick.

We tightened up our marking in the second half, but could pull only one goal back through Bryan Douglas. As we came off at the final whistle Baxter stuck the ball up his jersey and waddled off with a swagger that you became used to when you were on the wrong end of defeat against the Scots. Slim Jim had just given one of the finest individual performances by any Scot at Wembley. I expected Baxter to establish himself as one of the giants of the game during the 'sixties, but this was to prove the peak performance of a career that never quite lived up to its glittering promise. He broke a leg while playing with Rangers, and was never the same force again. In this match at Wembley he had looked as good as any attacking midfield player I have ever seen.

Two matches played, two defeats. The Ramsey Revolution had yet to get off the launching pad. He watched from the sidelines as Everton took over from his old Ipswich club as League champions...

THE LEAGUE CHAMPIONS

Everton sprinted to the League championship with an unbeaten run of 12 matches at the end of a season that would go down in the history books as the 'Ice Age' campaign. The season ran three weeks late after heavy snow and ice caused a virtual white-out of the League and Cup programme over a span of two months from late December. Everton's string of victories as they cleared their backlog of matches took them powering away at the top of the table, beating Spurs into second place by six points.

We had been conserving our main effort for the European Cup-Winners' Cup. That was my excuse, and I'm sticking to it. The Everton success story was a personal triumph for manager Harry Catterick, a former Goodison centre-forward whose playing career bridged the war. He had returned to Everton as the boss in succession to Johnny Carey in 1961 after steering Sheffield Wednesday back to the First Division.

Encouraged by a wealthy board, he adopted a money-no-object attitude, quickly shaping Everton into a championship-quality side. They became known as the 'chequebook champions' because all but two of their squad had been bought from other clubs. Aloof, calculating and an intelligent soccer strategist, Catterick was to suffer from being constantly compared with his larger-than-life Liverpool rival, Bill Shankly. But the fact that he was to win the League title twice and the FA Cup during his 12-year reign at Goodison was proof of his considerable ability as a manager.

Brian Labone was the rock round which Catterick built the Everton defence. He was a master of positioning at centre-half and quickly struck up a good understanding with the agile Gordon West, bought from Blackpool for a record fee for a goalkeeper of £27,500. Alex Parker and Mick Meagan were solid full-backs, with George Thomson coming into the back line for 19 matches.

Jimmy Gabriel and Brian Harris were strong and impressive half-back partners, but it was only when the dynamic Tony Kay arrived for a then club record £55,000 from Sheffield Wednesday that Everton really began to look championship class in midfield. Dennis Stevens, Alex Young and Roy Vernon often brought their skilful touches back into the midfield engine-room, but they were usually more concerned with attacking duties.

The inside-forward trio of Stevens, Young and Vernon were as lethal and creative a combination as there had been in the League. Young, the 'Golden Vision', was a master of subtle movements on and off the ball, in the finest traditions of classical Scottish centre-forwards who apply more brain than brawn. Skipper Vernon roamed as the chief architect of the attack and was also a deadly marksman who collected 24 goals in the championship season. Stevens was a superb passer of the ball, and a sharp-shooter if given just a glimpse of the goal. Physically they were all quite small, but they had a giant's share of talent.

Feeding them from the wings were Irish international Billy Bingham, an ageing but still dangerous outside-right who later made way for £40,000 newcomer Alex Scott; Johnny Morrissey, a full-of-tricks outside-left, who was a regular in the No. 11 shirt, with Ray Veall and Derek Temple in reserve.

Everton won the championship at Goodison, going through the season unbeaten at home. Their six defeats all came in away matches, and they established a club record of 61 points on their way to the title.

'We were labelled the big spenders, but people didn't realise that I was giving even more concentration that season to building for the future. That was a superb title-winning side with some marvellously talented players, but I was even more proud of a youth team that we were putting together which was to grow into my second championship-winning team.' – **Harry Catterick.**

THE FA CUP WINNERS

Manchester United were a Jekyll and Hyde team in the see-sawing 1962-63 season, blowing hot and cold like the weather. They scraped clear of relegation by just three points, but swept into the FA Cup final in style with victories over Huddersfield (5-0), Aston Villa (1-0), Chelsea (2-1), Coventry City (3-1) and, in the semi-final at Villa Park, Southampton (1-0).

They saved their best display of the season for the final in which Denis Law proved why he was worth every penny of the record £115,000 that it had cost United to bring him back from Italy in July, 1962. Denis loved a big stage, and Wembley was made for him. His electric reactions meant that he was always a thought and a deed ahead of a classy Leicester team which included players of the calibre of Gordon Banks, Frank McLintock, Graham Cross, Davie Gibson and John King.

United had a beautifully balanced side, and it was a mystery why they nearly slipped down and out of the First Division before clinching a place in the final. Dave Gaskell was a sound goalkeeper, and Tony Dunne and skipper Noel Cantwell were Irish international full-back partners who believed in skill ahead of the big boot. Rock-solid Bill Foulkes, a survivor of the Munich air crash, was dependable in the middle of the defence, and winning the ball with tigerish tackles that really bit was the 'Devilish Devonian' Maurice Setters (whose tactical knowledge in later years was to help Jack Charlton turn the Republic of Ireland team into a side to be respected). Pat (Paddy) Crerand was all style and silky skill in midfield, rarely getting above walking pace but pulling the Leicester defence this way and that with perfectly placed passes that were played all along the ground with the accuracy of a Jack Nicklaus putt.

The forward line had Johnny Giles as a ball-playing right-winger alongside Albert Quixall, the player known in the 'fifties as the 'Golden Boy' of football. David Herd, signed from Arsenal two years earlier, was a conventional centre-forward who learned all the tricks of the trade from his father, Alec, who had played for Manchester City in the FA Cup finals of 1933 and 1934. Firing in scorching shots from out on the left wing was blond

Denis Law *(above)* reacts in typical showman's style as Leicester City goalkeeper Gordon Banks catches the ball off a post during the 1963 FA Cup final, in which Law propelled Manchester United to a 3-1 victory.

Eusebio *(below),* playing for Benfica in the 1963 European Cup final, gets in a shot at goal despite a strong challenge from Milan's Maldini.

bomber Bobby Charlton, but it was the skinny player in the No. 10 shirt who ruled the roost – Denis Law, my favourite footballer of all time.

He was extrovert, flamboyant and spectacular, and never ever dull. An entertainer extraordinary, he had the sharpest reflexes of any player I've ever seen, and he could make a goal out of nothing. He had an uncanny ability to hover in the air when heading the ball, and he was a master of the bicycle kick.

Denis had always been a class above most other forwards since making his debut for Huddersfield Town at the age of 16, after arriving from his home town, Aberdeen, wearing national health glasses and with a squint in his eye that was corrected by an operation before his first League match. The son of a trawlerman, he was soon a big fish in the football pool. He became the youngest ever Scottish international, at the age of 18, and in 1960 was transferred to Manchester City for a British record £55,000. Torino bought him for £100,000 a year later, and he and Joe Baker were having a ball together in Italy when they were lucky to survive a smash in a sports car. United brought him back to the British stage where he belonged, and it was the FA Cup that brought the best out of him. The 40 goals he scored in the competition were an all-time record, and the total did not include the six goals he collected against Luton Town in an abandoned tie in 1961.

Denis, the 'Electric Heel', set the 1963 FA Cup final alight in the 30th minute. Crerand squared the ball to him, and the 'Lawman' dummied to his right as if going away from his target. This deceived the Leicester defenders into dropping their guard and he suddenly turned sharply back to hook the ball into the net past a startled Gordon Banks.

David Herd scored two victory-clinching goals in the second half, which sandwiched a goal from a brave diving header by Leicester centre-forward Ken Keyworth. United had the FA Cup to show off at the end of a season in which they might easily have been relegated. It was the beginning of a startling winning streak at Old Trafford, and for the next five seasons they would not be out of the top four in the First Division title race.

'Denis was in spectacular form in the final. I played against him many times, but I think this was his finest performance. He strolled round the pitch like an emperor, and was threatening something magical in almost every Manchester United attack. I would have really enjoyed watching him if I had not been on the receiving end of his brilliance.' – **Gordon Banks**.

CHAMPIONS OF EUROPE

AC Milan, the team I was so relieved to have left behind, missed me to such an extent that they won the Italian League championship and reached the European Cup final at I Wembley! Their opponents were reigning champions Benfica, who were expected to complete a hat-trick of European Cup victories.

But AC Milan had perfected the contain-and-counter game that had brought them 31 goals in eight matches on the way to the final. They had eliminated Union Luxembourg, Ipswich Town, Turkish champions Galatasaray and Dundee, for whom Alan Gilzean had scored nine goals in their European campaign.

Benfica were hardly stretched on the way to the final, beating IFK Norköpping, Dukla Prague and Feyenoord. In each tie they won the home leg and were then content to draw away.

Nereo Rocco had Milan playing a typically cautious game at the start of the final, but they were forced out of their shell when Eusebio shot the Cup-holders into the lead in the 18th minute after running on to a neat pass from towering centre-forward José Torres. Then a cynical foul by hatchet man Gino Pivatelli reduced Benfica's key midfield player Mario Coluna to a limping passenger, and from then on the pendulum of play started to swing Milan's way.

José Altafini, a really class act from Brazil who fed off the creative artistry of Italy's 'Golden Boy' Gianni Rivera, equalised early in the second half, and then scored a controversial winner in the 66th minute. Rivera sent a defence-splitting pass into Altafini's path and the Benfica defenders stood still appealing for off-side as he raced towards the penalty area. Goalkeeper Costa Pereira came off his line and parried the first shot, but the Brazilian collected the rebound and coolly fired the ball into the net for his 14th and most important goal of the tournament. It was the start of an Italian domination of the European Cup.

Valencia retained the European Fairs Cup, but not before a fright against Dunfermline in an astonishing second-round tie. Managed by Jock Stein, Dunfermline had crashed to a 4-0 defeat in the first leg in Spain. Stein used all the motivating powers for which he was to become famous with Celtic, and Dunfermline won the second leg 6-2 at East End Park. This was before the introduction of the rule of away goals counting double, and they travelled to Lisbon for a replay which Valencia won 1-0.

The Fairs Cup was almost Valencia versus Scotland. They had beaten Celtic 4-2 on aggregate in the first round and then accounted for Hibernian 6-2 in the quarter-finals. In the two-leg final the Spaniards beat Dynamo Zagreb 2-1 in Yugoslavia and 2-0 in the return match in Spain.

'For the first 20 minutes I feared that we had left our footballing skills at home in Italy, but once Gianni Rivera started to dominate in midfield I knew it was only a matter of time before we took control of the game. I cannot understand why there was any doubt about José Altafini's second goal. He was just inside our half when he collected the ball. We are so proud to be the first Italian club to win the European Cup, and now we intend to defend it successfully.' – **Nereo Rocco**.

THE EUROPEAN CUP-WINNERS' CUP

No British team had won a major trophy in Europe when Tottenham travelled to Rotterdam for the European Cup-Winners' Cup final, and hopes that we could break the duck were suddenly diminished when our main motivator, Dave Mackay, failed a fitness test on the day of the match.

The absence of Mackay was a devastating blow because he had been a major force in Tottenham's success. As it sank in that we would have to perform without his battering-ram backing we became less than confident about our chances of mastering Atletico Madrid. They were an outstanding side, as we had noted in the previous season when they won the Cup-Winners' Cup with a stylish victory over Fiorentina.

Mackay's absence plunged manager Bill Nicholson into a morose mood and he added to our depression when he ran through the strengths of the opposition during a tactical team talk. He made Atletico sound like the greatest team ever to run on to a football pitch, and bruised rather than boosted our confidence. Skipper Danny Blanchflower was so concerned about the mood of gloom and doom that descended on the team that he summoned all of us to a private players' meeting and made one of the most inspiring speeches I had ever heard.

Word-master Blanchflower, using a mixture of fact and blarney, pumped confidence back into us and made us believe in our ability to win. He countered every point that Bill Nicholson had made about the Madrid players by underlining Tottenham's strengths, and he convinced us that we were superior to the Spaniards in every department. It was a speech of Churchillian class, and we went into the final with renewed determination to take the trophy back to Britain. This was how we lined up for the game of our lives, with Tony Marchi stepping into Dave Mackay's place:

Tottenham Hotspur: Brown, Baker, Henry, Blanchflower, Norman, Marchi, Jones, White, Smith, Greaves, Dyson.

Atletico Madrid: Madinabeytia, Rivilla, Rodriguez, Ramiro, Griffa, Glaria, Jones, Adelardo, Chuzo, Mendonca, Collar.

Bill Nicholson, one of the finest tacticians in the game, deserved the credit for the fact that I was in position to give Spurs the lead in the 16th minute. He had spotted, during a spying mission to Madrid, that the Atletico defence were slow to cover down the left side and he instructed that full use should be made of the blistering speed of Cliff Jones. The Welsh international, moving with the pace and determination of a rugby wing-threequarter, sprinted to meet a neatly placed pass from Bobby Smith and I darted into the middle to steer his accurate centre into the net with my left foot. It was a real pickpocket job, and we could almost see the confidence draining out of the Atletico players.

It was on the wings that we were monopolising the match, with Jones and tiny Terry Dyson running the Spanish full-backs into dizzy disorder. Atletico, strangely enough, also had a winger called Jones, but he was not in the same class as our Welsh wizard. Dyson and Jones combined to set up goal number two in the 32nd minute, exchanging passes before releasing the ball to Smith who laid it back for John White to rifle a low shot into the net. It was a rare but crucial goal by John, who had made his reputation as a maker rather than a taker of goals. His signature was stamped on most of our attacks as he prised open the Atletico defence with beautifully weighted passes. Blanchflower, White and Marchi were working like Trojans in midfield to make up for the absence of the one and only Mackay. In most clubs, Marchi would have been an automatic choice for the first team and he played with such skill and determination that his contribution was in the Mackay class. There can be no higher praise.

Atletico Madrid revived their flickering flame of hope in the first minute of the second half when Collar scored from the penalty spot after Ron Henry fisted the ball off the goal-line. For 20 minutes there was a danger that we would lose our way as the Cup-holders forced a series of corner-kicks, but our defence managed to survive the Spanish storm. Goalkeeper Bill Brown took his life in his hands as he threw himself courageously at the feet of Mendonca to snatch the ball off his toes. Chuzo broke free and we sighed with relief as he sent his shot the wrong side of the post, and then Ramiro drove the ball just off target. This was when we started to wonder if we were going to get by without the great Mackay, who in a situation like this would have been breaking Spanish hearts with thundering tackles and brandishing a fist in a demand for extra effort from all of us.

It was Dyson, having the game of a lifetime, who dynamited the Atletico comeback when his hanging cross was fumbled into the net by goalkeeper Madinabeytia. Terry became a man inspired and he laid on a second goal for me before putting the seal on a memorable performance with a scorching shot at the end of a weaving 30-yard run. His first goal was something of a fluke, but the second was a masterpiece. As we trooped into the dressing-room after collecting the Cup Bobby Smith told Dyson in that blunt way of his: 'If I were you, mate, I would now hang up my boots. There's no way you can top that. You were out of this world'.

*"I simply persuaded the team to adopt a positive attitude. It struck me that Bill Nicholson, a marvellous manager, had allowed himself to become a little too obsessed by the strengths of Atletico. He did such a thorough job cataloguing their skills that he got us worrying whether we could live with them. I decided to balance all that Bill said by pointing out our many assets. It was particularly heartening to see Terry Dyson ha ving such an exceptional game. He rarely gets the credit that he deserves. He was our hero.' – **Danny Blanchflower**.*

GREAVSIE'S FOOTBALL DIARY
1962-63

1962

12 July: Denis Law comes home, joining Manchester United from Torino for a British record £115,000. Four days later his Torino team-mate Joe Baker was to join Billy Wright's Arsenal for £70,000.

1 August: Walter Winterbottom hands in his notice as England team manager and coach. He has been in charge since the war, but has always had his hands tied by an amateur selection committee. Walter is to become general secretary of the Central Council of Physical Recreation.

2 August: John Charles, the 'Gentle Giant', returns to Leeds United from Juventus for a fee of £53,000. Equally at home at centre-forward or centre-half, John is one of the greatest players ever produced in Britain and his performances with Juventus have made him a legend in Italian football. Leeds had sold big John to Juventus for £65,000 in 1957.

11 August: Tottenham beat Ipswich 5-1 in the Charity Shield match at Portman Road, and I bang in a couple of goals and play a part in the other three. A family holiday in the sun has helped restore my appetite for football after the slog of the World Cup.

13 August: Bobby Robson is sold by West Bromwich Albion to Fulham, the club where he started his League career. Jack Kelsey, Arsenal and Wales goalkeeper, is forced to quit at the age of 32 because of a back injury received playing for Wales against Brazil. Jack will always be remembered as a giant among goalkeepers.

22 August: Leeds alienate their fans by doubling their admission prices for the John Charles comeback match at Elland Road. They anticipate a crowd of 40,000, but only 14,000 show up. King John scores, but Leeds are beaten 4-1 by Rotherham.

23 August: Johnny Haynes is dragged from a wrecked car in Blackpool with serious knee and leg injuries. It signals the end of his distinguished England career after a run of 56 international matches, 22 of them as captain.

26 September: Arthur Rowley overtakes Jimmy McGrory's all-time British League goal-scoring record with his 411th goal. Rowley, 36-year-old player-manager of Shrewsbury, has collected his goals with Leicester City, Fulham and West Bromwich Albion. There are some sneering comments that he has scored most of his goals in the lower divisions, but goals are hard to come by no matter what the level of football and I respect his remarkable feat.

28 September: Spurs slam Nottingham Forest 9-2 at White Hart Lane. I score four against what has become my 'rabbit' team. During my career I was to notch 24 First Division goals against Forest (I don't think Cloughie would have allowed the Forest defence to be so charitable!).

29 September: Leeds United launch the League career of a 15-year-old Scottish winger called Peter Lorimer.

10 October: Allen Wade, a lecturer in physical education at Loughborough, is appointed the FA's director of coaching in succession to Walter Winterbottom. Me, I would happily see all coaches locked in a stadium and the key thrown away! Too many coaches squeeze the natural skill out of players.

24 October: Spurs pin Manchester United to the bottom of the First Division with a victory at White Hart Lane. I score a hat-trick and hit a post in the 6-2 win.

25 October: Alf Ramsey is named as England's new manager. The 40-year-old Ipswich manager will take over at the end of the year. I wonder how I'll get on with him. He likes hard workers, so I may not fit into his scheme of things.

29 October: We beat Rangers 5-2 at White Hart Lane in the second round of the European Cup-Winners' Cup, three of the goals coming from my inswinging corners from the right.

2 November: John Charles has struggled to settle back with Leeds and is sold to Roma for £65,000. I think John will always regret having left Juventus, where he was the king.

21 November: Walter Winterbottom's last match as England manager, and we give him a winning send-off with a comfortable 4-0 victory over Wales at Wembley. It gives me a lot of pleasure to score the final goal of Walter's reign. After the match we present Walter with a set of crystal-cut glasses. I shall miss him, even though I was never sure what he was talking about half the time. He is a real brain box, and the Football Association are brainless for letting him go. Many managers and coaches look up to him as their guru. He would eventually be knighted for his services to sport.

3 December: I score one goal and help create another two as the Football League beat the Italian League 3-2 at Highbury. It is one of my most satisfying games, and I now feel that the Italian affair is well and truly buried.

10 December: We finish Rangers off in the Cup-Winners' Cup with a 3-2 victory in the second leg at Ibrox. Bobby Smith scores two, and I manage to get the ball into the net after running from the halfway line with a pack of Rangers defenders snapping at my heels.

22 December: Harry Evans, 42-year-old assistant manager of Spurs, dies suddenly and plunges the club into mourning. He was a lovely cheerful man, who was the ideal foil for the more serious Bill Nicholson. Eddie Baily, a master inside-forward with the push-and-run Spurs, will become the new number two after Danny Blanchflower has a brief spell as Bill's right-hand man.

22-26 December: Snow and ice wipes out much of the Christmas football programme. It is the start of the worst spell of winter weather that I can remember, and for eight weeks our football world will be in turmoil. We play on a carpet of snow at Ipswich on Christmas Day and I give myself a present of a hat-trick of goals in the last five minutes. Alf Ramsey is saying his goodbyes at Portman Road ready to start his new job. It's nice to be able to give him a reminder that I am still hungry for England caps.

27 December: Everton sign Sheffield Wednesday's dynamo of a wing-half Tony Kay for £55,000, a British record fee for a midfield player. He will sadly make the headlines for all the wrong reasons in an earthquaking scandal that is set to rock British football to its foundations.

1963

22 January: It's brass monkey's weather, and with the snow wrecking the fixture list the Pools Promoters Association come up with the revolutionary idea of having a panel of experts deciding what the results of postponed matches would be.

28 January: Jackie Milburn, the idol of Tyneside, is named as the new Ipswich manager. Poor old Jackie's on a loser because he is inheriting an ageing team that has left its best behind.

6 February: Manchester United buy Pat Crerand from Celtic for £56,000, a record fee between English and Scottish clubs. I wonder if Pat will get a game. There has now been a total of 385 matches lost to the weather, and the season has been extended for two weeks.

27 February: Alf Ramsey's first match as England manager. France 5, England 2. *Sacré bleu!*

It was my privilege and pleasure to play with and against some of the finest footballers who have ever trodden the turf. This is the legendary Russian goalkeeper Lev Yashin *(above),* saving at my feet during the FA Centenary match at Wembley in 1963, and here *(left)* is the one and only Garrincha, giving the Brazilian samba treatment to England's greatest-ever left-back, Ray Wilson during the 1962 World Cup quarter-final, won 3-1 by Brazil.

5 March: Slovan Bratislava 2, Spurs 0 in the first leg of the Cup-Winners' Cup quarter-finals. As we come off the pitch at the end of a rough, tough battle, big Bobby Smith decides to start the pyschological war for the return. He gives an 'I'll have you at home' message with sign language to the centre-half who has given him a bit of a kicking. Bobby then puts a clenched fist under the goalkeeper's nose and says with a heavy northern accent: 'Londres...Londres...you'll get yours in Londres'. It may have lost something in its translation, but the message was not lost on the goalkeeper who literally turned white. This is in the days when goalkeepers are not an over-protected species, and I would not like to be in his boots when the 14-stone Smithy comes charging at him in the second leg.

6 March: Burnley sell Jimmy McIlroy to Stoke City for £30,000. At 32 he will be a young whippersnapper in an attack featuring the skills of 48-year-old Stanley Matthews.

9 March: For the first time since 8 December a complete Saturday League programme is possible. I can now take my long johns off. Tommy Cummings becomes Mansfield player-manager, and is succeeded as PFA chairman by Leyton Orient and former West Ham winger Malcolm Musgrove.

14 March: Spurs 6, Slovan Bratislava 0. The goalkeeper knows what is coming, and Bobby Smith does not disappoint him. He charges the petrified Czech into the back of the net in the first minute, and the poor bloke loses all his appetite for the game. We knock six past him because he is too busy looking for Smithy to worry about the ball.

6 April: Alf Ramsey's second match as England manager. England 1, Scotland 2. Och, mon, it's a terrible day to be an Englishman at Wembley.

15 April: Spurs top 100 League goals for the season with a 7-2 hammering of Liverpool at White Hart Lane, and I score four of them. Even Bill Shankly is speechless!

24 April: I am sent off for the one and only time in my career as a League club footballer. It is the first leg of the European Cup-Winners' Cup semi-final against OFK Belgrade in Yugoslavia. I retaliate with a punch that misses after their centre-half has taken a swing at me. The Hungarian referee sees the whole incident but chooses to pick on me. And with 70,000 Yugoslavs yelling blue murder who can blame him. The crowd are going mad, throwing bottles and abuse, as the referee points me in the direction of the dressing-room. Cliffie Jones, who has been sitting on the touchline bench, escorts me off the pitch with a protective arm around my shoulders. 'Come on, Jimbo,' he says, his eyes shining with excitement. 'I'll see you're all right, boyo. Let 'em come at us. We can take 'em.' Cliffie's Welsh blood is boiling and he's enjoying every second of it. Me, I'm frightened stiff. But we have the last laugh with a 2-1 victory. I will miss the second leg at White Hart Lane on 1 May, but we will storm through to the final with a 3-1 win.

8 May: The Battle of Hampden Park. Referee Jim Finney abandons a brawl between Scotland and Austria after 79 minutes. The Scots are leading 4-1, and the Austrians have had two players ordered off when Finney – one of the greatest of all referees – decides that the kicking has to stop. It's peaceful at Wembley where England and Brazil draw 1-1. Bryan Douglas scrambles a late equaliser after Pepe has beaten Gordon Banks with one of his famed and feared banana free-kicks. Alf Ramsey is still waiting for his first victory. He is furious over the Brazilian goal and tells Gordon: 'Don't say I didn't warn you exactly what Pepe would do. You fell for the three-card trick'. Out of Alf's hearing, Gordon says: 'The ball moved twice as violently as I had been led to believe. There is not a goalkeeper in the world who could have saved it'. We are learning that Alf is a perfectionist.

9 May: Stanley Matthews is named Footballer of the Year after scoring the goal that clinches Stoke City's promotion back to the First Division. It is a romantic story, but I feel that only one player deserves the award this year: Dave Mackay, who has been in barnstorming form for Spurs all season. And surely one of the Everton players who helped take the championship to Goodison deserves the award ahead of the old maestro, who has already been given the honour once?

15 May: Spurs win the European Cup-Winners' Cup. Amazingly, we manage it without the great Mackay. One man does not make a team, but Dave is worth two players to us.

25 May: Manchester United win the late-late FA Cup final at the end of the Ice Age season. United have come in out of the cold, and will light up the 'sixties with the sunshine of their style.

29 May: Czechoslovakia 2, England 4. Alf Ramsey's first victory as manager. Bobby Charlton and Bobby Smith score one apiece, and I collect a couple of goals. Chelsea right-back Ken Shellito, one of my best mates from my schoolboy footballing days, makes his international debut and looks a natural. But he is to be cruelly cut down at the peak of his career by a knee injury. Terry Paine, the Southampton winger, also makes his international bow against the Czechs and plays with pace and poise. The Czechs were runners-up in the World Cup finals only a year ago, and in midfield they have European Footballer of the Year Joséf Masopust. This is one of the most impressive performances by any England team on foreign soil. Even Alf has got a smile on his face.

2 June: I go down with tonsilitis and miss the match against East Germany in Leipzig. The lads do us proud, pulling back from a goal down to win 2-1 with goals from Roger Hunt and Bobby Charlton. Alf's smile is even broader. Alan Bass, the team doctor, tells me that they are going to have to leave me behind in East Germany while the rest of the party travel on to Switzerland. I plead to leave with them, even if it's on a stretcher. Believe me, East Germany is the pits. Doc Bass lets me sweat it out for an hour before I realise it's all a leg pull. He doses me up and for once in my life I am happy to be on a 'plane as we fly out of Leipzig. I have a laugh on Doc Bass, a lovely bloke, because on the bumpy flight back through the Berlin air corridor he turns green and becomes air sick. 'Get a doctor for the doctor', I shout. Doc Bass is not amused.

5 June: Switzerland 1, England 8, and I can't get my name on the scoresheet. Bobby Charlton scores a hat-trick and Budgie Byrne knocks in two. Alf is still smiling.

THE CHAMPIONS OF
1962-63

FIRST DIVISION:

1: Everton (61 points)

2: Tottenham Hotspur (55)

3: Burnley (54)

Championship squad:

Bingham (23 appearances), Dunlop (4), Gabriel (40), Harris (24), Heslop (1), Kay (19), Labone (40), Meagan (32), Morrissey (28), Parker (33), Scott (17), Sharples (2), Stevens (42), Temple (5), Thomson (19), Veall (11), Vernon (41), West (38), Wignall (1), Young (42).

Goalscorers: Vernon (24), Young (22), Morrissey (7), Stevens (7), Bingham (6), Gabriel (5), Scott (4), Parker (2), Harris (1), Kay (1), Veall (1), Wignall (1).

SECOND DIVISION:

1: Stoke City (53 points)

2: Chelsea (52)

3: Sunderland (52)

Championship squad:

Allen (41 appearances), Andrew (2), Asprey (42), Bebbington (19), Bridgwood (4), Clamp (32), Howitt (10), G. Matthews (3), S. Matthews (32), McIlroy (18), Mudie (40), Nibloe (1), O'Neill (42), Philpott (1), Ratcliffe (42), Ritchie (3), Skeels (38), Stuart (40), Thompson (5), Viollet (37), Ward (9), Wilson (1).

Goalscorers: Viollet (23), Mudie (20), McIlroy (6), Asprey (5), Ratcliffe (5), Skeels (4), Bebbington (4), Stuart (2), S. Matthews (1), G. Matthews (1), Thompson (1), 1 own goal.

THIRD DIVISION:

1: Northampton Town (62 points)

2: Swindon Town (58)

3: Port Vale (54)

Championship squad:

Ashworth (30 appearances), Branston (45), Brodie (46), Carr (1), Cockcroft (8), Etheridge (2), Everitt (28), Foley (43), Hails (25), Holton (21), Kurila (40), Large (20), Leek (42), Lines (46), Llewellyn (1), Martin (1), Mills (19), Reid (41), Robson (1), Sanders (15), Smith (14), Woollard (15).

Goalscorers: Ashworth (25), Large (18), Lines (16), Holton (14), Reid (11), Hails (5), Leck (5), Smith (4), Sanders (2), Everitt (1), Kurila (1), Mills (1), Foley (1), 5 own goals.

FOURTH DIVISION:

1: Brentford (62 points)

2: Oldham Athletic (59)

3: Crewe Alexandra (59)

Championship squad:

Anthony (33 appearances), Block (42), Brooks (39), Cakebread (28), Coote (46), Crowe (39), Dargie (3), Dick (38), Edgley (4), Fielding (7), Gelson (29), Gitsham (16), Hales (4), Hawley (2), Higginson (46), McAdams (34), McLeod (46), Rycraft (18), Scott (17), Summers (15).

Goalscorers: Dick (23), Brooks (22), McAdams (22), Block (8), Summers (6), McLeod (4), Fielding (3), Hales (2), Anthony (1), Edgley (1), Higginson (1), Scott (1), 4 own goals.

SCOTTISH FIRST DIVISION:

1: Rangers (57 points)
2: Kilmarnock (48)
3: Partick Thistle (46)

Championship squad:

Shearer (34 appearances), Ritchie (33), Baxter (32), Brand (32), McKinnon (32), Wilson (32), Millar (34), Greig (27), Henderson (27), Caldow (20), Davis (16), Provan (12), McMillan (12), McLean (9), Baillie (6), Watson (6), Forrest (4), Scott (4), Willoughby (3), Hunter (1), Martin (1). **Goalscorers:** Millar (27), Wilson (28), Brand (19), Greig (5), Henderson (5), Baxter (4), Davis (2), Willoughby (2), McLean (2), McMillan (1), Scott (1), 3 own goals.

SCOTTISH SECOND DIVISION:

1: St Johnstone (55 points)
2: East Stirling (49)
3: Morton (48)

FA CUP FINAL:

Manchester United 3 (Law, Herd 2)
Gaskell, Dunne, Cantwell, Crerand, Foulkes, Setters, Giles, Quixall, Herd, Law, Charlton.
Leicester City 1 (Keyworth)
Banks, Sjoberg, Norman, McLintock, King, Appleton, Riley, Cross, Keyworth, Gibson, Stringfellow.

LEAGUE CUP FINAL:

First leg:
Birmingham City 3 (Leek 2, Bloomfield)
Schofield, Lynn, Green, Hennessey, Smith, Beard, Hellawell, Bloomfield, Harris, Leek, Auld.
Aston Villa 1 (Thomson)
Sims, Fraser, Aitken, Crowe, Sleeuwenhoek, Lee, Baker, Graham, Thomson, Wylie, Burrows.
Second leg:
Aston Villa 0
Sims, Fraser, Aitken, Crowe, Sleeuwenhoek, Lee, Baker, Graham, Thomson, Wylie, Burrows.

Birmingham City 0
Schofield, Lynn, Green, Hennessey, Smith, Beard, Hellawell, Bloomfield, Harris, Leek, Auld.
Birmingham City win 3-1 on aggregate.

SCOTTISH FA CUP FINAL:

Rangers 3 (Wilson, Brand 2)
Ritchie, Shearer, Provan, Greig, McKinnon, Baxter, Henderson, McMillan, Millar, Brand, Wilson.
Celtic 0
Haffey, McKay, Kennedy, McNamee, McNeill, Price, Craig, Murdoch, Divers, Chalmers, Hughes.
Replay after 1-1 draw.

SCOTTISH LEAGUE CUP FINAL:

Hearts 1 (Davidson)
Marshall, Polland, Hope, Cumming, Barry, Higgins, Wallace, Paton, Davidson, Hamilton (W), Hamilton (J).
Kilmarnock 0
McLaughlin, Richmond, Watson, O'Connor, McGrory, Beattie, Brown, Black, Kerr, McInally, McIlroy.

EUROPEAN CUP FINAL:

Played at Wembley
AC Milan 2 (Altafini 2)
Ghezzi, David, Trebbi, Benitez, Maldini, Trapattoni, Pivatelli, Sani, Altafini, Rivera, Mora.
Benfica 1 (Eusebio)
Costa Pereira, Cavem, Cruz, Humberto, Raul, Coluna, Augusto, Santana, Torres, Eusebio, Simoes.

EUROPEAN CUP-WINNERS' CUP FINAL:

Played in Rotterdam
Tottenham 5 (Greaves 2, White, Dyson 2)
Brown, Baker, Henry, Blanchflower, Norman, Marchi, Jones, White, Smith, Greaves, Dyson.
Atletico Madrid 1 (Collar pen.)
Madinabeytia, RivillaRodrigues, Ramiro, Griffa, Glaria, Jones, Adelardo, Chuzo, Medonca, Collar.

EUROPEAN FAIRS CUP FINAL:

First leg:

Dynamo Zagreb 1 *(Zambata)*

Skoric, Belin, Braun, Biscam, Markovic, Perusic, Kobsnac, Zambata, Knez, Matus, Lamza.

Valencia 2 *(Waldo, Urtiaga)*

Zamora, Piquer, Chicao, Paquito, Quinocis, Sastre, Mano, Sanchez-Lage, Waldo, Ribelles, Urtiaga.

Second leg:

Valencia 2 *(Mano, Nunez)*

Zamora, Piquer, Chicao, Paquito, Quinocis, Sastre, Mano, Sanchez-Lage, Waldo, Ribelles, Nunez.

Dynamo Zagreb 0

Skoric, Belin, Braun, Raus, Markovic, Perusic, Kobsnac, Zambata, Knez, Matus, Lamza.

Valencia win 4-1 on aggregate.

Top Football League goalscorers:

Jimmy Greaves (Tottenham Hotspur)	37
Bobby Tambling (Chelsea)	36
KenWagstaff (Mansfield Town)	34
Colin Booth (Doncaster Rovers)	32
Roy Chapman (Mansfield Town)	31
Alan Peacock (Middlesbrough)	31
Joe Baker (Arsenal)	29
David Layne (Sheffield Wednesday)	29
Bert Lister (Oldham Athletic)	29
Frank Lord (Crewe Alexandra)	29
Dai Ward (Watford)	29

Top Scottish First Division marksman:

Jimmy Millar (Rangers) 27 goals

Highest average League attendance:

Everton (51,460)

Footballer of the Year:

Stanley Matthews (Blackpool)

European Footballer of the Year:

Lev Yashin (Moscow Dynamo)

World Club Championship:

Santos beat AC Milan 2-4, 4-2, 1-0

1963-64: HEARTBREAK SEASON

The 1963-64 season dawned with no hint that it was to see the break-up of the 'Super Spurs'. The heart would be ripped out of our team in a painful and tragic way, and a black cloud of despondency would envelop the club.

Our nightmare was slow and drawn out. It started on the evening of 10 December at Old Trafford when we were playing Manchester United in the second leg of a European Cup-Winners' Cup tie. Dave Mackay broke a leg in a collision with Noel Cantwell that would surely leave the United skipper losing sleep about the validity of his challenge.

Soon after, Danny Blanchflower was forced to retire because of a recurring knee injury. We had lost the brains of the team and the heart of the team, and worse was to follow at the end of the season. John White, the eyes of the team, was sitting under a tree sheltering from a storm on a North London golf course when he was tragically killed by lightning. We had lost the three most vital cogs in our machine.

Bill Nicholson got busy in the transfer market and bought Alan Mullery from Fulham, Laurie Brown from Arsenal, Cyril Knowles from Middlesbrough, Pat Jennings from Watford, Jimmy Robertson from St Mirren and Alan Gilzean from Dundee. He took a breather and then went shopping again, this time buying Mike England from Blackburn and Terry Venables from Chelsea.

Nick was trying to build another 'Super Spurs'. He never quite made it. The new Tottenham team had some memorable moments together in the mid-'sixties, but we never touched the peak performances of the Blanchflower-White-Mackay era.

I personally was sick when Nicholson failed in a bid to bring Johnny Haynes – recovered from his car-smash injuries – to White Hart Lane as John White's successor. The Blanchflower-White roles went to Alan Mullery and Terry Venables, and to be honest I was never really comfortable or content playing with either of them. It was not their fault, but I had become accustomed to the pace set by Danny and Dave and I struggled to adapt to their style of delivery. Both were given a tough time by the Spurs supporters, who – like me – had been spoiled over the years, and they unkindly yet understandably kept comparing them with their great idols. Venables was not always happy playing at Tottenham after his success as the midfield boss at Chelsea, and when he eventually moved on to Queen's Park Rangers he would not have taken any bets that one day he would return to White Hart Lane and buy the club! Yes, it's a funny old game.

It would come as no surprise to me when both Venners and Mullers went into management. Both were keen students of the game and, although neither of them actually said anything to me, I sensed they would have liked me to have been more conventional and conformist in my approach to football. I liked them both and thought they talked a lot of sense about the game, but I had always closed my ears to too much tactical theory. I thought that a lot of the individual flair and freedom of expression had been coached out of players, and I was determined not to let anybody stifle my game. I liked playing it off the cuff.

A player who shared my outlook was Alan Gilzean, the Scottish artist who was brought in from Dundee as my new playing partner after we had got this sad season out of our system. Gilly was a joy to play with, and I felt that he was never given sufficient credit for his delicate touch play and finishing finesse in the penalty area. He was a master of the flick header, and could bamboozle defences with deceptive changes of pace and clever ball control.

Missing the command of Blanchflower and the drive of Mackay, the 1963-64 season was relatively barren for Spurs after three years of non-stop success. We still managed to finish fourth in the League championship in a season that would be remembered for the start of the 'Red Revolution'...

THE LEAGUE CHAMPIONS

Liverpool clinched their first League title under the mesmeric Bill Shankly with a crushing 5-0 victory over Arsenal at Anfield in the last game of the season. It started a Mersey monopoly that was to spread across three decades.

It was the devastating double act of Ian St John and Roger Hunt that sent Liverpool charging to the championship. The Saint, the idol of the Kop, was the pilot of the Anfield machine. He was a superb touch player and a centre-forward who could dismantle defences by a mixture of intelligent positioning and powerful finishing. I would have loved to have played alongside him (years later I would have to be satisfied with sitting alongside him). Roger Hunt, strong, willing and a deadly finisher, was the hammer of the attack and scored goals with stunning consistency. He was a rival of mine for a place in the England attack, but we had an enormous respect for each other and never let our rivalry spill over into bitterness. Alf Arrowsmith plundered alongside Hunt, but Shanks was already planning changes to the formation to make way for a rugged youngster called Tommy Smith. Ouch!

Smith would wear a decoy No. 10 shirt, but would be detailed to a defensive, ball-winning role in midfield. It was a job he would do with ruthless efficiency and he would develop into one of the greatest of all anchormen and a hero of the Kop.

Dave Mackay *(left)* and John White, the heart and eyes of the Tottenham team. John was tragically struck down in his prime when hit by lightning on a golf course, and Dave showed his great fighting qualities by battling back to play at peak form after twice breaking a leg. Both have a special place in my personal hall of fame.

Out on the right wing, before his successful switch to midfield, was Ian Callaghan, a quick and clever player who tricked his way past markers and then created scoring chances with accurate centres. Out on the left, Peter Thompson was a destroyer of defences with mazy runs that were unpredictable but productive. He was an old-style dribbler, but performed at sprint speed rather than in the Stanley Matthews shuffling style.

Gordon Milne and Willie Stevenson, both inventive and imaginative players, were the wing-halves during the early Liverpool sweep of success. They combined determined defensive play with subtle support to the attack. Balding Jimmy Melia was the conductor, feeding the forwards with cunningly placed passes. Geoff Strong, bought from Arsenal for £40,000 as a goalscorer, would eventually be converted into a successful right-half when Melia moved on to Wolves. This was when Smith, the Liverpool iron man, was called in to bolster the midfield.

The defence was tight to the point of being miserly, dominating matches with a combination of skill and strength. Tommy Lawrence, nicknamed 'The Flying Pig' by the Kopites, took over from Jim Furnell in goal, and was always safe and sound and at times spectacular as he came racing off his line to act as a 'sweeper' at the back of the defence. In front of him like a man mountain stood the giant Ron Yeats, an inspiring captain and commanding centre-half around whom Shanks built his Liverpool resistance movement. Gerry Byrne and Ronnie Moran were skilful and effective full-backs, with the cultured Chris Lawler taking over from Moran in 1964.

While it was the players who took the eye, it was Shanks who claimed the ear. He had a Chuchillian gift for motivating men. He could be hard, humorous, stern, soothing, ruthless, responsive and, above all, demanding. All this in the space of a ten-minute prematch team talk during which he inspired his players to go beyond the call of duty. He was totally devoted and dedicated to football in general and Liverpool Football Club in particular, and he injected everybody who played for him with this mood. He said: 'Whoever said that football was a matter of life and death has got it wrong. It's much more important than that'. This captured his fanatical approach to the game.

In his playing days Shanks was a driving wing-half with Carlisle, Preston and Scotland before serving his managerial apprenticeship with Carlisle, Grimsby, Workington and Huddersfield. But it was at Liverpool that he became larger than life and inspired one Kopite to carry a huge banner to every match that read: 'Some say God ... we say Shankly'. Shanks would never have to walk alone.

> 'Everybody is proud to play for Liverpool Football Club. Pride. That's our secret. We will settle only for the best. It is what our supporters deserve because they are the best in the world. No player dare put on the Liverpool shirt in front of them and give anything less than 100 per cent. That would be unforgivable. Unforgivable.' – **Bill Shankly.**

A MATCH TO REMEMBER

Which of the hundreds of matches touched with the magic of Pele – Brazil's superman for all seasons – should we feature in this walk down memory lane into the 'sixties? It is like trying to choose the best of Beethoven or the greatest work of Van Gogh. The Aladdin's Cave of choices is made easier because I was fortunate to witness from close range his first ever performance against England during a prestige international tournament in Brazil in the summer of 1964. Even by Pele's sky-scraping standards it was an exhibition of exceptional brilliance.

Brazil were the current world champions and in opponents England they were facing the team that would take over their crown in 1966. Manager Alf Ramsey was still searching for his World Cup players and formation. Only four of the players selected for this match against Brazil in Rio would survive for the World Cup final at Wembley Stadium two years later – full-backs George Cohen and Ray Wilson, skipper Bobby Moore and Manchester United goal hunter Bobby Charlton, who had yet to make the transition to a scheming role. I was surprised that for such a crucial contest, Alf decided to leave regular first-choice goalkeeper Gordon Banks on the sidelines and to call in debutant Tony Waiters, who was a lifeguard on Blackpool beach when not keeping goal for the local club. Brazil relied on a mixture of the old and the new. Goalkeeper Gylmar and gifted striker Vava were survivors of the 1958 and 1962 World Cup winning squads, along with the incomparable Pele, and among the newcomers were full-backs Carlos Alberto and Brito, and a gazelle of a forward called Gerson, all of whom would write their names into World Cup history in the 1970 finals. This was how we lined up:

Brazil: Gylmar, Carlos Alberto, Brito, Diaz, Joel, Rildo, Julinho, Gerson, Vava, Pele, Rinaldo.

England: Waiters, Cohen, Wilson, Milne, Norman, Moore, Thompson, Greaves, Byrne, Eastham, Charlton.

Alf Ramsey decided not to give any detailed marking instructions for Pele. 'Whoever is closest to him at set pieces can take responsibility for him', Alf told us in a team meeting before the kick-off. 'Let's try to stop the ball getting through to him and if it does whichever defender is nearest must pick him up.' There was plenty of time for tactical talking because Brazil arrived at the ground an hour late with a fuming Ramsey about to call the match off. He saw it as a deliberate ploy to unsettle the England players before we had to go out in front of 100,000 frenzied fans who were filling the night air with rockets and firecrackers.

Ramsey's plan of virtually ignoring Pele seemed to work in the first half, during which centre-forward Johnny Byrne had a shot cleared off the goal-line and I was just a coat of paint off target with a shot on the turn. At half-time only a goal by left-winger Rinaldo separated us, but the fact that it had been created by a run from Pele in which he glided past four tackles was a warning of what was to come.

We had sudden brief hope of taking command when I stole a goal from close range midway through the second half, but then Pele took over. He pulverised us with a purple patch that produced three goals in five minutes. Twice he earned free-kicks just outside the penalty area while dancing through the England defence, juggling the ball like a circus performer. Poor old Waiters was completely deceived by swerving free-kicks that brought spectacular goals from wingers Rinaldo and Julinho. Pele also contributed a magical goal of his own, pushing the ball through the legs of first Bobby Moore and then Maurice Norman before sending a shot screaming into the England net from 25 yards. Suddenly a scoreline that had read a healthy 1-1 was now a Pele-inspired 4-1. Yet the master was not finished. He ran our defence into such a state of confusion that they failed to spot Diaz coming through from a deep position to score goal number five two minutes from the end.

Edson Arantes do Nascimento – the one and only Pele – was born in near poverty in Três Corações (Three Hearts), Bauru, on 23 October, 1940. He had come under the influence of former Brazilian World Cup player Waldemar de Brito while playing for his local team, Noroeste. De Brito had recommended him to Santos, where he quickly emerged as an international star, making his debut for Brazil at the age of 16 and getting world acclaim the following season for his magnificent performances in the 1958 World Cup finals.

Wearing the No. 10 shirt that was to become his trademark, Pele averaged 94 goals a season in his first three years with Santos and rival coaches tried to mark him out of games by putting as many as four defenders on him. Santos, using Pele as their calling card, toured the world playing exhibition matches.

His World Cup record is second to none. He is the only player to have been a member of three World Cup-winning teams (1958,1962 and 1970), although he missed the final stages of the 1962 tournament because of a pulled muscle. His total World Cup appearances, including his two matches in 1966, were 14, and he scored in the 1958 and 1970 finals. He was to be brutally hacked out of the 1966 tournament, the victim of the sort of vicious tackling that he'd had to contend with throughout his career.

Although usually a sporting opponent, he had a touchpaper temperament if defenders deliberately fouled him and there were several times in his career when he was guilty of retaliating against players of lesser ability who tried to literally chop him down to size. The worst demonstration of Pele's ugly temper came in Brazil's second match of the 1964 tournament after the 5-1 victory over England. And we England players got too close a look at it. Brazil were playing arch rivals Argentina in Rio, and we were assigned to touchline benches just two yards from the pitch and eight yards from the fenced-in capacity crowd. It was far too close for comfort. Right from the first whistle defender Messiano made it clear that his one intention was to stop Pele from playing. He kicked him, tripped him, spat at him, wrestled him to the floor and pulled his shirt any time he seemed likely to get past. Finally, after about 30 minutes of this almost criminal assault, Pele completely lost his temper. He took a running jump at Messiano and butted him full in the face. The Argentinian was carried off with a broken nose and, incredibly, the Swiss referee – fearing a violent crowd reaction – let Pele play on. I have never seen anything like it.

But Pele was usually a perfect sportsman. He scored 1,216 goals in 1,254 matches from 1956 until his retirement in 1974. His peak year for goals was 1958, when he scored 139 times. In 1975 he was to make a comeback with New York Cosmos, kicking soccer in the United States into life. He made a farewell appearance against Santos in New Jersey on 1 October, 1977. It was his 1,363rd match and he naturally marked it with a goal to bring his career total to 1,281. In a word, Pele was a genius. I was sure he could have been a world-class gymnast. He had wonderful spring, perfect balance, could shoot with either foot, was as brave as a lion and had tremendous vision. We held the Brazilians for an hour in the match in Rio and were just beginning to think in terms of trying to win the game when Pele ran riot. He sold our defence more dummies than Mothercare and won the match on his own.

'What people have never realised about Pele is the speed of the man. He Had unbelievable skill that we could all see, but it was only when you were chasing him that you realised that he could motor like an Olympic sprinter. I was running back after him when he was on a run through the England defence and it was all I could do to keep pace with him – and he had the ball at his feet. He had left two of our defenders standing and then fired a right-footed shot while in full stride. The ball whistled into the net from 25 yards, and as it left him Pele shouted, 'G-o-a-l'. He was as enthusiastic about his football as a young kid. I felt it a privilege to be on the same pitch.' – **Johnny Byrne**.

THE FA CUP WINNERS

West Ham United's contribution to football in the 'sixties stretched far beyond the boundaries of the domestic scene. They won the FA Cup and the European Cup-Winners' Cup with stylish soccer that was tactically a decade ahead of its time. The three main motivators, Bobby Moore, Geoff Hurst and Martin Peters, would knit West Ham-designed moves into the England playing pattern and would be influential in the 1966 World Cup victory. There have been more successful and resilient sides but rarely one as attractive and entertaining.

In the 1964 FA Cup final at Wembley they were given a thorough examination of their class and staying power by a Second Division Preston team that played football right out of the top drawer. Neutral fans would have felt great sympathy for Preston, who were level or in front for all but the last 90 seconds of the match. West Ham's victory provided the foundation for greater triumphs that lay ahead.

There were sneers that West Ham manager Ron Greenwood inherited so much young talent when he took over at Upton Park in 1961 that he could not have failed to capture major honours. But Greenwood, a master of soccer strategy, had the vision and the perception to mould and shape the team into a winning unit. He spotted the true potential of Geoff Hurst, for instance, and converted him from an ordinary wing-half into a world-class striker. Ron was a man of high principle who stood for all that was good and proper about football, and even when West Ham started to slide as other less talented teams concentrated on kicking their way to success, he continued to preach that the game should be played with style, panache and sportsmanship.

Bobby Moore was the kingpin of the West Ham defence, which was sometimes suspect under pressure. Bobby, in my view the greatest defender ever to pull on an England shirt, was a superb reader of situations alongside the strong and reliable Ken Brown at centre-half. Jim Standen was an agile goalkeeper, and at full-back the flamboyant John Bond was partnered by the stylish Jack Burkett.

Ronnie Boyce was the heart of the Hammers in midfield. He was nicknamed 'Ticker' because his non-stop running and precise passing made the team tick. An unobtrusive player, he was always to be found where the action was – rarely taking the eye of the spectators, but his team-mates always knew he was exactly where he was most needed. Eddie Bovington played the role of anchorman, winning the ball and then distributing it with sensible rather than spectacular passes. He was keeping a youngster called Martin Peters on the sidelines.

Johnny Byrne, creative and with a nose for goals, was the perfect partner for the more positive Hurst in the middle of the West Ham attack, with Peter Brabrook and John Sissons providing width as orthodox wingers who could deliver pin-pointed centres. Sissons was just 18, and would have been the youngest ever Wembley finalist but for the fact that his England youth team-mate Howard Kendall was on the other side,

Howard Kendall, 17-year-old Preston protégé, looks on helplessly *(left, above)* as West Ham celebrate an equaliser by Geoff Hurst in the 1964 FA Cup final. Ronnie Boyce *(right, below)* scored a late winner for the Hammers, and skipper Bobby Moore collected the FA Cup for the first leg of a unique treble. In the next two years he was to climb the famous Wembley steps to collect, first, the European Cup-Winners' Cup and then, the peak prize, the World Cup.

playing for Preston, and was still only 17.

'Kid' Kendall was at left-half in a Preston team that had a balanced mixture of youth and experience. Their forward line of David Wilson, Alec Ashworth, Alex Dawson, Alan Spavin and Doug Holden had been impressive all season, and they had narrowly missed promotion to the First Division after being pipped for second place by Sunderland. Dawson, a powerful, no-nonsense centre-forward out of the old school, had learned his trade with Manchester United, along with driving right-half Nobby Lawton.

Alan Kelly was on his way to a club appearances record in the Preston goal, and full backs George Ross, Jim Smith and centre-half Tony Singleton completed a sound defence.

Preston got off to a flying start with a goal after nine minutes. Holden slid the ball into the net after goalkeeper Jim Standen failed to hold a low shot from the bulldozing Dawson. West Ham hit back with an instant equaliser a minute later when an angled shot from Sissons out on the left made him the youngest scorer in an FA Cup final at Wembley.

It was Preston who were looking more a First Division team than West Ham, and five minutes before half-time Dawson hurled himself forward to head in a Wilson corner.

There was more than a touch of good fortune about West Ham's second equaliser seven minutes into the second half. Hurst got his head to a corner from Peter Brabrook on the right, and the ball had just enough power behind it to roll over the line after hitting both the crossbar and goalkeeper Alan Kelly. Geoff would get another lucky bounce off that crossbar a couple of years later!

It was only after the Hurst goal that West Ham started to unfurl the classic football for which they were to become famous in the 'sixties, but the proud Preston defence refused to buckle. Just as it seemed as if it would take extra-time to break the deadlock old twinkle-toes Brabrook, a good pal of mine from schoolboy days, made a darting run down the right and Boyce came through the middle like a train to head in his lofted centre. This winning goal came two minutes into injury-time. Most neutrals thought that poor Preston deserved at least the reward of a replay.

'I had only netted six goals in the League that season, and manager Ron Greenwood kept encouraging me to come through from midfield to get into scoring positions. It was like a dream come true to score the winning goal in a Wembley Cup final, and I think I would have run all the way out of the stadium if my team-mates had not caught up with me!' – **Ronnie Boyce**.

CHAMPIONS OF EUROPE

The European Cup stayed in Milan – passing from AC Milan to their great rivals Internazionale, who shared the same San Siro Stadium. Inter were under the intoxicating influence of Helenio Herrera, an imaginative, dogmatic and excitable coach from Argentina via France, Casablanca and Spain, where he had been a reasonably good player before switching with great success to coaching.

When he first arrived at Inter from Barcelona in 1960 Herrera was keen to build an attacking team, but his principles were broken on the back of the defensive football that was polluting the Italian game. Helenio decided he could not beat the system, and so he joined it and with a determination to do it better than anybody in history. I was flirting briefly with Italian football with AC Milan while he was getting his defensive formation off the launching pad, and it was one of the reasons I wanted to get out of Italy as fast as possible.

He introduced a stifling style known as *catenaccio,* hiding the Inter goal behind a wall of defenders and relying on just two forwards to feed off the creative work of Luis Suarez, a genius of an attacking midfield player who had followed him to Milan from Barcelona.

The Herrera system made football dull to watch and frustrating to play. It turned defenders into robots, but it could not be denied that it brought results. Herrera had brought together a squad of exceptional players who had the skill to put his theories into practice. There has rarely been a more gifted left-back than Giacinto Facchetti or a sweeper with the composure and control of skipper Armando Picchi. Mario Corso and the Brazilian Jair da Costa were both quick and clever, and in Sandrino Mazzola Inter had a quality player with a thoroughbred pedigree. His father, Valentino Mazzola, had been the most famous of the Torino team wiped out by an aircrash in 1949 when Sandrino was just a lad.

Inter had their toughest time on their way to the final in the preliminary round. They were held to a goalless draw by Everton at Goodison, and then squeezed a 1-0 win in Milan thanks to a freak goal from a mis-hit centre by Jair.

The black-and-blue stripes on the Inter shirts looked like prison bars to forwards as they broke their hearts against a massed defence, and French champions Monaco, Yugoslav champions Partizan Belgrade and Borussia Dortmund were eliminated on the way to the final in Vienna, where the Italian misers were to meet the old masters, Real Madrid.

Di Stefano, Puskas and Gento were now slowed-down veterans, but they had dug back into their memories to produce a vintage display in the quarter-finals when beating holders AC Milan 4-1 in the first leg in Spain. Milan won 2-0 in the San Siro Stadium, but could not pull back the deficit.

Inter's double-parked defence put a stranglehold on the Real attack in the final, and the match became a midfield muddle. It took a sniper shot from Mazzola to break the deadlock two minutes before half-time. Two defensive errors let Milani and Mazzola in for Inter goals in the second half, sandwiching a headed goal by Felo. The final score-line of 3-1 flattered Inter-Milan, who had been in a negative mood for much of the match.

'We came to Vienna with a plan, and we carried it out to perfection. I cannot understand the criticism of our tactics. There is an art in defensive football, particularly when you can use it to launch swift and incisive counter attacks like we have throughout the European Cup competition.'– **Helenio Herrera**.

THE EUROPEAN CUP-WINNERS' CUP

Tottenham's chances of retaining the European Cup-Win-ners' Cup disappeared with Dave Mackay, who was stretchered off with a broken leg in the return match of our first round tie with Manchester United at Old Traf-ford. Our hearts went off with him, and United powered on to a 4-1 victory to wipe out the 2-0 advantage we had held from the first leg at White Hart Lane. David Herd and Bobby Charlton each scored two goals.

United looked destined for the semi-finals when they hammered Sporting Lisbon 4-0 at Old Trafford, with Denis Law scoring a hat-trick which included two penalties. Denis had also netted a hat-trick in the first round tie against Dutch team Willem II. Amazingly, United lost 5-1 in the second leg of their quarter-final against Sporting Lisbon in Portu-gal. Perhaps United should have taken more notice of a result in the previous round: Sporting had beaten Apoel Nicosia 16-1 in their home leg.

Celtic suffered a similar shock to Manchester United in the semi-final. They had beaten MTK Budapest 3-0 in the first leg in Glasgow, when a Jimmy Johnstone goal and two from Steve Chalmers had seemed to have put them into an unassailable lead. But they crashed 4-0 in Hungary, where the MTK fans had so little faith in their team's ability to survive that only 10,000 turned out to support them. Sporting Lisbon needed a replay before they conquered Olympic Lyon 1-0 on neutral territory in Madrid.

The final also went to a replay after a 3-3 draw in Brussels. Sporting Lisbon won by the only goal of the match in Antwerp when Morais scored with an inswinging corner from the left.

In the European Fairs Cup, Valencia came agonisingly close to completing a hat-trick of victories. For the first time it was to be a one-match final, and once again it was an all-Spanish affair. Valencia faced Real Zaragoza in Barcelona and the holders were beaten by a second-half goal from centre-forward Marcelino after an even first half during which Villa scored for Zaragoza and Urtiaga for Valencia.

It was a miserable Fairs Cup for British challengers. Hearts had gone out to Lausanne in the first round after a play-off, and Arsenal, Sheffield Wednesday and Partick Thistle had all fallen at the second-round hurdle.

GREAVSIE'S FOOTBALL DIARY
1963-64

1963

9 August: John Charles, the Gentle Giant, returns to the land of his fathers. Cardiff sign him from Roma for £20,000.

14 August: Liverpool buy Peter Thompson from Preston for £40,000. The ball-playing left winger is to become an important piece in the Bill Shankly jigsaw.

23 August: Arsenal shell out £62,500 for Dundee and Scotland international centre-half Ian Ure. It's a British record fee for a half-back.

29 August: Johnny Giles joins Leeds United from Manchester United for £32,000 three months after he collected an FA Cup-winners' medal at Wembley. There are a lot more medals to come his way.

31 August: A First Division hat-trick for Spurs against my 'rabbit' team Nottingham Forest.

4 September: Norwich City sign Luton Town centre-forward Ron Davies for £35,000. I cannot understand why a major club has not jumped in for the Welsh international centre-forward.

30 September: Chelsea chairman Joe Mears is elected chairman of the Football Association. I like and respect Joe, and I hope he wakes up the old duffers at Lancaster Gate.

1 October: A First Division hat-trick against Birmingham City puts Tottenham on top of the table.

12 October: Bobby Smith scores twice and Bobby Charlton and I grab a goal apiece as England wallop Wales 4-0 at Wembley. It's a milestone goal for Bobby Charlton. His 31st goal for England takes him above Nat Lofthouse and Tom Finney as England's top marksman.

23 October: One of my most memorable matches for England. I score the winning goal against the Rest of the World in a match at Wembley to mark the FA Centenary. In the first half I have four shots saved by magnificent Russian goalkeeper Lev Yashin. I then get the ball into the net after surviving a trip and skipping past four tackles, but Scottish referee Bobby Davidson awards England a free-kick for the trip. He later apologises for not having played the advantage rule. All the players who take part are presented with a gold watch. I give mine to my dad. The honour of playing in the showpiece game is sufficient reward for me. The Rest of the World team reads like a 'Who's Who' of football: Yashin, Djalma Santos, Schnellinger, Pluskal, Popluhar, Masopust, Kopa, Law, di Stefano, Eusebio, Gento. Subs: Soskic, Eyzaguirre, Baxter, Seeler, Puskas.

20 November: The first match under the Wembley floodlights, and I score four and Terry Paine three as we hammer Northern Ireland 8-3.

7 December: I score my 200th League goal at Bolton, and the statisticians tell me I have at the age of 23 years and 290 days – achieved the feat at exactly the same age at which Dixie Dean reached the same milestone with Everton. Not a lot of people want to know that!

10 December: Dave Mackay, the man we call 'indestructible', is carried off with a broken leg in Tottenham's European Cup-Winners' Cup tie against Manchester United at Old Trafford.

26 December: Football goes goal crazy. Thirty-nine League matches in a Boxing Day blitz produce 157 goals. Sixty-six of them come in the First Division. Biggest win – Fulham 10, Ipswich 1. John Cobbold, Ipswich chairman, cracks: 'Only our goalkeeper was sober'. Graham Leggat (Fulham), Andy Lochhead (Burnley) and Roger Hunt (Liverpool) each score four goals.

1964

8 January: Chelsea beat Spurs 2-0 in an FA Cup third round replay. The attendance at Stamford Bridge: 70,123.

11 January: A First Division hat-trick for Spurs against Blackburn Rovers. Tottenham are back on top of the table, but we have lost Dave Mackay and it is looking increasingly unlikely that our skipper Danny Blanchflower – the poet of the team – will be able to play again because of a recurring knee injury.

6 February: Leeds buy England centre-forward Alan Peacock from Middlesbrough for £53,000.

Three footballers of the 'sixties who went on to managerial careers: Bobby Robson *(left, above)* playing for Fulham with West Ham's Geoff Hurst about to challenge, and young Ron Atkinson *(left),* who is leading out Oxford United. Hurst, England's hat-trick hero in the 1966 World Cup, briefly managed Chelsea before getting out of the rat race to set up a car insurance business with Martin Peters. There were so many changes on the managerial roundabout in the 'sixties that it is doubtful if anybody could have sold the bosses any insurance!

15 February: Oxford United, driven from midfield by Ron 'The Tank' Atkinson, conquer First Division Blackburn Rovers 3-1 to become the first Fourth Division side to reach the quarter-finals of the FA Cup.

10 March: Everton buy Blackburn's England Under-23 centre-forward Fred Pickering for £80,000, a record fee between British clubs. He scores a hat-trick in his debut.

14 March: Bill Nicholson, accepting that Danny Blanchflower's career is coming to an end, buys Alan Mullery from Fulham for £72,500 – a British record for a half-back.

5 April: Danny Blanchflower announces his retirement at the age of 37. A light has gone out at Tottenham.

11 April: A rare mistake by Gordon Banks costs a goal as Scotland beat England 1-0 at Hampden for their third successive win over the 'auld enemy'. Alan Gilzean heads the winner after Gordon is deceived by a Davie Wilson lob as the ball suddenly dips in the swirling wind. I'm relieved to be sitting this one out.

18 April: Liverpool slam Arsenal 5-0 at Anfield to become League champions for the sixth time. Shankly's Army are on the march.

20 April: Good old Bobby Moore is elected Footballer of the Year. Charlie Hurley, Sunderland centre-half, is runner-up, with Denis Law in third place.

21 April: Don Howe, West Bromwich Albion's 28-year-old England international right-back, joins Arsenal for £45,000 – a British record fee for a full-back. He is signed by his old England chum and captain Billy Wright.

22 April: Leicester City clinch victory in the two-leg League Cup final, beating Stoke City 4-3 on aggregate.

25 April: Rangers win the Scottish FA Cup for a record 18th time to complete the treble of Cup, League championship and League Cup.

9 May: Johnny Byrne scores both England goals in a 2-1 win over Uruguay at Wembley. The Uruguayan tackles are so high it's a wonder they don't get snow on their boots.

17 May: Portugal 3, England 4 in Lisbon. It's one of the most exciting internationals in which I have ever played. 'Budgie' Byrne clinches an astonishing victory when completing his hat-trick in the last minute, and he does it in style with a beautiful chip shot. 'Budgie' and I were among seven players Alf had threatened to leave behind in England after we had gone out for a late-night drink in London on the eve of the tour. He put our passports on each of our beds to show he had spotted that we had broken the curfew. Naughty boys!

20 May: I dash from Lisbon to Copenhagen where I am honoured to be selected by West German manager Helmut Schoen for the Rest of Europe team for a showpiece match against Scandinavia. I have the satisfaction of popping in a couple of goals.

24 May: On to Dublin and a goal for England in their 3-1 victory over the Republic of

Ireland. Then on to the 'plane from Shannon to New York.

27 May: Alf gives me a welcome breather, and I watch England destroy the United States 10-0. Fred Pickering bags a hat-trick in his international debut, and Roger Hunt scores four goals.

30 May: England 1, Pele 5, in Rio. Pele is the only difference between England and Brazil. And what a difference!

4 June: Another Roger Hunt goal earns us a draw with Portugal in 'The Little World Cup' in Sao Paulo. Brazil and Argentina are the other two teams taking part in this tournament. Both Terry Paine and I hit the bar, and José Torres hits the referee! Portugal's towering six foot seven inch centre-forward is sent off after clumping the referee when his goal is ruled off-side.

6 June: Argentina beat us 1-0 in Rio to lift the trophy with three wins in three matches. We reckon they will be the biggest danger to us in the World Cup finals in England in 1966. Their strutting skipper, Antonio Rattin, looks a particularly talented player.

21 July: John White, Tottenham's cultured midfield schemer, is killed when lightning strikes him while he is sheltering under a tree on a golf course in Enfield. Football has lost a great player. I have lost a good friend. Rest easy, pal.

THE CHAMPIONS OF
1963-64

FIRST DIVISION:
1: Liverpool (57 points)
2: Manchester United (53)
3: Everton (52)

Championship squad:
Arrowsmith (20 appearances), Byrne (33), Callaghan (42). Ferns (18), Furnell (2), Hunt (41), Lawler (6), Lawrence (40), Melia (24), Milne (42), Moran (35), St John (40), Stevenson (38), Thompson (42), Thomson (2), Wallace (1), Yeats (36).
Goalscorers: Hunt (31), St John (21), Arrowsmith (15), Callaghan (8), Thompson (6), Melia (4), Milne (2), Moran (2), Stevenson (1), Yeats (1), 1 own goal.

SECOND DIVISION:
1: Leeds United (63 points)
2: Sunderland (61)
3: Preston North End (56)

Championship squad:
Beal (35 appearances), Bremner (39), Charlton (25), Collins (41), Cooper (2), Giles (39), Goodwin (11), Greenhoff (2), Hair (8), Henderson (2), Hunter (42), Johanneson (37), Lawson (25), Madeley (3), Peacock (14), Reaney (42), Sprake (41), Storrie (15), Williamson (1), Wright (1), Weston (35).
Goalscorers: Johanneson (13), Weston (13), Lawson (11), Peacock (8), Giles (7), Collins (6), Storrie (3), Charlton (3), Hunter (2), Bell (2), Bremner (2), Henderson (1).

THIRD DIVISION:
1: Coventry City (60 points)
2: Crystal Palace (60)
3: Watford (58)

Championship squad:
Barr (13 appearances), Bruck (10), Curtis (46), Farmer (44), Gould (2), Hale (39), Hill (40), Hudson (32), Humphries (40), Kearns (42), Kirby (9), Kletzenbauer (9), Machin (17), Meeson (5), Mitten (4), Newton (8), Rees (46), Sillett (41), Smith (9), Wesson (41), Whitehouse (9).
Goalscorers: Hudson (25), Hale (15), Rees (13), Farmer (11), Humphries (10), Kirby (5), Barr (3), Machin (3), Newton (3), Whitehouse (3), Hill (2), Kletzenbauer (1), 4 own goals.

FOURTH DIVISION:
1: Gillingham (60 points)
2: Carlisle United (60)
3: Workington Town (59)

Championship squad:
Arnott (43 appearances), Ballagher (17), Burgess (46), Campbell (1), Farrall (45), Francis (16), Gibbs (46), Godfrey (13), Hunt (43), Hudson (36), Moss (2), Newman (37), Pulley (31), Ridley (7), Simpson (46), Stringfellow (25), Stacey (12), Taylor (1), Waldock (6), White (11), Yeo (11).
Goalscorers: Gibbs (17), Newman (11), Francis (7), Pulley (6), Ballagher (4), Hunt (3), Godfrey (2), Ridley (2), Burgess (1), Farrall (1), Hudson (1), White (1), 1 own goal.

SCOTTISH FIRST DIVISION:
1: Rangers (55 points)
2: Kilmarnock (49)
3: Celtic (47)

Championship squad:
Greig (34 appearances), Ritchie (34), Brand (31), McKinnon (31), Provan (31), Shearer (31), Henderson (30), Baxter (26), Forrest (24), Millar (22), McLean (19), Wilson (16), McMillan (10), Watson (7), Willoughby (6), Baillie (4), Davis (4), Wood (4), Caldow (3), Trail (3), Hynd (1).
Goalscorers: Forrest (21), Brand (19), McLean (10), Millar (6), Wilson (6), Baxter (4), Greig (4), Henderson (3), Provan (3), Willoughby (3), McMillan (1), 1 own goal.

SCOTTISH SECOND DIVISION:
1: Morton (67 points)
2: Clyde (53)
3: Arbroath (46)

FA CUP FINAL:
Wesf Ham United 3 *(Sissons, Hurst, Boyce)*
Standen, Bond, Burkett, Bovington, Brown, Moore, Brabrook, Boyce, Byrne, Hurst, Sissons.
Preston North End 2 *(Holden, Dawson)*
Kelly, Ross, Smith, Lawton, Singleton, Kendall, Wilsoon, Ashworth, Dawson, Spavin, Holden.

LEAGUE CUP FINAL:
First leg:
Stoke City 1 *(Bebbington)*
Leslie, Asprey, Allen, Palmer, Kinnell, Skeels, Dobing, Viollet, Ritchie, McIlroy, Bebbington.
Leicester City 1 *(Gibson)*
Banks, Sjoberg, Appleton, Dougan, King, Cross, Riley, Heath, Keyworth, Gibson, Stringfellow.
Second leg:
Leicester City 3 *(Stringfellow, Gibson, Riley)*
Banks, Sjoberg, Appleton, Dougan, King, Cross, Riley, Heath, Keyworth, Gibson, Stringfellow.

Stoke City 2 *(Viollet, Kinnell)*
Leslie, Asprey, Allen, Palmer, Kinnell, Skeels, Dobing, Viollet, Ritchie, McIlroy, Bebbington
Leicester City win 4-3 on aggregate.

SCOTTISH FA CUP FINAL:
Rangers 3 *(Millar 2, Brand)*
Ritchie, Shearer, Provan, Greig, McKinnon, Baxter, Henderson, Willoughby, Millar, Brand, Wilson.
Dundee 1 *(Cameron)*
Slater, Hamilton, Cox, Seith, Ryden, Stuart, Penman, Cousins, Cameron, Gilzean, Robertson.

SCOTTISH LEAGUE CUP FINAL:
Rangers 5 *(Forrest 4, Willoughby)*
Ritchie, Shearer, Provan, Greig, McKinnon, Baxter, Henderson, Willoughby, Forrest, Brand, Watson.
Morton 0
Brown, Boyd, Mallan, Reilly, Kiernan, Strachan, Adamson, Campbell, Stevenson, McGraw, Wilson.

EUROPEAN CUP FINAL
Played in Vienna
Inter-Milan 3 *(Mazzola 2, Milani)*
Sarti, Burgnich, Facchetti, Tagnin, Guarneri, Picchi, Jair, Mazzola, Milani, Suarez, Corso
Real Madrid 1 *(Felo)*
Vicente, Isidro, Pachin, Müller, Santamaria, Zoco, Amanco, Felo, di Stefano, Puskas, Gento

EUROPEAN CUP-WINNERS' CUP FINAL:
Played in Brussels
Sporting Lisbon 3 *(Figueiredo 2, Dansky own goal)*
Carvalho, Gomez, Baptista, Carlos, Geo, Mendes, Oswaldo, Mascarenhas, Figueiredo, Morais.
MTK Budapest 3 *(Sandor 2, Kuti)*
Kovalik, Keszei, Dansky, Jenei, Nagy, Kovacs, Sandor, Vasas, Kuti, Bodor, Halapi.

Replayed in Antwerp
Sporting Lisbon 1 *(Morais)*
Carvalho, Pendes, Baptista, Carlos, Geo, Mendes, Oswaldo, Mascarenhas, Figueiredo, Morais.
MTK Budapest 0
Kovalik, Keszei, Dansky, Jenei, Nagy, Kovacs, Sandor, Vasas, Kuti, Bodor, Halapi.

EUROPEAN FAIRS CUP FINAL:
Played in Barcelona
Real Zaragoza 2 *(Villa, Marcelino)*
Yarza, Cortizo, Reija, Isasi, Santamaria, Pepin, Canario, Duca, Marcelino, Villa, Lapetra.
Valencia 1 *(Urtiaga)*
Zamora, Arnal, Videgany, Paquito, Quinocis, Roberto, Suco, Guillot, Waldo, Urtiaga, Ficha.

Top Football League goalscorers:

Hugh McIlmoyle (Carlisle United)	39
Jimmy Greaves (Tottenham Hotspur)	35
Ron Saunders (Portsmouth)	33
Andy McEvoy (Blackburn Rovers)	32
Roger Hunt (Liverpool)	31
Alfie Biggs (Bristol Rovers)	30
Alex Dawson (Preston North End)	30
Derek Kevan (Manchester City)	30
Denis Law (Manchester United)	30
Rodney Green (Bradford City)	29
Ken Wagstaff (Mansfield Town)	29
Denis Coughlin (AFC Bournemouth)	28
Alan Spence (Southport)	27

Top Scottish First Division marksman:
Alan Gilzean (Dundee) 32 goals

Highest average League attendance:
Everton (49,401)

Footballer of the Year:
Bobby Moore (West Ham United)

European Footballer of the Year:
Denis Law (Manchester United)

World Club Championship:
Inter Milan beat Independiente 0-1, 2-0

1964-65: ARISE, SIR STANLEY!

Stanley Matthews, arguably the greatest player of any time, became the first footballer to be knighted on 1 January, 1965. In a way this was a demotion. The king of soccer had been turned into a knight. Arise, Sir Stanley!

When he helped Stoke City beat Fulham on 6 February, 1965 – five days after his 50th birthday – he broke Billy Meredith's long-standing record by becoming the oldest footballer to play in the League. A masterof football in the 'thirties, the 'Wizard of Dribble' was still weaving his spells in the 'sixties.

Sir Stanley, the son of a professional boxer known as Jack Matthews, the 'Fighting Barber of Hanley', had joined Stoke as an amateur when he was a 15-year-old England schoolboy international. Two years later he signed professional forms, and was established in the England team at the age of 19.

There were so many events that turned Matthews into a legend in his own lifetime. For instance, there was the day he brought the city of Stoke to a stop when thousands of workers downed tools and demonstrated in the streets when he announced that he wanted to leave Stoke. He was eventually transferred to Blackpool in 1947 for a fee of £11,500. There were his 54 England appearances and another 24 in wartime internationals, and – above all – his amazing match-winning performance when he inspired Blackpool to come from behind to beat Bolton 4-3 in the 1953 FA Cup final, winning his first medal at the age of 38. Most people had thought that would be his swansong, but nine years later he was brought 'home' to Stoke by City's bold and imaginative manager, Tony Waddington, and he helped inspire them back into the First Division, doubling their gates in the process.

Matthews was unique not only because of his astonishing dribbling skills, but also because of his model behaviour on the pitch. Never in a career spanning 33 years did he have his name taken. It was my good fortune to play at the back-end of both his career and that of the player who would always be bracketed with him, Preston's one and only Tom Finney. With these two wonder wingers hanging up their boots, the face of football would never be quite the same. They don't make them like that any more.

I was thrilled to partner Sir Stanley in his farewell match at Stoke on 28 April, 1965. The Stanley Matthews All Stars were beaten 6-4 by a World X1, and at the end of an enjoyable exhibition match emotions took over as we linked hands and sang *Auld Lang Syne.* Sir Stanley was chaired around the pitch on the broad shoulders of Ferenc Puskas and Lev Yashin. For the record, these were the teams that were honoured to take part in Sir Stanley's passing out parade:

Stanley Matthews All Stars: Waiters, Cohen, Thomson, Haynes, Flowers, Baxter; Matthews, Greaves, Gilzean, Douglas, Jones. Sub: Ritchie.

World XI: Yashin (USSR), Johansen (Denmark), Schnellinger (West Germany), Pluskal (Czechoslovakia), Popluhar (Czechoslovakia), Masopust (Czecho-slovakia), Henderson (Scotland), Kubala (Spain), di Stefano (Spain), Puskas (Spain), Van den Borg (Belgium). Sub: Sorensen (Denmark).

An era ended with the retirement of Matthews. The ball had now passed to the feet of the 'new Matthews'...an Irish wizard of dribble called George Best ...

THE LEAGUE CHAMPIONS

Matt Busby's Manchester United team that had captured the FA Cup in 1963 had taken on a new look. Pat Dunne had replaced Dave Gaskell in goal, his brother, Tony Dunne, was now partnering fellow-Irishman Shay Brennan at fullback, and Nobby Stiles was snapping and snarling in the No. 6 shirt in place of Maurice Setters. Bobby Charl-ton was starting to play more of a withdrawn role, with the wizardry on the wings being provided by my England partner, John Connelly, and a precocious young Irishman called George Best.

If any individual was to symbolise football in the 'sixties it was George, the man I consider the greatest British footballer of my lifetime – yes, even ahead of Sir Stanley Matthews. His career was like a mirror image of what was hap-pening off the pitch. He became known as 'the Fifth Beatle' – a leader of fashion, irreverent, undisciplined, a playboy who was rarely without a beautiful, mini-skirted blonde on his arm; and above all he was a sparkling showman for whom the football pitch was a stage on which to parade his stunning skills. In this season of 1964-65 he was building the foundation to a ten-year career with United, during which he was to touch dazzling peaks of perfection with his play and hit the basement with his behaviour. He would become a folk hero, thrilling everybody with his flamboyant performances on the pitch and hitting the headlines with his controversial antics off it.

At the pinnacle of his career with United and Northern Ireland, George was a phe-nomenal player. He had amazing balance, total control of the ball even at top speed, was as brave as a lion and could conjure his way past defenders in confined space. He had that rare ability to be able to invent something out of nothing, and he created openings no matter what defences tried to do to block his path.

He, and the less spectacular but nearly as effective John Connelly, brought a new di-mension to the United attack, and on the way to their fourth First Division championship

Stanley Matthews *(left)* was taking his final bow with Stoke City at the same time as precocious young Irishman George Best *(right)* was building the foundation to his sensational career with Manchester United. Matthews was knighted shortly before his final League appearance with Stoke at the age of 50. Sir Stanley, who gave me the honour of playing alongside him in his farewell testimonial match, was a footballing master of the 'thirties, 'forties, 'fifties and 'sixties.

since the war United were top scorers with 89 goals in an age when defences were beginning to become much tighter and more disciplined. They won the championship at Old Trafford, losing only one home match while scoring 52 goals.

In a nail-biting, neck-and-neck climax to the season United pipped Don Revie's Leeds United on goal average, with both clubs amassing 61 points. The championship was decided in Manchester United's final home match of the season when they beat Arsenal 3-1 – rich consolation for their 1-0 defeat by Leeds in an FA Cup semi-final replay five weeks earlier.

Denis Law and David Herd, United's Scottish connection at the front of the attack, collected 48 League goals between them to clinch the championship a mere fraction ahead of Leeds, who got themselves involved in a lot of friction. I was among those who felt that Leeds were too hungry for success. Their win-at-all-costs methods would lose them lots of friends.

'I have known few nights as memorable as when we beat Arsenal in our final match to clinch the championship. We proved we have great character to go with all the ability running through the team, and I am very optimistic of hitting our main target next season ...the European Cup.' – **Matt Busby**.

THE FA CUP WINNERS

Leeds had a remarkable season when they almost won everything and finished with nothing. Just five days after the heartbreak of losing the League title race on goal average they took on Bill Shankly's wonderfully balanced Liverpool team in the FA Cup final at Wembley. They struggled to get out of a defensive mode, and were fortunate to take the match into extra-time after a goalless 90 minutes in which the Merseysiders were always looking the side most likely to score.

Wembley had witnessed better matches, but had never known anything quite like the atmosphere generated by the crowd. The Liverpool fans filled the stadium with their 'ee-aye-addio' chants that had brought a sound revolution to the terraces, and the players could almost warm their hands on the passion pouring from their supporters.

Willie Stevenson and Tommy Smith were stifling the midfield movement of the

Scottish duo Bobby Collins and Billy Bremner, who had been mainly responsible for the Leeds success since motoring up as Second Division champions the previous season. Another disappointment for Leeds was the performance of their black South African winger, Albert Johanneson, who made no impact against the tight marking of Liverpool right-back Chris Lawler. And, surprisingly, Leeds could not take advantage of the fact that left-back Gerry Byrne was struggling from early in the match with a broken collarbone.

Three minutes into extra-time Liverpool at last created the goal they richly deserved. Byrne bravely worked the ball down the by-line before sending over a knee-high centre. Roger Hunt stooped low to nod the ball wide of goalkeeper Gary Sprake. Leeds, a side of tremendous character and courage, struck back almost immediately and equalised in a rare raid on the Liverpool goal. Jack Charlton headed the ball down into the path of Bremner, who crashed a shot on the half-volley into the roof of the net.

Just as most people were thinking in terms of a replay the king of the Kop, Ian St John, came up with an unusual but welcome winner. Ian Callaghan fired over a cross from the left. The ball seemed to be going behind The Saint, whose socks were down to his ankles as he tried to combat cramp. Ian corkscrewed backwards and managed to get his head to the ball, steering it into the net from six yards. Nobody could deny that Liverpool deserved their victory, but you got the feeling that Leeds would not be empty handed for much longer.

> *'It would have been a travesty of justice if we had left Wembley without a victory. We were always sharper and more decisive, and it was a mystery how we did not have it all sewn up long before extra-time. The goal was one of the most satisfying of my career. Our supporters were unbelievable. It sounded as if we were playing at Anfield.'* - **Ian St John**.

CHAMPIONS OF EUROPE

The Milan stranglehold on the European Cup continued, with Inter retaining it with a 1-0 victory over Benfica on their own territory at the San Siro Stadium. It completed an incredibly successful season for Helenio Herrera's tightly disciplined side. They finished three points clear of AC Milan in the Italian championship race and beat Independiente 3-0 on aggregate to win the world club championship.

The Italians survived two tough European Cup matches

against British opponents. In the quarter-final against Rangers they lost 1-0 at Ibrox, but were comfortable 3-1 victors in Milan. I wonder if the result might have been different had Rangers not lost their midfield master, Jim Baxter, with a broken leg in the previous round against Rapid Vienna.

Inter were then lucky to scramble through the semi-final against Liverpool, who produced a magnificent performance just four days after the FA Cup final to win the first leg 3-1 at Anfield. They went down 3-0 in the return leg in Milan, and Bill Shankly's protests about the refereeing rumbled on for years. The goal that knocked Liverpool out came after goalkeeper Tommy Lawrence caught the ball, and he could not believe it when Joaquim Peiro was allowed to get away with kicking it out of his hands and into the net. It would not be the last time that Inter were linked with debatable decisions, and allegations of bribery and corruption involving referees and linesmen deposited a stench over Milan that was to hang around for years.

Benfica were furious that the European Cup final was to be played in Milan, but in fairness to the UEFA organisers the ground was selected before the competition started. At one point Benfica were theatening to send their youth team, until warned that they would be heavily fined.

Jair gave Inter an early lead on a rain-saturated pitch, but instead of opening up the game in a search for more goals they retreated into their defensive shell. Even when Benfica goalkeeper Costa Pereira was injured and replaced by centre-half Germano Inter refused to drop their neurotic, negative approach and one of the dreariest of all finals ended with the champions retaining the trophy with a 1-0 victory.

There was another dull final in the European Fairs Cup, Ferencvaros beating Juventus 1-0 on their home ground in Turin. The Hungarians had scraped through on replays in three rounds, including the semi-final against Manchester United, who had piled up the goals in the early stages. Denis Law and Bobby Charlton each scored eight in the competition.

'This European Cup final was one of the most frustrating matches in which I've played. Inter were interested only in defending their goal once they had taken a lucky lead. It is not good for the game that Inter are so successful with this negative style.' – **Eusebio**.

THE EUROPEAN CUP-WINNERS' CUP

West Ham's peak performance in the 'sixties came, fittingly, in front of their biggest audience, when 100,000 spectators at Wembley and millions more watching on Eurovision saw them come close to perfection in a memorable European Cup-Winners' Cup final against Munich 1860.

Manager Ron Greenwood selected a side showing four changes from the team that had pipped Second Division Preston in last season's FA Cup final. Joe Kirkup replaced the veteran John Bond at right-back. The elegant Martin Peters took Eddie Bovington's place in midfield, and virtual unknowns Alan Sealey and Brian Dear came into the attack for injured England internationals Johnny Byrne and Peter Brabrook.

Munich, who had eliminated Cup favourites Torino in the semi-final, had just finished third in the fiercely contested Bundesliga and fielded four West German internationals. It looked an evenly balanced contest, and Greenwood told his players: 'We must adopt a positive attitude. Let's go out there to win and to win in style'. Across the concrete corridor separating the dressing-rooms at Wembley respected Munich coach Max Merkel was giving almost identical instructions. He, too, wanted victory in style. It would have all been quite foreign to Helenio Herrera.

West Ham fans feared that their attack would not be firing on all cylinders because of the absence of dribbling winger Peter Brabrook and highly-skilled centre-forward 'Budgie' Byrne, but within minutes their home-produced stand-ins, Alan Sealey and Brian Dear, were making daring inroads deep into the Munich defence. Radenkovic, a colourful goalkeeper from Yugoslavia, made a string of superb saves for Munich, and at the opposite end the immaculate Bobby Moore shepherded his defence into keeping composed under the pressure of swift counter attacks. Hammers goalkeeper Jim Standen, a summertime cricketer with Worcestershire, held two magnificent catches from point-blank snap shots by Rudi Brunnenmeier, Munich's roving centre-forward and skipper.

From first kick to last, both teams produced adventurous and imaginative football and there could easily have been a shoal of goals at either end before Sealey at last made the breakthrough in the 69th minute. It was Ronnie Boyce who set up the goal moments after the jinking John Sissons crashed a shot against a post to interrupt a tide of Munich raids. Boyce sent a defence-splitting pass arrowing through to Sealey, who instantly converted it into a goal with a low right-footed shot from 12 yards. Sealey, born within goal-kicking distance of West Ham's Upton Park ground, cartwheeled with delight, and just 90 seconds later had even more reason for celebration. Moore flighted a free-kick to Peters, who smartly flicked it into the goalmouth where Sealey charged forward to force the ball over the goal-line from two yards.

In the final moments of a glorious game Sissons again smashed a shot against the woodwork. It was sad for the gifted winger but justice for Munich, who certainly did not deserve a three-goal defeat. They played a proud part in a classic contest.

Bobby Moore led his team up the Wembley steps to collect the trophy a year and 17 days after making the same journey to receive the FA Cup. He would complete an historic hat-trick in 1966.

The game would be remembered as one of the finest footballing displays ever seen at Wembley, and a lot of the credit must go to Munich for matching West Ham's spirit of adventure. Moore was his usual reliable and ice-cool self. West Ham and England have not had a finer servant. He was a refined defender, stamping his authority on every match, and he had the gift of being able to read situations ahead of anybody else.

There had rarely been a better 'big occasion' player than Bobby, who would collect 108 caps for England and equal the Billy Wright record of captaining the team in 90 matches. The one and only Pele would pay him the ultimate compliment of calling him 'the greatest defender in the world'. Born in Barking on 12 April, 1941, Bobby had skippered the England youth team while winning a record 18 caps. He had made his West Ham debut in 1958, replacing his great pal Malcolm Allison, whose career was cut short by tuberculosis. In 1962 he had succeeded Bobby Robson in the England team and he'd taken over from Jimmy Armfield as captain in 1963-64. He would play 545 League matches for West Ham before switching to Fulham late in his career. In his first season at Craven Cottage he would play a major part in steering Fulham to their first ever FA Cup final. Ironically they would be beaten at Wembley by West Ham.

There was a happy sequel to the Cup-Winners' Cup final. Hammers and Munich shared a United Nations Fair Play Award for their sportsmanship and skill in the Wembley classic.

> *'If anybody wants to know what my thinking on football was all about I would like to be judged on this match. It was close to perfection and presented the game in the best possible light. We had worked for this for four years and for us it was like reaching the summit of Everest.' – **Ron Greenwood.***

My winning goal against Hungary at Wembley in 1965 *(above)* brought a rare smile to the face of manager Alf Ramsey, who at last felt avenged for the 6-3 hammering of England by Hungary in 1953 when he was playing at right-back. Bobby Moore skippered the team that beat the Hungarians 1-0 and two weeks later led the West Ham team *(below)* that won the European Cup-Winners' Cup. The Moore-Hurst-Peters trio in the middle of this picture had golden times waiting for them at Wembley a year later.

GREAVSIE'S FOOTBALL DIARY
1964-65

1964

22 August: Liverpool beat Arsenal 3-2 at Anfield in the first 'Match of the Day' television programme, on BBC2. Derek Forster, at 15 years and 185 days, becomes the youngest First Division player in League history when he plays in goal for Sunderland. Blimey, they'll be wearing nappies next!

4 September: Jackie Milburn resigns as manager of struggling Ipswich Town. I feel sorry for Jackie, who inherited an over-the-top team from Alf Ramsey.

12 September: Dave Mackay, making his comeback in a reserve match for Spurs, breaks his leg for a second time in nine months. It plunges all of us at the club into a mood of gloom.

29 September: Bill McGarry leaves Watford to succeed Jack Milburn at Ipswich. Bill, a former England international half-back, will have his hands full.

30 September: Jeff Astle leaves Notts County to join West Bromwich Albion. What a bargain at £25,000.

3 October: A hat-trick for England against Northern Ireland in 11 minutes at Windsor Park gives us a 4-3 victory and takes my tally to a record 35 goals. The most memorable thing about the match is the wizardry of a young winger making his first international appearance against England. His name: George Best. He is certain to become a giant of the game. What a prospect!

5 October: Arsenal buy Frank McLintock from Leicester City. The fee of £80,000 is a British record for a half-back. He will prove to be one of Arsenal's finest ever signings.

21 October: Alf Ramsey experiments with a new left-wing combination of Terry Venables and Alan Hinton against Belgium at Wembley. We scramble a 2-2 draw thanks to a scorching shot from Hinton that is deflected into the net by a Belgian defender. Venners sets a unique record. He is the only player in the history of the game to have won England international caps at five levels – schoolboy, youth, amateur, Under-23 and full.

7 November: Everton and Leeds go over the top with their competitive spirit in a bitterly contested First Division match at Goodison Park, and the referee orders both teams off the pitch for a cooling-down period. Geoff Strong makes his debut as an inside-forward for Liverpool after his £40,000 transfer from Arsenal. His best days at Anfield will come when he moves to midfield.

18 November: Sadly, I have to report that the seeds of hooliganism are being sewn on the terraces, where behaviour standards are beginning to drop (it will be the 'seventies and 'eighties when they get out of control), and on the pitch the tackling is becoming reckless and often vicious. The Football League and the FA set up a joint committee to discuss the problems on and off the pitch, and they issue a toothless statement that future offenders will be punished with tougher disciplinary measures. This should be the time for strong action before things get out of hand.

8 December: Jim Baxter breaks a leg in the final seconds of the Rangers European Cup tie against Rapid of Vienna in Austria.

9 December: I score a goal four minutes from the end to give England a 1-1 draw with Holland in Amsterdam. In the old days we would have expected to outclass the Dutch, but we now see that they are closing the gap at a rate of knots. They have made incredible advances with their individual technique, and they are developing a fine passing game.

16 December: Spurs buy Alan Gilzean from Dundee for £72,500 – a record fee for Scottish football. It's like an early Christmas present for me, and Gilly and I hit it off on the pitch from the moment he pulls on a Tottenham shirt.

16 January: Jimmy Dickinson plays his 750th League match for Portsmouth against Southampton at The Dell. Jimmy is 'Mr Pompey' and was a stalwart in the England team that I idolised as a schoolboy. He wore the No. 6 shirt in the half-back line, the names of which roll off the tongue like old friends: Wright, Franklin, Dickinson.

17 January: A hat-trick as Spurs beat Torquay 5-1 in an FA Cup third round replay at White Hart Lane. I also miss three sitters!

26 January: A black day for football. Ten current and former professional footballers are found guilty of 'fixing' matches, and all are given prison sentences at Nottingham Assizes. They include two of my England team-mates, Tony Kay and Peter Swan. It is proved that they were part of a betting ring while at Sheffield Wednesday between 1960 and 1963, and both are banned from football for life. What they have done is wrong, but I consider their punishment far too severe. Surely a prison sentence is enough, without taking away from them the right to play football anywhere in the world. Theirs is the folly of fools rather than villains. Both Kay and Swan are excellent players who would, I am sure, have been in England's 1966 World Cup squad.

30 January: I bag a hat-trick and Alan Gilzean two goals as Spurs thump Ipswich 5-0 in the fourth round of the FA Cup at White Hart Lane. Gilly is a joy to play with, and has a delicate touch that is not always appreciated by the spectators but admired by his fellow-professionals.

6 February: Sir Stanley Matthews bows out of football after helping Stoke City beat Fulham 3-1. He celebrated his 50th birthday six days ago.

14 February: I score after 75 seconds against Sheffield United, and I am later informed that I have completed some sort of record by getting the ball into the net against every club currently in the First Division. It's news to me. I believe in leaving the counting to others, and just concern myself with trying to score my next goal.

25 February: Arthur Rowley retires with a record 434 League goals to his name. Nobody will catch him.

16 March: Roy Vernon, Everton's Welsh goal master, joins the 'Old Boys' Academy' at Stoke where talent is measured by ability, not by age.

9 April: Bobby and Jack Charlton set a record by becoming the first brothers to play together for England this century. Bobby and I score the goals in a 2-2 draw against Scotland at Wembley. 'Budgie' Byrne picks up a crippling knee injury.

4 May: Alf Ramsey is a happy man when I score the only goal of the match to beat Hungary 1-0 at Wembley. Alf was in the England team humbled 6-3 by the Hungarians back in 1953.

George Graham, playing for Chelsea, beats Leeds United centre-half Jack Charlton in an aerial duel at Stamford Bridge *(above)* in the 1964-65 season, during which big Jack made his breakthrough into the England team. Jack and 'kid' brother Bobby *(right)* set a record by becoming the first brothers to play together for England this century.

THE CHAMPIONS OF
1964-65

FIRST DIVISION:
1: Manchester United (61 points)
2: Leeds United (61)
3: Chelsea (56)

Championship squad:
Aston (1 appearance), Best (41), Brennan (42), Cantwell (2), Charlton (41), Connelly (42), Crerand (39), A. Dunne (42), P. Dunne (37), Foulkes (42), Fitzpatrick (2), Gaskell (5), Herd (37), Law (36), Moir (1), Setters (5), Sadler (6), Stiles (41).
Goalscorers: Law (28), Herd (2), Connelly (15), Charlton (10), Best (10), Crerand (3), Sadler (1), Cantwell (1), 1 own goal.

SECOND DIVISION:
1: Newcastle United (57 points)
2: Northampton Town (56)
3: Bolton Wanderers (50)

Championship squad:
Allen (1 appearance), Anderson (41), Burton (2), Clark (42), Craig (40), Cummings (24), Hilley (34), Hockey (24), Iley (38), Knox (9), Marshall (42), Moncur (11), McGarry (31), McGrath (42), McKinney (2), Penman (22), Robson (20), Suddick (21), Taylor (9), Thomas (7).
Goalscorers: McGarry (16), Hilley (12), Anderson (8), Cummings (8), Penman (7), Robson (7), Suddick (6), Iley (5), Thomas (3), Taylor (2), Hockey (2), Knox (1), Burton (1), 3 own goals.

THIRD DIVISION:
1: Carlisle United (60 points)
2: Bristol City (59)
3: Mansfield Town (59)

Championship squad:
Blain (29 appearances), Brayton (22), Caldwell (46), Carlin (28), Dean (26), Evans (44), Garbutt (8), Harland (46), Johnstone (10), Kirkup (13), Large (36), Livingstone (11), McConnell (44), McIlmoyle (15), Neil (43), Oliphant (1), Passmoor (44), Ross (20), Simpson (22).
Goalscorers: Evans (18), Large (16), McConnell (7), Blain (5), Carlin (5), Brayton (4), Simpson (4), Harland (3), Kirkup (3), Livingstone (3), Johnstone (2), Caldwell (1), McIlmoyle (1), Neil (1), Oliphant (1), 2 own goals.

FOURTH DIVISION:
1: Brighton & Hove Albion (63 points)
2: Millwall (62)
3: York City (62)

Championship squad:
Baxter (39 appearances), Bertolini (24), Burtenshaw (2), Cassidy (25), Collins (45), Donnelly (3), Gall (4), Goodchild (43), Gould (43), Hennigan (4), Hopkins (34), Knight (3), McGonigal (5), McQuarrie (2), Oliver (5), Powney (41), Rees (12), Sanders (16), J. Smith (35), R. Smith (31), Turner (39), Upton (10), Webb (1).
Goalscorers: Gould (21), R. Smith (19), J. Smith (17), Collins (17), Cassidy (10), Goodchild (10), Turner (2), McQuarrie (2), Knight (1), Rees (1), Hopkins (1), Gall (1), 1 own goal.

SCOTTISH FIRST DIVISION:

1: Kilmarnock (50 points)
2: Heart of Midlothian (50)
3: Dunfermline Athletic (49).

Championship squad:

Murray (34 appearances), King (33), McGrory (32), McInally (32), Beattie (31), McIlroy (29), Watson (29), Hamilton (28), Sneddon (28), Forsyth (26), McFadzean (26), McLean (19), Black (9), Ferguson (8), Mason (2), Dickson (4), Malone (2), Brown (1), O'Connor (1).
Goalscorers: Hamilton (16), McInally (32), McIlroy (8), Black (6), Sneddon (5), Murray (4), McFadzean (3), McLean (3), Mason (2), Beattie (1), King (1), O'Connor (1), Watson (1).

SCOTTISH SECOND DIVISION:

1: Stirling Albion (59 points)
2: Hamilton Academicals (50)
3: Queen of the South (45)

FA CUP FINAL:

Liverpool 2 (Hunt, St John)
Lawrence, Lawler, Byrne, Strong, Yeats, Stevenson, Callaghan, Hunt, St John, Smith, Thompson.
Leeds United 1 (Bremner)
Sprake, Reaney, Bell, Bremner, Charlton, Hunter, Giles, Storrie, Peacock, Collins, Johanneson.
After extra-time.

LEAGUE CUP FINAL:

First leg:
Chelsea 3 (Tambling, Venables pen,. McCreadie)
Bonetti, Hinton, Harris, Hollins, Young, Boyle, Murray, Graham, McCreadie, Venables, Tambling.
Leicester City 2 (Appleton, Goodfellow)
Banks, Sjoberg, Norman, Chalmers, King, Appleton, Hodgson, Cross, Goodfellow, Gibson, Sweenie.

Second leg:
Leicester City 0
Banks, Sjoberg, Norman, Chalmers, King, Appleton, Hodgson, Cross, Goodfellow, Gibson, Sweenie.
Chelsea 0
Bonetti, Hinton, Harris, Hollins, Young, Boyle, Murray, Graham, McCreadie, Venables, Tambling.
Chelsea win 3-2 on aggregate.

SCOTTISH FA CUP FINAL:

Celtic 3 (Auld 2, McNeill)
Fallon, Young, Gemmell, Murdoch, McNeill, Clark, Chalmers, Gallagher, Hughes, Lennox, Auld.
Dunfermline Athletic 2 (Melrose, McLaughlin)
Herriot, Callaghan, Lunn, Thomson, McLean, Callaghan, Edwards, Smith, McLaughlin, Melrose, Sinclair.

SCOTTISH LEAGUE CUP FINAL:

Rangers 2 (Forrest 2)
Ritchie, Provan, Caldow, Greig, McKinnon, Wood, Brand, Millar, Forrest, Baxter, Johnstone.
Celtic 1 (Johnstone)
Fallon, Young, Gemmell, Clark, Cushley, Kennedy, Johnstone, Murdoch, Chalmers, Divers, Hughes.

EUROPEAN CUP FINAL:

Played in Milan
Inter-Milan 1 (Jair)
Sarti, Burgnich, Facchetti, Bedin, Guarneri, Picchi, Jair, Mazzola, Peiro, Suarez, Corso.
Benfica 0
Pereira, Cavem, Raul, Cruz, Germano, Neto, Coluna, Augusto, Torres, Eusebio, Simoes.

EUROPEAN CUP-WINNERS' CUP FINAL:
Played at Wembley
West Ham United 2 (Sealey 2)
Standen, Kirkup, Birkett, Peters, Brown, Moore, Sealey, Boyce, Hurst, Dear, Sissons.
Munich 1860 0
Radenkovic, Wagner, Kohlars, Bena, Reich, Luttrop, Heiss, Kuppers, Brunnenmeir, Rebele.

EUROPEAN FAIRS CUP FINAL:
Played in Turin
Ferencvaros 1 (Fenyvesi)
Geczi, Novak, Horath, Juhasz, Matrai, Orosz, Karaba, Varga, Albert, Rakosi, Fenyvesi.
Juventus 0
Anzolin, Gori, Sarti, Bercellino, Castano, Leoncini, Stachini, Del Sol, Combin, Mazzia, Menichelli.

Top Football League goalscorers:

Alick Jeffrey (Doncaster Rovers)	36
Terry Harkin (Crewe Alexandra)	35
Ken Wagstaff (Hull City & Mansfield Town)	34
George O'Brien (Southampton)	32
Robin Stubbs (Torquay United)	31
Barry Dyson (Tranmere Rovers)	29
Jimmy Greaves (Tottenham Hotspur)	29
Kevin Hector (Bradford City)	29
Andy McEvoy (Blackburn Rovers)	29
Denis Law (Manchester United)	28
Gary Talbot (Chester City)	28
Mike Metcalfe (Chester City)	27
Fred Pickering (Everton)	27
Laurie Sheffield (Newport County)	27

Top Scottish First Division marksman:
Jim Forrest (Rangers) 30 goals

Highest average League attendance:
Manchester United (45,990)

Footballer of the Year:
Bobby Collins (Leeds United)

Scottish Footballer of the Year:
Billy McNeill (Celtic)

European Footballer of the Year:
Eusebio (Benfica)

World Club Championship:
Inter-Milan beat Independiente 3-0, 0-0

1965-66: THE WINGLESS WONDERS

I could be accused of wearing rose-coloured glasses on this walk back through the 'sixties, but I am prepared to accept that all was not sweetness and light. There were the darker sides, such as the gradual swing towards more violent play, and the first hooligans were beginning to raise their ugly heads. And even during England's finest hour – the winning of the 1966 World Cup – there was a price to pay. Wingers, those specialist players who brought excitement and adventure to football, were suddenly all but wiped out of the game.

Alf Ramsey was wrongly saddled with the blame for making wingers redundant, but he was merely playing to England's strengths at the time when he settled for a 4-3-3 formation without any recognised flank players. It was not his intention to turn wingers into a dying breed, but England's success in the 1966 World Cup spawned an army of imitators and suddenly the majority of clubs were playing the 4-3-3 way with the emphasis heavily on defence.

I speak from painful memory when I say that it made life harder for goalscorers. Penalty areas became as packed as Piccadilly in the rush hour and goals, the lifeblood of the game, were suddenly much harder to come by. There was now, too often, spite as an added ingredient to go with the strength of tackles. The rule that banned tackling from behind had yet to be introduced, and the ankle-tap and the boot in the calf were two of the nastier fouls that became commonplace. It was now that new phrases were starting to creep into the language of the game. Work-rate ... the overlap ... tackling back ... running off the ball ... centre-backs ... sweepers ... ball-watching ... midfield anchormen. When I first came into the game I was an inside-forward, pure and simple. Now I was described as a striker. The coaches were in charge, and their tactics started to squeeze the goals out of football just as I had seen happening during my brief spell in Italy. It was all much more technical and efficient. But in my view it was from about the time of these mid-'sixties that the fans started to get less of a good deal.

Of course, money was at the root of many of the game's growing problems. It was in the years immediately following the lifting of the maximum wage that the 'Fear Factor' started to take a grip at all levels. Everyone was suddenly frightened of failure - the manager because his job was in danger; the player because he could lose his first-team place and the bonus money that went with it; the director, desperate to cling on to his boardroom place which gave him one-upmanship over his business associates, and the fan because of the 'stick' he had to take from work-mates if the team with which he was identified lost. You could almost reach out and feel the pressure and tension at First

Division matches. We were now not only entering the era of the big boot but also of big business. Football had lost it innocence.

For me, personally, it was a season that I would prefer to forget. I was to be put out of action by a strength-draining bout of hepatitis, and I would then miss out on the 'dream match' World Cup final at Wembley. In a domestic season that would be dominated by thoughts of the World Cup finals, the Anfield Army were again on the march ...

THE LEAGUE CHAMPIONS

It was a testimony to the character as well as the ability of Bill Shankly's Liverpool team that not once in this 1965-66 season did they lose two consecutive matches on their way to their second championship triumph in three seasons; and their consistency was underlined by the fact that only 14 players were called on during the campaign, and one of them – Bobby Graham – appeared only in the final away game at Nottingham Forest, which Liverpool won 4-0 to give themselves a comfortable six-point cushion over the eternal runners-up Leeds United. The marvellous Merseysiders went close to a memorable double, losing in extra-time to Borussia Dortmund in the European Cup-Winners' Cup final.

The only major changes in the Liverpool team compared with the one which captured the championship two seasons earlier was that Tommy Smith and Geoff Strong made their mark in midfield, and Chris Lawler was now a permanent fixture at right-back. Smith wore the No. 10 shirt, but his duties were mainly defensive. He won the ball with tackles that were always fierce and usually fair. Scouser Smith looked as if he had been quarried out of the Scotland Road pavement on which he had first started to kick a ball, and his toughness and competitive spirit would lift him into the land of legend at Liverpool. Geoff Strong had arrived at Anfield from Arsenal as a respected goal-scorer, but had struggled to settle. Then Shanks had the brainwave of playing him in a creative midfield role following an injury to England international Gordon Milne, and it worked so well that he became something of a key man in the Anfield engine-room.

Leeds were looking good for the championship until Liverpool beat them during the Christmas programme. It started a remarkable run for the Reds, who lost only two more League matches in the rest of the season.

Once again it was the goal plundering of the dynamic duo Roger Hunt and Ian St John that destroyed defences. It was a vintage season for Hunt, who scored 30 First Division goals as Liverpool won the League title for the seventh time in their history, equalling the all-time record set by Arsenal. Hunt scored his goals in 19 matches, every one of which Liverpool won, and that underlined that he was a born match-winner.

Roger would go on to amass a club record 245 League goals for Liverpool, until

The Liverpool team *(above)* that illuminated the mid-'sixties, back row: Gordon Milne, Gerry Byrne, Tommy Lawrence, Ron Yeats, Chris Lawler, Willie Stevenson; front row: Ian Callaghan, Roger Hunt, Ian St John, Tommy Smith, Peter Thompson. And *(below)* the man who created the team and started the Liverpool dynasty, the 'man of the people', Bill Shankly.

winding down his career with Bolton in 1969 before retiring to concentrate on his family road haulage business. While his selfless running off the ball made him an invaluable team member, it was his control and killer instinct in the penalty box that pin-pointed him as a devastating individual player. He was strong, brave, quick and totally committed to every match - a true star of the 'sixties.

Sir Alf Ramsey paid Liverpool a great compliment by choosing seven Anfield players in his provisional squad of 40 for the World Cup: Gerry Byrne, Gordon Milne, Chris Lawler, Tommy Smith, Ian Callaghan, Peter Thompson and, of course, Roger Hunt.

> 'The secret of our success under Bill Shankly was that we all played for each other. There were no prima donnas in the team, and we did not care who put the ball into the net as long as it counted for Liverpool. I was lucky to have Ian St John as a partner. He created many goals for me by his fine positional play and his superb passes.' – **Roger Hunt**.

THE FA CUP WINNERS

Cornishman Mike Trebilcock had the sort of FA Cup final of which dreams are made. In only his second Cup match for Everton, he dug the Goodison club out of trouble with two goals against Sheffield Wednesday in a thriller of a final at Wembley.

Wednesday were the underdogs, but dictated the pace and the pattern of the play in the first half after Jim McCalliog – once a young star at Chelsea – shot them into an early lead. He collected a square pass from David Ford in the fourth minute and his snap shot took a deflection that deceived diving goalkeeper Gordon West.

Everton had clambered over the city of Manchester to get to Wembley, beating Second Division champions City in the quarter-finals after two replays, and then United in the semi-finals. They had a balance of youth and experience at full-back, with England master Ray Wilson partnering promising Tommy Wright, and Colin Harvey was now established as a power in midfield. But Everton looked doomed to defeat against Wednesday when Ford added a second goal on the half-hour to give the Yorkshiremen a 2-0 stranglehold on the game.

Then Trebilcock took centre stage. Called into the team at the last moment as a surprise replacement for England centre-forward Fred Pickering, he struck twice in five

Everton, the 'other team' on Merseyside, also had a memorable 1965-66 season, coming from behind to win the FA Cup final against Sheffield Wednesday. Skipper Brian Labone (third left) and Brian Harris proudly hoist the trophy *(above)* as a young, tearful Colin Harvey gets a congratulatory pat on the head. Ray Wilson (extreme left) returned to Wembley two months later as a key member of England's World Cup-winning team. Everton manager Harry Catterick *(left)* had to live in the shadow of the larger-than-life Bill Shankly, but still managed to capture his fair share of trophies.

minutes to bring the scores level.

Extra-time was looming when Wednesday defender Gerry 'Mr Reliable' Young made a rare error that would haunt him into old age. He lost control of the ball in midfield and suddenly flying Everton winger Derek Temple was set free with only goalkeeper Ron Springett to beat. He raced deep into Wednesday's half before firing a shot low and true past the advancing Springett.

> 'I could hardly believe it when manager Harry Catterick told me I was playing. Fred Pickering was the first choice and I thought I would be sitting in the stand as a spectator. My selection came so late that I did not even have my name in the programme. As long as I live I will never forget my two goals. It really was like something out of a dream.' – **Mike Trebilcock**.

CHAMPIONS OF EUROPE

Rebuilt Real Madrid, with only Gento remaining of the great side of the 'fifties, captured the European Cup for a record sixth time in eight finals. This all-Spanish Real team was workmanlike and efficient rather than spectacular when compared to their peerless predecessors, but then which team could possibly find successors in the class of Puskas and di Stefano? How do you replace gods of the game?

Real had battled through to the final in Brussels by eliminating Feyenoord, Kilmarnock, Anderlecht and then – in the semi-finals – the Cup-holders, Inter-Milan.

Partizan Belgrade were to be their opponents in the final after accounting for Nantes and then Werder Bremen, a tie that was scarred by a pitch riot. In the quarter-final against Sparta Prague, Partizan had been trailing 4-1 in the first leg but scored four goals in 30 minutes in their home leg in Belgrade on the way to a 6-4 victory and a semi-final tie against Manchester United. After a magnificent 8-3 aggregate win over Benfica in the quarter-finals, United were confident they could reach their first European Cup final. But they were outfought by Partizan, who won 2-0 in Belgrade and then barricaded their goal behind an eight-man defence at Old Trafford to squeeze through despite a 1-0 defeat in the second leg.

Real had to come from behind to win in the final after Vasovic headed in from a corner in the 55th minute. Amancio equalised and then, with six minutes to go to extra-time, Real right-winger Serena scored the winner with a scorching shot from 20 yards.

For the maestro Francisco Gento it was his eighth appearance in a final – surely a record that would never be beaten. Paco – as he was known to his team-mates – was one of the fastest players I have ever seen. He streaked down the left wing like an Olympic sprinter, and even when at full pace managed to retain control of the ball. A small, compact man with powerful thighs.Paco packed a thundering left foot shot, and his passes were always pin-pointed. He took over from di Stefano as skipper, and he played on into his late 30s to add ten Spanish League championship medals to his collection of eight European Cup-winners' medals. What a player.

> '*I could truthfully say that this win over Partizan has given me as much satisfaction as any of our European Cup final victories. Many people said when Alfredo and Ferenc were no longer with the team that we would not be a power any longer. We have proved all those people wrong, and the European Cup is back where it belongs with Real Madrid.*' – **Gento**.

THE EUROPEAN CUP-WINNERS' CUP

Three British teams reached the semi-finals, but it was the German club Borussia Dortmund who carried off the Cup after a tense final against Liverpool at Hampden Park.

Borussia, with international striker Lothar Emmerich banging in 14 goals on the way to the final, had beaten Cup-holders West Ham 5-2 on aggregate in the semi-finals. Liverpool had cleared four tough hurdles, beating Juventus, Standard Liege, Honved and then – in the semifinals – Celtic after trailing 1-0 from the first leg in what had been an unofficial British championship match.

The game in Glasgow had been marred when spectators pelted the pitch with bottles after a Celtic goal was ruled offside. The incident led to Liverpool becoming something less than popular in the Celtic half of Glasgow and there was a lot of support from the locals for Borussia when the final was staged at Hampden. Ziggy Held put the Germans into the lead, but old faithful Roger Hunt equalised, despite Borussia defenders arguing that the referee should rule it out because of an infringement during the build-up to the goal. Liverpool had done most of the attacking, but they went down to defeat in extratime when a cross from Reinhard Libuda thumped into the net off Ron Yeats.

> '*It is a disappointing way to end a memorable season. But mark my words, Liverpool will win a major European trophy ... and it will be sooner rather than later. We are in the European Cup next season. Don't bet against us winning it. We will make this defeat work for us. It has made us all the more determined to show that we are the best in Europe.*' – **Bill Shankly**.

THE 1966 WORLD CUP FINAL

England team manager Alf Ramsey, who was usually as mean with his quotes as a miser with his money, stepped out of character three years before the 1966 World Cup finals when he stated quite categorically: 'England will win the World Cup'. He had tossed aside his customary cloak of caution to go against history because it was 32 years since the host country had won the tournament. I agreed with Alf's assessment, and I was delighted to get into the World Cup squad after shaking off the hepatitis that had put me out of the game for three months during the build-up to the finals.

Outsiders found it difficult to understand Ramsey's confidence during the group matches, when we made heavy work of a goalless draw with a totally negative Uruguayan team, and we had hardly set the world alight with victories over Mexico and' France. In the game against the French I got a nasty gash on my shin, and it would cost me my place against Argentina in the quarter-finals. Geoff Hurst would take over on his way into the history books.

In a bitterly fought match England eliminated a talented but temperamental Argentinian side 1-0 after skipper Antonio Rattin had been ordered off because of his contemptuous attitude towards the referee. The winning goal against Argentina was scored by Hurst – a beautifully directed header from a perfectly placed ball by his West Ham team-mate Bobby Moore. Alf Ramsey got himself into hot water for describing the Argentinians as 'animals' because of their loutish behaviour. I felt that Alf should have issued an immediate apology – to animals!

For the first time in the tournament England played without a recognised winger. England's 'Wingless Wonders' were born and their 4-3-3 formation was to change the face of football.

Ramsey's 'We will win' prediction gathered a bandwagon of support when England purred to a 2-1 victory over Eusebio-inspired Portugal in a high quality semi-final that erased the memory of much of the tedium and tantrums of the early matches. This was the performance that convinced Alf that he should select the same side for the final,

Two heart-stopping moments during the 1966 World Cup. Argentinian skipper Antonio Rattin *(third from right, above)* has just been given his marching orders in the quarter-final against England because of his contemptuous attitude towards referee Rudolf Kreitlin.

Skipper Bobby Moore is appealing unsuccessfully for handball *(below)* as Wolfgang Weber scrambles the last-minute equaliser for West Germany that sent the World Cup final into extra-time. England went on to win 4-2.

which meant there was no place for me. I will not pretend that I was pleased to miss what would be the match of a lifetime, but Alf was the guv'nor and had to do what he thought was right.

At Wembley England would meet a powerful West German team that had reached the final with a quarter-final elimination of Uruguay and a semi-final win over the USSR.

In Uwe Seeler, Ziggy Held and Helmut Haller the Germans had a striking force that could devastate any defence if given freedom of movement, and lurking out on the left was the tricky but unpredictable Lothar Emmerich, who had one of the fiercest left-foot shots in the game.

Motivating the team from midfield were the composed, 20-year-old Franz Becken-bauer and elegant, left-footed pass-master Wolfgang Overath. They had strength in depth in defence with Horst Höttges and Karl-Heinz Schnellinger giving them flair at full-back while Willie Schulz and Wolfgang Weber were solid and reliable partners at the heart of the defence. The one big question mark was against goalkeeper Hans Tilkowski, whom the England players had nicknamed 'Dracula' because he seemed so frightened of crosses. Both teams would line up in 4-3-3- formations:

England: Banks, Cohen, Jack Charlton, Moore, Wilson, Stiles, Bobby Charl-ton, Peters, Ball, Hunt, Hurst.

West Germany: Tilkowski, Höttges, Schulz, Weber, Schnellinger, Haller, Beck-enbauer, Overath, Seeler, Held, Emmerich.

Two sharp showers just before the kick-off had made the surface of the Wembley pitch quick and treacherous. Players on both sides showed nerves that were as ex-posed as barbed wire on a wall, and there was so much tension around that it was inev-itable that a goal was going to be born out of an error. What nobody expected was that the mistake would be made by the most dependable of all England's players – the cool, commanding Ray Wilson, who had not put a foot wrong throughout the tournament.

The game was into its 13th minute when Wilson looked to have time and room in which to clear a Ziggy Held cross. But instead of his usual accuracy, he pushed the ball to the feet of Helmut Haller, a deadly enough marksman without need of such charitable assistance. He turned and gleefully squeezed a low shot just inside the left post from 12 yards, with goalkeeper Gordon Banks looking on helplessly. England 0, West Germany 1.

All of us looking on willing an England victory consoled ourselves with the fact that the World Cup had not been won by the side which scored first in any of the four pre-vious post-war finals.

It was after this startling goal that England revealed the discipline and determina-tion that Alf Ramsey had drilled into them during the build-up to the finals. There was no hint of panic or loss of composure. The unflappable Wilson carried on in his usual immaculate style with a poker-face manner that was to serve him well in his later profession as a funeral director.

If anything, the goal acted as an inspiration to England and they began to settle into their stride. They were rewarded for their professional attitude with an equaliser just six minutes later. Overath tripped Bobby Moore and the England skipper took an instant free-kick while the German defenders were still regrouping. He floated the ball in from the left and Geoff Hurst drifted behind the German defence to glide a header wide of Tilkowski, who was still feeling the effects of an early collision with Hurst in which he had been knocked out. It was a made-in-West-Ham goal.

The action was fast and fluctuating, with neither side able to claim domination. West German team manager Helmut Schöen had watched England's victory against Portugal in the semi-final and was so impressed by a phenomenal display from Bobby Charlton that he delegated Beckenbauer a man-to-man marking job on the Manchester United schemer. This meant that the two most creative players on the pitch were cancelling each other out.

Roger Hunt squandered a good chance to give England the lead, but England were gradually getting on top – particularly down the right side of the pitch where Alan Ball, the 21-year-old 'baby' of the England team, was providing action to go with his words. He had told room-mate Nobby 'The Toothless Tiger' Stiles before the match in that 'Clitheroe Kid' voice of his: 'That Schnellinger's made for me. I'll give him such a chasing that he won't know what day it is'.

It was fitting that the red-shirted, red-haired Ball – covering every inch of the right side of the Wembley pitch like the fire from a flamethrower – should set up what most people thought was the match-winning goal 12 minutes from the end. His shot was pushed out by Tilkowski for a corner that the Blackpool marathon runner took himself. The ball dropped at the feet of Hurst, whose shot was deflected by Hottges into the path of Martin Peters. He almost had enough time to pick his spot as he clinically buried the ball into the back of the net from six yards. Another made-in-West-Ham goal.

The Germans looked out on their feet and there was a growing victory roar rolling around Wembley. The cheers died in thousands of throats when, with less than a minute to go, Swiss referee Gottfried Dienst harshly ruled that Jack Charlton had fouled Germany's spring-heeled skipper, Uwe Seeler.

Emmerich, who had hardly been allowed a kick by his marker George Cohen, crashed the free-kick towards goal with his feared left foot. The ball was deflected – Bobby Moore argued that it was by a German hand – to Held, who half hit the ball across the face of the goal. Gordon Banks, the outstanding goalkeeper in the tournament, was wrongfooted because he had reacted for a clean shot from Held. The ball bobbled loose to defender Wolfgang Weber who bundled it into the England net with the last kick of ordinary time.

Players of both sides tumbled to the ground in exhaustion as the referee's whistle signalled extra-time. Alf Ramsey came striding purposefully on to the pitch and did a quick walkie-talkie tour of his players, offering them encouragement and advice. He pointed to the drained West German players. 'Look at them', he said. 'They're finished. You've beaten them once. Now go and do it again.' I was just watching and I felt exhausted.

The fiercely competitive Nobby Stiles, socks rolled down to his ankles and teeth removed, flourished a fist at his team-mates. 'Come on, lads,' he yelled in his Mancunian accent, 'let's stoof the booggers.' Battling Alan Ball responded with a run and a shot in the second minute of extra-time that brought a fine save from Tilkowski, who had shaken off his early indecision.

Eight minutes later, after a Bobby Charlton shot from a pass by brother Jack had been turned on to a post, Ball tore past the exhausted Schnellinger yet again. This time his centre found Geoff Hurst, who span round and crashed a shot against the underside of the bar. As the ball bounced down, Roger Hunt – the England player closest to the net – immediately whirled round in celebration of a goal. His opinion was supported after a heart-stopping delay by Russian linesman Tofik Bakhramov, who signalled that the ball had crossed the line, a decision that will always be disputed by the Germans.

Skipper Seeler called for one more effort from team-mates who had run themselves to the edge of exhaustion. Beckenbauer, at last released from his negative containment of Bobby Charlton, pushed forward from midfield and was shaping to shoot when he was dispossessed by a tigerish tackle from the resolute Stiles, who was displaying the brand of courage and willpower for which medals were awarded in the field of battle. Then Haller battled his way through the middle only to be foiled by the long legs of Jack Charlton. The Germans were so committed to all-out attack that they were leaving inviting gaps in their own penalty area.

Celebrating England fans were trespassing over the touchline in anticipation of the final whistle when hero-of-the-hour Hurst ended all arguments in the closing seconds of the match. He chased a measured pass from the majestic Moore and hammered in a left-foot shot that left Tilkowski rooted in front of his goal like a man facing a firing squad. With the last kick of the match Hurst had became the first man to complete a World Cup hat-trick, and for the first time the World Cup had come to the birthplace of organised football.

The son of a non-League professional, Hurst was born in Ashton-under-Lyne, Lancashire, on 8 December, 1941. He had been selected for the England squad for the first time in this 1965-66 season, making his debut in a 1-0 victory over West Germany in a friendly international at Wembley on 23 February, 1966. He went on to score 24 goals in 49 matches for England. His League goals haul for West Ham would reach 180, and he would then add 22 League goals for Stoke before closing his career with West Bromwich Albion.

Alf Ramsey was honoured with a knighthood and Bobby Moore with an OBE in the honours list following England's victory. Other players who had taken part in early

A golden kiss from skipper Bobby Moore seals the greatest moment in English football history *(above)* as George Cohen and Jack Charlton wait their turn to get their hands on the World Cup. Geoff Hurst, whose three goals won the trophy for England, appears to be trying to do a Nobby Stiles impression.

The triumphant World Cup team *(below),* back row: trainer Harold Shepherdson, Nobby Stiles, Roger Hunt, Gordon Banks, Jack Charlton, George Cohen, Ray Wilson, Alf Ramsey; front: Martin Peters, Geoff Hurst, Bobby Moore, Alan Ball, Bobby Charlton.

matches in the tournament were wingers Terry Paine, Ian Callaghan, John Connolly and myself. Eusebio was top scorer with nine goals, including four in the quarter-final against North Korea when he had inspired a comeback from 3-0 down to a 5-3 victory. Portugal beat the USSR 2-1 in the third-place play-off.

> *'I was not sure whether my third goal counted until I saw it go up on the score-board. I noticed some fans running on the pitch as I shot and I wondered if the final whistle had gone. I am completely overwhelmed by what has happened. A couple of weeks ago I didn't think I was going to get a game in the World Cup. Now this. It's just incredible.'* – **GEOFF HURST**.

GREAVSIE'S FOOTBALL DIARY
1965-66

1965

3 July: The Football Association – by 43 votes to 19 – sanction the Football League proposal to allow one substitute for each team to re-place any injured player during the coming season. Twelve-a-side foot-ball is with us.

13 July: Joe Mercer is appointed manager of Manchester City. His first signing as coach and assistant manager is Malcolm Allison. City are about to have a ball.

19 July: Sir Stanley Matthews retains his links with the Potteries by becoming gen-eral manager of Port Vale.

27 July: Ivor Allchurch, 35-year-old Cardiff and former Newcastle inside-forward, re-joins his first club, Swansea, for £6,500. The most-capped Welsh international with 68 appearances behind him, Ivor is a true artist of the game and he and his brother, Len, have made the name Allchurch one of the most respected of all in Welsh football.

21 August: Charlton forward Keith Peacock gets into the record books by becoming the first ever substitute in League football when he comes on wearing the No 12 shirt against Bolton Wanderers at Burnden Park.

10 September: Jeff Astle has made a cracking start to the season with West Brom-wich Albion. He notches his third hat-trick in eight days.

2 October: England are held to a goalless draw by Wales at Ninian Park in our first match of the World Cup season. Alf Ramsey has recently repeated his 'We will win the World Cup' statement, so we take a lot of stick. I feel the press should have given more credit to Wales, and particularly to centre-half Mike England, who is outstanding in the middle of the Welsh defence; and Terry Hennessey, who gives a barnstorming performance at right-half.

6 October: A sickening blow for Leeds. Wee Bobby Collins, the veteran Scottish architect of their attack, is carried off with a fractured thigh in a European Fairs Cup tie in Turin. One of the great masters of the game, who believes in living by the sword, Bobby will confound the medical experts by battling back from the crippling injury to play again.

9 October: Hooliganism is reported at several First Division grounds. This is when the problem, still in its infancy, should be stamped on with tough disciplinary measures, but it will be allowed to become a cancer that will gnaw away at the game for the next two decades.

16 October: A hat-trick in Tottenham's 5-1 win over Manchester United at White Hart Lane. It includes a goal that people tell me is the greatest I have ever scored when I manage to slip past five tackles before steering the ball into the net. Happy days!

20 October: England 2, Austria 3 at Wembley! Nine months to go to the World Cup finals and we are not exactly filling our fans with confidence. Mind you, this is a freak result. We should have won by at least two goals. Ron Springett is back in goal for England, but Ron apart this will be England's defence in the World Cup: George Cohen, Ray Wilson, Nobby Stiles, Jack Charlton and, of course, Bobby Moore.

27 October: Brian Clough starts his managerial career down in the Fourth Division with Hartlepool. Peter Taylor joins him as his right-hand man.

5 November: I am lighting a bonfire for my kids when suddenly I feel as if somebody has chopped me off at the legs. I go to bed with what I think is pneumonia and am then carted off to hospital with what is diagnosed as hepatitis. Horrible days!

18 November: Lying in hospital, I get the distressing news that Tottenham centre-half Maurice Norman has broken a leg in a meaningless friendly against Hungary at White Hart Lane. It is a double fracture, and it will end big Mo's distinguished career during which he has won 23 England caps as a commanding centre-half who played a key role in the glory glory days of 'Super Spurs'.

19 November: Nottingham Forest sign Birmingham City's driving Welsh international half-back Terry Hennessey for £30,000.

8 December: Stan Cullis, so cruelly sacked by Wolves, is brought back into football as Birmingham City manager. Alf Ramsey launches his 'Wingless Wonders', playing without a recognised winger for the first time in an international match. England beat Spain 2-0 in Madrid with goals from Joe Baker and Roger Hunt. When Norman 'Bites

Yer Legs' Hunter comes on for his international debut as a substitute for the injured Baker, Alan Ball puts his hands together, looks up to the heavens and says: 'For what they are about to receive ...'

1966

3 January: Dick Graham, who has been a consistent headline maker since taking over as manager of Crystal Palace, leaves Selhurst Park. Arthur Rowe, the grand old man of football who guided the push-and-run Spurs of the 'fifties to the League championship in 1951, will take over as caretaker manager until Bert Head arrives from Swindon via Bury.

5 January: A rare goal by skipper Bobby Moore gives England a 1-1 draw with Poland on a mud heap of a pitch at Goodison Park. Bobby Charlton is injured and joins me on the sidelines. Burnley's quick and direct Gordon Harris makes a satisfactory debut in Bobby's place, and helps set up Moore's late equaliser.

27 January: Billy Wright gets tough at Highbury and drops his two star players, George Eastham and Joe Baker, and both ask to be placed on the transfer list.

28 January: I return to football with a goal for Spurs in a 4-0 victory over Blackburn at White Hart Lane. It's great to be back, but I have lost a vital half a yard of pace.

2 February: Jack Charlton blows his top during a bad-tempered Fairs Cup tie against Valencia at Leeds. As he chases an opponent around the pitch the police come on and intervene, and Dutch referee Leo Horn orders both teams off. When the match is restarted 11 minutes later Jack is left behind in the dressing-room on the orders of the referee. Valencia have two players sent off.

23 February: England beat West Germany 1-0 at Wembley thanks to a goal by, of all people, Nobby Stiles. He wears the No. 9 shirt, but plays his usual tigerish role in midfield. Geoff Hurst makes his debut for England in a match that we do not realise is to prove a dress-rehearsal for the World Cup final in five months' time.

25 February: Joe Baker joins Nottingham Forest from Arsenal for a club record £65,000.

28 February: Mike Bailey, England international right-half, joins Wolves from Charlton for £40,000. A born leader, Bailey has battled back from a broken leg that threatened to end his career.

5 March: Arsenal skipper Don Howe breaks a leg playing against Blackpool. It will signal the end of his career, and he will become one of the game's outstanding coaches.

17 March: Manchester City buy Colin Bell from Bury for £45,000 as Joe Mercer and Malcolm Allison put the finishing touches to one of the most exciting teams in Maine Road history. Fulham buy Allan Clarke from Walsall for £35,000 and on the same day sell local hero Rodney Marsh to Queen's Park Rangers for £15,000.

20 March: England have lost the World Cup without a ball being kicked! The gold Jules Rimet trophy is stolen while on show at an exhibition at Caxton Hall in London.

27 March: The World Cup is found by a dog called Pickles while going for 'walkies' with his owner in Norwood, Middlesex. Pickles is sniffing around a front garden when he comes across the trophy lying undamaged and wrapped in newspaper.

2 April: Scotland 3, England 4 in a thriller at Hampden Park. England lead 2-0, 3-1 and 4-2, but each time the Scots battle back. Geoff Hurst bags his first goal for England, Bobby Charlton scores with a 25-yard screamer and Roger Hunt nets two goals. Denis Law and two-goal Jimmy Johnstone score for Scotland, who are celebrating a fourth goal when Nobby Stiles brilliantly heads the ball off the line. The game is watched by a crowd of 134,000, willing Scotland on in the search for a victory that would give them some consolation for not having qualified for the World Cup finals.

26 April: Charlie Cooke joins Chelsea for £72,000 from Dundee. This leaves the way clear for Terry Venables to move from Stamford Bridge to Tottenham for £80,000.

4 May: I make my England comeback and score in England's 2-0 victory over Yugoslavia at Wembley. This will be our last match at Wembley before the World Cup and there is a growing confidence that we can make Alf Ramsey's prediction come true. Bobby Charlton scores England's second goal.

10 May: John Atyeo, playing in the final match of his career for Bristol City, takes his club goalscoring record to 350 – a magnificent collection that has taken him 15 years. A school teacher when he is not playing football, John has been a fine ambassador for the sport.

24 May: England Under-23 international goalkeeper Alex Stepney joins Chelsea from Millwall for £50,000. It seems an odd buy by Tommy Docherty who, in Peter Bonetti, has already got one of England's finest goalkeepers on his books.

10 June: Billy Wright's four-year reign as Arsenal manager ends in confusion. The Highbury board say that he has resigned, but Billy – as honest as the day is long – says: 'I've never walked out on anything in my life. I have been sacked'. Bertie Mee, 46-year- old club physiotherapist, will take over, with Dave Sexton as his coach.

26 June: Finland 0, England 3. This is the first of four tour matches to get us tuned up for the World Cup finals. Martin Peters, Roger Hunt and Jack Charlton score the goals. Bobby Moore and I look on from the sidelines.

29 June: Norway 1, England 6. I bang in four goals. This will be the team that will line up in the World Cup final at Wembley in a month's time, with one exception – Geoff Hurst will be in my place.

1 July: A shadow is cast over our tour when Joe Mears, the 61-year-old chairman of the Football Association and of Chelsea, collapses and dies of a heart attack while strolling through an Oslo park. Joe was a true gentleman whom I looked on as a friend ever since my days at Chelsea. He will be greatly missed in football.

3 July: Denmark 0, England 2. It is my 50th match for England, and the Danish FA kindly present me with a silver salver before the kick-off. Peter Bonetti makes his international debut in goal.

5 July: Poland 0, England 1. Our last match before the World Cup finals. Roger Hunt settles it with a superb shot.

THE CHAMPIONS OF 1965-66

FIRST DIVISION:
1: Liverpool (61 points)
2: Leeds United (55)
3: Burnley (55)

Championship squad:
Arrowsmith (3 appearances), Byrne (42), Callaghan (3), Graham (1), Hunt (37), Lawler (40), Lawrence (42), Milne (28), St John (41), Smith (42), Stevenson (41), Strong (21), Thompson (40), Yeats (42).
Goalscorers: Hunt (30), St John (10), Milne (7), Callaghan (5), Lawler (5), Stevenson (5), Strong (5), Thompson (5), Smith (3), Yeats (2), Arrowsmith (1), Byrne (1).

SECOND DIVISION:
1: Manchester City (59 points)
2: Southampton (54)
3: Coventry City (53)

Championship squad:
Bacuzzi (15 appearances), Bell (11), Brand (17), Cheetham (12), Connor (29), Crossan (40), Dowd (38), Doyle (19), Gray (3), Gomersall (1), Heslop (34), Horne (15), Kennedy (35), Murray (11), Oakes (41), Ogley (4), Pardoe (40), Sear (19), Summerbee (42), Wood (1), Young (35).
Goalscorers: Young (14), Crossan (13), Pardoe (9), Doyle (7), Murray (7), Summerbee (7), Bell (4), Connor (3), Brand (2), Gray (1), Kennedy (1), Oakes (1), Sear (1), 6 own goals.

THIRD DIVISION:
1: Hull City (69 points)
2: Millwall (65)
3: Queen's Park Rangers (53)

Championship squad:
Brown (5 appearances), D. Butler (37), I. Butler (45), Chilton (45), Collinson (2), Davidson (45), Greenwood (1), Heath (11), Henderson (38), Houghton (45), Karvis (33), Milner (46), Sharpe (4), Simpkin (46), Summers (11), Swan (36), Wagstaff (46), Wilkinson (1), Williams (10).
Goalscorers: Wagstaff (27), Chilton (25), Houghton (22), I. Butler (13), Henderson (13), Jarvis (3), Simpkin (1), 5 own goals.

FOURTH DIVISION:
1: Doncaster Rovers (59 points)
2: Darlington (59)
3: Torquay United (58)

Championship squad:
Broadbent (8 appearances), Chapman (5), Coleman (32), Dawson (7), Durrant (11), Fearnley (15), Finney (14), Fairhurst (3), Grainger (5), Gilfillan (29), Jeffrey (38), Kelly (45), Leivers (5), Lovell (2), McMinn (1), Nicholson (39), Ogden (11), Potter (19), Ricketts (46), Ripley (14), Robinson (17), Sheffield (43), Watton (31), Wilkson (20), Wylie (46).
Goalscorers: Sheffield (28), Jeffrey (22), Gilfillan (6), Ricketts (6), Coleman (5), Ogden (4), Broadbent (3), Robinson (1), Ripley (1), Finney (1), Kelly (1), Wylie (1), Durrant (1).

SCOTTISH FIRST DIVISION:
1: Celtic (57 points)
2: Rangers (55)
3: Kilmarnock (45)

Championship squad:
Clark (34 appearances), Gemmell (34), Johnstone (32), Murdoch (31), McBride (3), Simpson (30), McNeill (25), Lennox (24), Hughes (23), Chalmers (22), Gallagher (19), Auld (17), Young (17), Craig (15), Cushley (12), Fallon (4), Divers (3), Brogan (2), Cattenach (1).
Goalscorers: McBride (31), Lennox (15), Chalmers (14), Hughes (14), Auld (8), Johnstone (8), Murdoch (5), Gallagher (5), Gemmell (4), Young (2), Divers (1).

SCOTTISH SECOND DIVISION:
1: Ayr United (53 points)
2: Airdrieonians (50)
3: Queen of the South (47)

FA CUP FINAL:
Everton 3 (Trebilcock 2, Temple)
West, Wright, Wilson, Gabriel, Labone, Harris, Scott, Trebilcock, Young, Harvey, Temple.
Sheffield Wednesday 2 (McCalliog, Ford)
Springett, Smith, Megson, Eustace, Ellis, Young, Pugh, Fantham, McCalliog, Ford, Quinn.

LEAGUE CUP FINAL:
First leg:
West Ham 2 (Moore, Byrne)
Standen, Burnett, Burkett, Peters, Brown, Moore, Brabrook, Boyce, Byrne, Hurst, Dear.
West Bromwich Albion 1 (Astle)
Potter, Cram, Fairfax, Fraser, Campbell, Williams, Brown, Astle, Kaye, Lovett, Clark.
Second leg:
West Bromwich Albion 4 (Kaye, Brown, Clark, Williams)
Potter, Cram, Fairfax, Fraser, Campbell,

Williams, Brown, Astle, Kaye, Lovett, Clark.
West Ham 1 (Peters)
Standen, Burnett, Burkett, Peters, Brown, Moore, Brabrook, Boyce, Byrne, Hurst, Dear.
West Bromwich Albion win 5-3 on aggregate.

SCOTTISH FA CUP FINAL:
Rangers 1 (Johansen)
Ritchie, Johansen, Provan, Greig, McKinnon, Millar, Wilson, Watson, Forrest, Johnston, Henderson.
Celtic 0
Simpson, Young, Gemmell, Murdoch, McNeill, Clark, Johnstone, McBride, Chalmers, Gallagher, Hughes.
Replay after a 0-0 draw.

SCOTTISH LEAGUE CUP FINAL:
Celtic 2 (Hughes 2 pens.)
Simpson, Young, Gemmell, Murdoch, McNeill, Clark, Johnstone, McBride, Chalmers, Gallagher, Hughes.
Rangers 1 (Young own goal)
Ritchie, Johansen, Provan, Wood, McKinnon, Greig, Henderson, Willoughby, Forrest, Wilson, Johnston.

EUROPEAN CUP FINAL:
Played in Brussels
Real Madrid 2 (Amancio, Serena)
Araquistain, Pachin, Sanchis, Pirri, De Fekipe. Zoco, Serena, Amancio, Grosso, Velasquez, Gento.
Partizan Belgrade 1 (Vasovic)
Soskic, Jusufi, Milhailovic, Becejac, Rasovic, Vasovic, Bakic, Kovacevic, Hasanagic, Galic, Primajer.

EUROPEAN CUP-WINNERS' CUP FINAL:
Played at Hampden Park, Glasgow
Borussia Dortmund 2 (Held, Yeats own goal)
Tilkowski, Cyliax, Redder, Kurrat, Paul, Assauer, Libuda, Schmidt, Held, Sturm, Emmerich.

Liverpool 1 *(Hunt)*
Lawrence, Lawler, Byrne, Milne, Yeats,
Stevenson, Callaghan, Hunt, St John, Smith,
Thompson.
After extra-time

EUROPEAN FAIRS CUP FINAL:

First leg:

Barcelona 0
Sadurni, Benitez, Eladio, Motesinos, Gallego,
Torres, Zaballa, Muller, Zaldua, Fuste, Vidal.

Real Zaragoza 1 *(Canario)*
Yarza, Irusquieta, Reija, Pais, Santamaria,
Violeta, Canario, Santos, Marcelino, Villa,
Lapetra.

Second leg:

Real Zaragoza 2 *(Marcelino 2)*
Yarza, Irusquieta, Reija, Pais, Santamaria,
Violeta, Canario, Santos, Marcelino, Villa,
Lapetra.

Barcelona 4 *(Pujol 3, Zaballa)*
Sadurni, Foncho, Eladio, Motesinos, Gallego,
Torres, Zaballa, Mas, Zaldua, Fuste, Pujol.
*Extra-time played in 2nd leg. Barcelona win 4-3
on aggregate.*

Top Football League goalscorers:

Kevin Hector (Bradford City)	44
Les Allen (Queen's Park Rangers)	32
John O'Rourke (Luton Town)	32
Martin Chivers (West Ham United)	30
John Dyson (Tranmere Rovers)	30
Roger Hunt (Liverpool)	30
Willie Irvine (Burnley)	29
Lawrie Sheffield (Doncaster Rovers)	28
Matt Tees (Grimsby Town)	28
Tony Hateley (Aston Villa)	27
Ken Wagstaff (Hull City)	27
Chris Chilton (Hull City)	25

Top Scottish First Division marksmen:
Alex Ferguson (Dunfermline) 31 goals
Joe McBride (Celtic) 31 goals

Highest average League attendance:
Liverpool (40,000)

Footballer of the Year:
Bobby Charlton (Manchester United)

Scottish Footballer of the Year:
John Greig (Rangers)

European Footballer of the Year:
Bobby Charlton (Manchester United)

World Club Championship:
Penarol beat Real Madrid 2-0, 2-0

1966-67: THE TEAM THAT JOCK BUILT

A big man in every way. That was Jock Stein, manager of Celtic, the club that monopolised the season of 1966-67 in a manner so magnificent that it made even we cynical Englishmen proud to call them British. Jock was big in physique, personality and ideas. He was the driving force that transformed Celtic into one of the world's greatest teams within a matter of months of taking over as manager in 1965 after serving his apprenticeship with Dunfermline and Hibernian.

A former Celtic centre-half and captain, he had always passionately believed that football should be played with a positive attitude. He demanded an attacking approach at Parkhead where Celtic – the team that Jock built – provided testimony to his enormous talent as a master creator.

Celtic's record under the mesmerising management of Stein was unparalleled in British football. In his first six full seasons in charge at Parkhead, the Glasgow club were to win six Scottish League titles and lose only 17 of 204 League games while scoring 597 goals. They reached five Scottish FA Cup finals, winning three; and they won five out of six League Cup finals. Celtic polished and perfected their teamwork in a Scottish League where they were so dominant that even Rangers fans had to applaud their achievements.

There were dismissive remarks heard south of the border that the Scottish League was not a real test of a team's quality, but those sort of sniping comments were silenced as Celtic set out to try to become the first British club to win the European Cup. They barnstormed into the final with a brand of exciting, attacking football that put to shame those clubs becoming addicted to the drug of defensive football that paralysed so many games in the mid-to-late 'sixties. In the final they were to meet the great architects of defence-dominated football, Internazionale Milan, who had captured the European Cup in successive seasons in 1964 and 1965 from the springboard of their sterile *catenaccio* defensive system. As we have learned in previous chapters, Helenio Herrera's Inter built a human fortress around their goal and then relied on three or four jet-paced forwards to make maximum capital out of carefully constructed counter attacks.

Celtic's style and attitude was the exact opposite. The team that Jock built was geared to flair and adventure. Many years later I would get a reputation for being anti-Scottish football because of some of my biting criticisms as a television know-all. The truth is that I have always been an admirer of the way the Scots in general, and Celtic in particular, play the game. At their best they are as good as any footballers in the world. To prove how highly I rate the Jock footballers here is a team I have selected from Scottish international players who were established with their clubs in the 'sixties. It is a combination that would beat most permutations you could come up with from the same era:

Ronnie Simpson (Newcastle and Celtic), Sandy Jardine (Rangers), Eddie McCreadie (Chelsea), Pat Crerand (Celtic and Manchester United), Billy McNeill (Celtic), Dave Mackay (Hearts and Tottenham), Jimmy Johnstone (Celtic), Denis Law (Manchester United), Ian St John (Motherwell and Liverpool), Jim Baxter (Rangers), Willie Johnston (Rangers). Subs: John Greig (Rangers), Billy Bremner (Leeds).

I hope that clears up the nonsense of me being anti-Jocks. There are few better sights in football than a Scottish team playing the traditional way with carpet passes and the emphasis on ball skill. This must be an exceptional team if I cannot get my Tottenham side-kick Alan Gilzean in, because he was a marvellous player.

I had no hesitation in selecting Ronnie Simpson, son of a former Rangers captain, as goalkeeper. He was a remarkable last line of defence for Jock Stein's Celtic, and disproved the theory that Scottish goalkeepers cannot even catch colds. Ronnie had won two FA Cup-winners' medals with Newcastle in 1952 and 1955. Over a decade later, at the age of 36, he was still as agile and alert as ever. Jim Craig, skipper Billy McNeill, John Clark and power-shooting left-back Tommy Gemmell made up a formidable back line in front of Simpson. They were encouraged to keep pushing forward as auxiliary attackers.

Taking responsibility for the supply of passes from the midfield engine-room in Celtic's 4-2-4 formation were the skilful and competitive Bertie Auld and the industrious and inventive Bobby Murdoch.

The four-man firing line was one of the most effective goal machines in football. Jinking Jimmy Johnstone was unstoppable on his day as a quick and clever right winger who could destroy defences with his darting runs. Bobby Lennox patrolled the left wing with a mixture of cunning and power, cutting in to shoot or to feed delicate passes to central strikers Willie Wallace and Steve Chalmers.

CHAMPIONS OF EUROPE

The 1967 European Cup final was to be a contest between Inter-Milan's negative, smothering tactics and the up-and- at-'em cavalier charges of Celtic. Neutrals hoped that the positive would beat the negative. The Milan method was tried and tested. They liked to search for a quick goal and then sit back and barricade their goal behind a fortress defence. So it was no surprise to Celtic when the Italians opened with a burst of attacking football that could have come out of the Jock Stein manual. Sandro Mazzola, Milan's key player following the late withdrawal of injured schemer Luis Suarez, headed against Ronnie Simpson's legs in the opening raid.

Then, in the seventh minute, Mazzola triggered an attack that led to the early goal on which Milan had set their sights. He put Corso clear on the left with a penetrating pass. The wingman released the ball to Cappellini, who was in the process of trying to shoot when a crunching Jim Craig tackle knocked him off the ball. It was judged a foul by German referee Herr Tschenscher, and Mazzola coolly scored from the penalty spot.

It had been a magnificent opening spell by the Italians, but by force of habit they shelved their attacking talents and pulled all but two forwards back to guard their goal. It was an invitation to Celtic to attack – and they gladly accepted.

The Scottish champions pushed full-backs Craig and Gemmell forward on virtually permanent duty as extra wingers, and the Milan defensive wall buckled and bent under an avalanche of attacks.

Goalkeeper Sarti made a procession of brilliant saves, and when he was beaten the woodwork came to his rescue as first Auld and then Gemmell hammered shots against the bar. Any other team might have surrendered with broken hearts as the Milan goal miraculously survived the onslaught, but skipper McNeill kept brandishing his fist as he urged his team-mates to greater efforts. The word 'surrender' was not part of the Celtic vocabulary.

At last, after an hour of sustained attack, Celtic were rewarded with an equaliser, and it was the exclusive creation of overlapping full-backs Craig and Gemmell. First of all Craig brought the ball forward along the right side of the pitch. The retreating Italian defenders tightly marked every player in a green-hooped shirt, but there was one man that they missed. Craig spotted Gemmell coming through like a train on the left side and angled a pass into his path. Sarti had managed to stop everything to date, but no goalkeeper on earth could have saved Gemmell's scorching shot, which was smashed high into the net from 20 yards.

Propelled by panic, Milan tried to get their attacking instincts working, but they were so accustomed to back-pedalling that they could not lift the pace and pattern of their play. Celtic maintained their momentum and created the winning goal they so richly deserved six minutes from the end of an emotion-draining match. Gemmell came pounding forward along the left touchline. The Italians were not sure whether to mark his team-mates or to try to block his route to goal in case he was tempted to take another pot shot. Caught in two minds, they gave too much room to Bobby Murdoch, who accepted a pass from Gemmell and unleashed a shot. The diving Sarti was confident he had the ball covered, but Steve Chalmers managed to deflect it out of his reach for a winning goal that made Celtic the first British winners of the major prize in club football.

At the final whistle thousands of Celtic fans came chasing on to the pitch to parade their heroes like trophies. Jock Stein waited anxiously in the dressing-room, counting

Tommy Gemmell strikes the goal that put Celtic in charge of the 1967 European Cup final against Inter-Milan *(above)*, and Jock Stein returns home to Glasgow to a hero's welcome *(left)*. Bill Shankly told Stein in the dressing-room after the stunning victory: 'You've become bloody immortal!'

his players as they battled their way through the thronging supporters on the night that Lisbon belonged to Glasgow.

Following on behind the last of the Celtic players was Liverpool's larger-than-life manager Bill Shankly, one of the few people who could put his record up against his old Scottish pal Stein. As he entered the dressing-room Shankly summed up Stein's achievement with one of his typically direct and appropriate statements. 'John,' he boomed, using Stein's Christian name, 'you've just become a bloody legend.'

Skipper Billy McNeill epitomised the spirit and style of Celtic. He was an extension of Jock Stein on the pitch, the driving force who made the team tick and the opponents quiver. There were few harder men in the tackle, and for a big man he was surprisingly quick on his feet and a master of positioning. It was rare for anybody ever to beat him in the air, and his amazing consistency made him Celtic's man-for-all-seasons as he went on to collect a record nine successive League championship medals, seven Scottish Cup-winners' medals and 29 full international caps.

For six years, Celtic would be the 'Great Untouchables', winning everything in sight, apart from an infamous world championship match with Racing Club of Buenos Aires in which tempers and tantrums over-ruled the talent of both teams. In 1970 they won the unofficial crown as champions of Britain when they conquered Football League champions Leeds United in the semi-final of the European Cup. In the final they would be beaten 2-1 by Feyenoord after extra-time, with Gemmell scoring their goal. Jock Stein, the man who masterminded Celtic's greatest triumphs, sadly died 'in harness' in 1985. Aged 62, he collapsed and died in the players' tunnel moments after Scotland had eliminated Wales from the World Cup in a qualifying match in Cardiff. A light went out in British football. The game had lost one of its finest managers and greatest characters.

'There is not a prouder man on God's earth than me at this moment. Winning was important, aye, but it was the way that we won that has filled me with satisfaction. We did it by playing football. Pure, beautiful, inventive football. There was not a negative thought in our heads. Inter played into our hands. It's so sad to see such gifted players shackled by a system that restricts their freedom to think and to act. Our fans would never accept that sort of sterile approach. Our objective is always to try to win with style.' – *Jock Stein*.

THE LEAGUE CHAMPIONS

Manchester United once again won the right to carry England's challenge in the European Cup campaign with what was to prove to be, astonishingly, their final League championship triumph for more than a quarter of a century. The turning point in United's season came in February, 1967, when they were tumbled out of the FA Cup by Second Division Norwich City in a fourth round tie at Old Trafford. Manager Matt Busby called a team meeting and it was agreed that an all-out effort must be made to capture the championship as consolation for the undignified FA Cup defeat. 'We are disgusted with the way we played against Norwich', said fiery Scot Denis Law. 'We owe it to our supporters to make up for it by making an extra effort to win the First Division title.'

Liverpool led the way in the championship race, but with Roger Hunt having one of the quietest seasons of his career they lost their impetus in the last third of the season and United took over with a sequence of storming performances following their humiliation by Norwich.

The only major changes in the United team that won the championship in 1963-64 were that Alex Stepney had taken over in goal, and John Aston had established himself on the left wing. Bobby Noble was just beginning to make a name for himself in the United defence when his career was wrecked by injury. It was again the 'Fearsome Threesome' – Best, Law and Charlton – who combined to create havoc in rival defences, and it was the goal power of Law (23) and Herd (16) that pushed them ahead of a spirited challenge from Nottingham Forest. This was the 'nearly' season for Forest, who finished runners-up in the League and fell at the semi-final hurdle in the FA Cup to Spurs. They would have to wait for the arrival of one Brian Clough before they would at last get among the glittering prizes.

United clinched the championship with a crushing 6-1 victory over West Ham at Upton Park on 9 May. Sadly, their triumph was scarred by hooliganism in the crowd, but even this growing problem could not overshadow the fact that United had a team equipped to bring the European Cup to England at last.

'There is a quietly confident mood at Old Trafford that we can go on and win the European Cup. Celtic have shown that it can be done. Now every player on the staff wants to do it for the boss, Matt Busby. That has got to be our number one target for next season. I am not a betting man, but I certainly would not advise anybody to bet against us.' – *George Best.*

THE FA CUP WINNERS

While Celtic, Liverpool, Everton and Manchester United had been grabbing the headlines and the major honours, Bill Nicholson had quietly been rebuilding his Tottenham team. We proved that his jigsaw was complete by reaching the FA Cup final at Wembley, led by the remarkable Dave 'Miracle Man' Mackay, who had made an astonishing recovery after twice breaking a leg.

Of the side that won the FA Cup in 1962, only Dave, Cliffie Jones and I were still with the team. Goalkeeper Pat Jennings was building himself into a legend as our last line of defence, and baby-faced Irish international Joe Kinnear had come in at right-back in place of the energetic Phil Beal, who was unlucky to break an arm after playing an important part in our season. Joe, a neat, controlled player, was partnered at full-back by Cyril Knowles, a former Yorkshire miner who took the eye with sharp tackling and some polished, if at times eccentric, skills. Standing like a Welsh mountain in the middle was Mike England, one of the finest centre-halves ever produced in Britain. He was a class player from head to toe. Dave Mackay was the immoveable link between defence and the midfield engine- room where Alan Mullery and Terry Venables were forging a productive partnership. They never quite touched the sort of peaks we had seen from the Blanchflower-White-Mackay combination of the 'Super Spurs' era, but not many midfield players have ever reached that sky-scraping standard.

Jimmy Robertson was a flying Scot on the right wing, where his speed was a vital asset for Alan Gilzean and I as we loitered with intent in the middle. I had rarely felt more comfortable playing with anybody than with Gilly, and we had a radar-like understanding of where to be to get the best out of each other. For the final, Bill Nicholson preferred Frank Saul to Cliff Jones for the No.11 shirt, and my old mate Jonesie had to settle for a place on the substitute's bench. Frank was more of a central striker than a winger, but he was a direct player with a good nose for goal.

Facing us in the first all-London final were Tommy Docherty's elegant but unpredictable Chelsea team. They had gone through an even more drastic rebuilding programme than us, and Terry Venables was part of the upheaval when he moved on to Tottenham to make room the previous year for the arrival of Scotland's 'Wizard of Dribble', Charlie Cooke.

Peter 'Catty' Bonetti was their goalkeeper, as good a catcher of the ball as I've ever seen. Allan Harris, preferred to substitute Joe Kirkup, was a solid right-back and an ideal balance for the marvellously skilled Eddie McCreadie, who had the ball control of a winger to go with his scything tackle. Marvin 'Lou' Hinton was a sound centre-half with a good footballing brain, and making the earth tremble alongside him was poker-faced Ron 'Chopper' Harris, one of the most feared ball-winners in the game. I always got the impression that Ron would kick his granny if it meant him getting the ball. His challenges are a bruise on my memory, and of all my opponents he was the one I least liked to face.

Tottenham goalkeeper Pat Jennings *(above)* shows his authority as he punches clear under pressure from Tony Hateley and John Boyle during the 1967 FA Cup final against Chelsea. The ever-alert Cyril Knowles guards the goal-line. Nice one, Cyril.

Terry Venables *(below),* not yet considering buying the club, parades the FA Cup with Jimmy Robertson. Also on show here, left to right, Cyril Knowles, Joe Kinnear, Alan Gilzean (half hidden by Robertston) and Frank Saul.

He was a great man to have on your side.

Young John Hollins was a bundle of atomic energy at right-half, and aggressive John Boyle played a utility role in midfield while wearing the No.11 shirt. Filling the schemer's role that had belonged to Venables was the dance master Cooke, a charismatic character known to his fans as 'Bonny Prince Charlie'. All the people who tried to compare Charlie with his predecessor Venners were wasting their breath. They were as alike as grass and granite. Charlie liked to hang on to the ball and run with it as if it was tied to his bootlaces, while Terry let the ball do the work with precise passes.

Chelsea relied on three main marksmen to get the ball into the net. Bobby Tambling, a faithful Stamford Bridge servant who had recently overtaken my Chelsea goalscoring record, had terrific speed and was a deadly finisher. Tommy Baldwin, who had joined Chelsea in a part-exchange deal that took George 'Stroller' Graham to Arsenal eight months earlier, was nicknamed 'Sponge' because of the way he soaked up work (Tommy could also match me when it came to soaking up liquid!). Then there was Tony Hateley, a master of the airways whom Tommy Docherty had bought from Aston Villa for £100,000 after his silkily-skilled centre-forward Peter Osgood had broken a leg. While weak on the ground, Tony was a powerhouse header of the ball who learned a lot from the old head master Tommy Lawton. One day he would pass on all he knew to his son, Mark Hateley.

Masterminding the Chelsea team was manager Tommy Docherty, one of the game's great personalities. He had a razor-sharp Glaswegian wit and also the fastest tongue in the west, and barely a day went by without the Doc making the headlines with an outrageous quote. Behind the joker's mask there was an ambitious and competitive character who demanded total effort from his team, and he had proved that he could be ruthless if they ever let him down. Tommy, more than most people, was missing the guidance of the late Chelsea chairman Joe Mears, and we heard on the grapevine that the spirit at the club was low because of rows over ticket allocation and bonuses.

I have to be honest and admit that we did not produce a particularly memorable final. The whole day fell a bit flat, mainly because both teams were from London. That robbed the match of much of its atmosphere because the supporters were not in that bubbling 'Up f'the Cup' day-out mood.

Skipper Dave Mackay had a personal mission to win after having been inactive for so long, and he was driving us on like a man possessed. We deserved our lead when Jimmy Robertson crashed a shot wide of Bonetti after Alan Mullery's long-range piledriver had been blocked just before half-time.

Robertson, one of the the most effective of all the forwards, set up our second goal in the 68th minute when he steered a typical long throw-in from Dave Mackay into the path of Frank Saul, who pivoted and hooked the ball high into the net.

We then slowed the game down to suit ourselves, playing possession football so that Charlie Cooke could not get the ball to take command with his mesmerising control.

Bobby Tambling was allowed in for a goal five minutes from the end, but we tightened up at the back and held out for a victory that was more comfortable than the scoreline suggests.

'A lot of people wrote me off when I broke my leg for a second time, and nobody is happier than me to prove them all wrong. It was one of the most satisfying moments of my career when I collected the Cup.' – **Dave Mackay**.

FOOTBALL LEAGUE CUP WINNERS

Queen's Park Rangers, Third Division in status but First Division in the quality of their play, completed a remarkable double in April 1967 when they clinched the Third Division championship by 12 points from runners-up Middlesbrough. Just a month earlier they had won the first League Cup final staged at Wembley as that competition came of age and was finally established as a major trophy. They were the first Third Division club to make it to a Wembley final.

In a classic contest, Rangers pulled back a 2-0 deficit against First Division West Bromwich Albion to win 3-2. It could easily have been 3-0 to Albion at half-time but for a magnificent save from Jeff Astle by Peter Springett – younger brother of Ron, England and Sheffield Wednesday goalkeeper (they were later to be involved in a unique swap deal).

The undoubted Wembley star was Rodney Marsh, a supreme entertainer who moved skilfully and stealthily around the pitch as if he owned it. His second-half equalising goal, which knocked the heart out of Albion, was considered as good as any ever witnessed at Wembley. Rodney secured possession on the halfway line and set off on a twisting, turning run which left three Albion defenders tackling his shadow. While his opponents and team-mates were waiting for him to either pass or continue his run, Marsh looked up almost casually, took aim and fired a snaking right-foot shot from 20 yards that cannoned into the net off the left-hand post.

It was a goal of splendour by one of the game's most talented players. Rodney had many detractors among the blinkered coaches, and there were those who dismissed him as a clown because of his ball-conjuring tricks. But Marsh – who had an army of fans who continually chanted Rod-nee, Rod-nee – stamped his class and authority on that League Cup final.

While it was Marsh who inspired the stirring Rangers revival movement on the pitch, it was manager Alec Stock who was the hidden motivator off the field. Alec, as much an impresario as a manager, injected the Rangers players with new confidence in the dressing-room at half-time when they were trailing 2-0 to goals from former QPR winger Clive 'Chippy' Clark. Stock took centre stage in the dressing-room and gave a Churchillian call to arms. 'You are the better side,' he told them. 'You have got to believe it because it is true. They will be sitting in their dressing-room now feeling satisfied and complacent. They think they have got the game won. What a shock they've got coming because you are going to go out there and play them off the park. And you, Rodney, are going to show that they are not fit to tie your bootlaces. Go out and dazzle them with your skill. Hear me? Dazzle them.'

It was almost as if Stock was hypnotising his players, and – as had so often happened in Stock's long and distinguished career in football management – his psychology worked. Rodney and Rangers duly produced a second-half exhibition of dazzling football that devastated the West Bromwich defence.

Roger Morgan – who along with identical twin Ian was later to join Tottenham – pulled one back for Rangers 18 minutes into the second half. Mark Lazarus, the Jewish rightwinger who was affectionately known as the 'Kosher Garrincha', was brought down as he made deep inroads into the Albion defence. Les Allen, enjoying a bonanza in the autumn of his career with Rangers after distinguished service with Chelsea and Spurs, lofted a free-kick into the penalty area and Morgan climbed high to head the ball into the back of the net.

Twelve minutes later Marsh stitched his memorable goal into the fabric of what was becoming the greatest match in the history of the Shepherds Bush club. Suddenly Albion were rocked back on their heels, and you could almost see the confidence seeping out of them. Rangers skipper Mike Keen started bossing the midfield alongside the industrious Frank Sibley, and veteran Jim Langley – 'stolen', like Rodney, from neighbours Fulham – was playing with the pace and passion of a spring-heeled youngster.

There were eight minutes left when Lazarus snatched a controversial goal which lifted Rangers to an astonishing victory. Rangers centre-half Ron Hunt collided with goalkeeper Dick Sheppard as he collected the ball. Sheppard was knocked out in the clash and as the ball ran loose Lazarus clipped it into the net with the Albion defenders screaming for a foul. The referee ruled that the collision was accidental, and the goal stood.

It was an incredible triumph for a Rangers team that was a collection of inexperienced youngsters like right-back Tony Hazell, veterans like Jim Langley and Les Allen, several rejects from other clubs and even a part-timer in computer programmer Keith Sanderson, who provided full-time effort in midfield. Albion felt sick in defeat, but they would be back within a year much wiser for the experience.

Rodney Marsh *(above)* watches as his shot threads past West Bromwich Albion defenders and into the net to put Queen's Park Rangers in charge of the 1967 League Cup final at Wembley, then *(left)* turns to celebrate. It was a goal that turned Rodney into a folk hero at Queen's Park Rangers, who became the first Third Division club to win a major final at Wembley.

'The important thing to us that season was winning promotion. The League Cup was just the icing on the cake. Our second-half performance against Albion was out of this world, and Rodney was in a class of his own. He rivals George Best as being the nearest thing there is to a genius in this game of ours.'–**Alec Stock**.

THE EUROPEAN CUP-WINNERS' CUP

Rangers came close to making it a great Scottish double in Europe by reaching the Cup-Winners' Cup final. They showed they were in impressive form in the second round when they knocked out holders Borussia Dortmund 2-1 on aggregate.

This was the first year in which away goals were to be counted double in the event of the teams being level on aggregate. It was intended to get rid of the farce of deciding tied matches by the toss of a coin. Ironically when Rangers and Real Zaragoza each won their home leg 2-0 in the third round they had to resort to the coin routine, and skipper John Greig called correctly for Rangers. Zaragoza had knocked out English representatives Everton in the second round.

In the two-leg semi-final goals from wingers Davie Wilson and Willie Henderson lifted Rangers to a 2-0 aggregate victory over Slavia Sofia. At Ibrox they were suddenly wondering if they could slip out of the shadow being cast across Rangers by Jock Stein's rampaging Celtic team.

The final against Bayern Munich was staged in Nuremburg a week after Celtic's triumph in the European Cup, and the whole of Scotland held its breath as they hoped and prayed for a remarkable double. But Rangers, missing the creative skill of injured Jim Baxter, wasted a hatful of chances before Volker Roth scored the winner for Bayern in extra-time of a disappointing final. I felt particularly sorry for Rangers centre-half Ron McKinnon, who kept Bayern's Gerd 'Der Bomber' Müller under lock and key. Not many defenders could claim to have got the better of Müller, who was to prove over the next few years to be one of the all-time great goal hunters.

'We were weakened by injuries to key players, otherwise I am convinced we would have pulled off a great double for Scotland. It was heartbreaking to lose in extra-time. So near, yet so far. We had fantastic support from thousands of fans who made the trip out to Germany, and we feel we let them down. ' – **John Greig.**

THE FAIRS CUP FINAL

Leeds United added to their growing reputation as the team that could win everything but the games that mattered by finishing runners-up in the Fairs Cup. Leeds, who had reached the semi-final in the previous season, before going out to eventual Cup-winners Real Zaragoza, played magnificently on the way to the final. They hammered DWS Amsterdam 8-2 on aggregate, and then produced the performance of the tournament against Valencia, the team with whom they had been involved in a riotous match the previous season. It looked like curtains for Leeds when they were held to a 1-1 draw at Elland Road, but in the return leg they conjured an inspired display to beat the Spaniards 2-0. It was a particularly memorable match for Johnny Giles. Just minutes before the kick-off he was handed a telegram telling him that his wife had given birth to a baby daughter. The little Irish ball master celebrated by scoring the first Leeds goal, and he then monopolised the midfield with a procession of accurately placed passes, one of which set up a late victory-clinching goal for young Scot Peter Lorimer.

A toss of a coloured disc put Leeds into the semi-finals after a 1-1 deadlock against Bologna. 'This is a farcical way to decide a game of such importance', said manager Don Revie. 'It would make much more sense to settle it on alternate penalties. At least that way football skill is being used rather than reducing it to a lottery.' (The Russian roulette system of penalty deciders would be introduced in the 'seventies, but even then there would be people complaining that this put too much pressure on players. In my view it was at least an improvement on the farce of tossing a coin or a disc).

In the semi-final Leeds eliminated Kilmarnock 4-2 on aggregate after the Scottish First Division club had accounted for Antwerp, La Gantoise and Locomotive Leipzig.

At last Leeds seemed set to end their run of collecting second prizes, but they froze in the first leg of the final against Dynamo Zagreb, which was postponed until the start of the following season because of a fixture pile-up. Playing without field marshal Giles in Zagreb, Leeds tumbled to a 2-0 defeat. The Yugoslavs then closed up shop in the goalless return leg at Elland Road.

But people who felt sorry for Leeds were wasting their sympathy. There was so much character and determination running through the team that it could only be a matter of time before they started capturing the major prizes ... and there was not long to wait before the bridesmaids got their chance to lead rather than follow down the aisle.

> *'Don Revie must get the credit for picking us up after the shattering disappointment of losing out yet again. He told us to think positively and reminded us that most other clubs had not got within sniffing distance of any trophies while we were in contention every season . Don made us believe in our ability and stressed that our time would come. ' –* **Billy Bremner.**

GREAVSIE'S FOOTBALL DIARY
1966-67

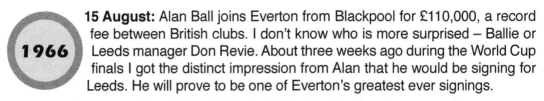

1966

15 August: Alan Ball joins Everton from Blackpool for £110,000, a record fee between British clubs. I don't know who is more surprised – Ballie or Leeds manager Don Revie. About three weeks ago during the World Cup finals I got the distinct impression from Alan that he would be signing for Leeds. He will prove to be one of Everton's greatest ever signings.

10 September: Kevin Hector, top Football League scorer last season with 44 goals, joins Derby County from Bradford for £40,000.

13 September: Goalkeeper Alex Stepney signs for Manchester United from Chelsea for £55,000, a British record fee for a goalkeeper. He has spent only four months at Chelsea after joining them from Millwall, and he has played just one League game for the Stamford Bridge club.

21 September: Johnny Byrne scores four goals as the Football League bury the Irish League under an avalanche of 12 goals in an inter-League match at Plymouth. It's good to see 'Budgie' among the goals, but I do not feel these inter-League games serve any purpose.

29 September: George 'Stroller' Graham joins Arsenal from Chelsea in exchange for

£50,000 plus Tommy 'The Sponge' Baldwin. It is the start of a mutual love affair between George and the Gunners.

1 October: Arsenal manager Bertie Mee continues his rebuilding programme by buying left-back Bob McNab from Huddersfield Town for £50,000. It's a British record fee for a full-back.

5 October: Peter Osgood, the new young idol of Stamford Bridge, breaks a leg in a League Cup tie at Blackpool.

22 October: England beat Northern Ireland 2-0 at Windsor Park in their first match since winning the World Cup. It's a bitterly fought game, and Billy Ferguson is ordered off for a foul on Alan Ball. Roger Hunt and Martin Peters score a goal in each half to sink the Irish.

26 October: With Peter Osgood sidelined for several months, Chelsea manager Tommy Docherty shells out £100,000 for the aerial power of Aston Villa centre-forward Tony Hateley. It's a world record fee for a non-international player.

27 October: The transfer roundabout continues to spin, with Bolton's Welsh international centre-forward Wyn Davies moving to Newcastle for £85,000.

2 November: England are held to a goalless draw by Czechoslovakia in their first international at Wembley since the World Cup triumph.

9 November: Johnny Morrissey, Everton's quick and clever left winger, is ordered off as Everton go down to a 2-0 defeat against Real Zaragoza in the first leg, first round European Cup-Winners' Cup tie. Everton will win the return leg at Goodison, but will go out 2-1 on aggregate.

11 November: Sheffield Wednesday pay out a club record £70,000 for Stoke City striker John Ritchie.

16 November: Geoff Hurst nets two goals and both Charlton brothers, Bobby and Jack, get on the scoresheet as England beat Wales 5-1 at Wembley.

18 November: Malcolm Allison, the outspoken Manchester City coach, is banned from football for a month for swearing at a referee. Big Mal says: 'This will be the longest month of my life. I will say no more otherwise they may hang me'.

14 December: Liverpool are knocked out of the European Cup after drawing their first round, second leg match 2-2 with Ajax at Anfield. A young Dutchman called Johan Cruyff scores two goals at Anfield to go with the one he netted when Ajax slammed Liverpool 5-1 in the first leg in Amsterdam.

17 December: Two goals by Bobby Tambling in a 5-5 draw with West Ham at Stamford Bridge lift him above my Chelsea goalscoring record. Bobby, one of the nicest blokes in the game, who is equally effective coming through the middle or from wide on the wing, now has 129 League goals to his name.

1967

1 January: Arise Sir Alf! Alf Ramsey is knighted in the New Year's Honours List, and there is an OBE for England's World Cup skipper Bobby Moore.

9 January: Sheffield Wednesday chairman Dr Andrew Stephen is elected chairman of the Football Association in succession to the late Joe Mears. Sir Stanley Rous, the world's number one administrator, wanted the job but his rivals block his bid on a technicality.

28 January: Glasgow Rangers 0, Berwick Rangers 1 in the Scottish Cup! It is the shock of the season.

14 February: Johnny Byrne returns to his local club Crystal Palace in a £45,000 transfer from West Ham. 'Budgie' has not been quite the same power since he suffered a crippling knee injury when playing for England against Scotland in 1965.

18 February: Ron Suart, likeable, unflappable manager of Blackpool, leaves Bloomfield Road. He will become a key member of the Chelsea backroom team. Stan Mortensen, the old Blackpool bomber, is summoned to take over as manager of the seaside club where he and Stanley Matthews wrote themselves into footballing legend.

27 February: Blackpool sell buccaneering midfield star Emlyn Hughes to Liverpool for £60,000.

10 March: Everton buy a youngster called Howard Kendall from Preston for £80,000. It completes one of the great midfield trios at Goodison: Kendall, Ball, Harvey.

15 March: I play alongside Allan 'Sniffer' Clarke for the first time and I'm impressed as he scores two goals to help the Football League beat the Scottish League at Hampden Park. Geoff Hurst scores the other goal in a 3-0 victory. And I still say these inter-League matches prove nothing, but it's lovely to beat the Jocks!

16 March: Derek Dougan, the 'Long Fella', joins Wolves from Leicester City for £50,000. Doog is about to have his day.

2 April: Leicester City appear to have gone potty. They let England goalkeeper Gordon Banks move to Stoke for £52,500, and will trust his job to an unknown kid called Peter Shilton.

15 April: Scotland beat England 3-2 at Wembley and claim that they are the world champions. They could not care less that we are reduced to eight fit men, with Jack Charlton breaking a toe and Ray Wilson and I both hobbling. The Scots really mean business, and it's the first time any of us can remember Denis Law wearing shinpads. Denis has a marvellous game, and he scores their first goal after 28 minutes. Bobby Lennox and Jim McCalliog also find the net. Jack Charlton, limping at centre-forward, gets one back for England and Geoff Hurst makes it 3-2 in a dramatic finish. Substitutes are not yet allowed in international matches, and Leeds manager Don Revie is quite understandably upset that his key defender Jack Charlton is allowed to play on and so risk further damage to an already serious injury. This is my first match back in the England team, and it is the only change that Sir Alf has made to the side since the World Cup. I come in for out-of-form Roger Hunt. It is a game that I would have preferred to have missed. There are incredible scenes at the finish when Scottish fans invade the pitch and start digging it up. Wembley, they have decided, belongs to them. About half a dozen of them swing on the crossbar until it snaps in half.

3 May: Jack Charlton is elected Footballer of the Year. It completes a unique double for the Charlton family. Bobby won the award last year.

13 May: Ron Greenwood completes one of his most important transfer deals for West Ham when he buys Billy Bonds from Charlton. 'Bonzo' arrives at Upton Park as an adventurous right-back, but will develop into a magnificent midfield player. He will become the heart of the Hammers.

24 May: Roger Hunt and I grab a goal each as England beat Spain 2-0 at Wembley. The game is played in torrential rain, and our biggest challenge is keeping our feet. It might have made a better spectacle if we had played wearing water skis. John Hollins makes a promising England debut, wearing the No.11 shirt but playing his usual dashing role in midfield.

27 May: Austria 0, England 1 in Vienna. Alan Ball scores the winner in the 20th minute with a neatly taken goal. The match is a remarkable milestone for England trainer Harold Shepherdson. It is his 100th international, and his 98th in succession as England's 'sponge' man. Harold has been a loyal and conscientious right-hand man to Walter Winterbottom and Alf Ramsey. The Middlesbrough man is excellent at his job, and also has the sort of pleasant personality that is good for team morale. Everybody likes Shep.

THE CHAMPIONS OF
1966-67

FIRST DIVISION:
1: Manchester United (60 points)
2: Nottingham Forest (56)
3: Tottenham Hotspur (56)

Championship squad:
Aston (26 appearances), Best (42), Brennan (16), Cantwell (4), Charlton (42), Connelly (6), Crerand (39), Dunne (40), Fitzpatrick (3), Foulkes (33), Gaskell (5), Herd (28), Law (36), Noble (29), Ryan (4), Sadler (35), Stepney (35), Stiles (37).
Goalscorers: Law (23), Herd (16), Charlton (12), Best (10), Aston (5), Sadler (5), Crerand (3), Stiles (3), Connelly (2), 5 own goals.

SECOND DIVISION:
1: Coventry City (59 points)
2: Wolverhampton Wanderers (58)
3: Carlisle United (52)

Championship squad:
Bruck (38 appearances), Clements (40), Coop (2), Curtis (42), Farmer (32), Glazier (41), Gould (38), Gibson (31), Glover (1), Hill (15), Kearns (41), Key (21), Lewis (13), Lowes (3), Machin (34), Mitten (8), Morrissey (1), Pointer (7), Rees (39), Thomas (1), Tudor (16).
Goalscorers: Gould (24), Machin (10), Gibson (8), Tudor (8), Key (6), Clements (4), Rees (3), Bruck (2), Curtis (2), Farmer (2), Mitten (2), Pointer (2), Kearns (1).

THIRD DIVISION:
1: Queen's Park Rangers (67 points)
2: Middlesbrough (55)
3: Watford (54)

Championship squad:
Allen (42 appearances), Clement (1), Collins (1), Hazell (37), Hunt (44), Keen (46), Keetch (1), Langley (40), Lazarus (44), Leach (2), Marsh (41), Morgan I. (10), Morgan R. (44), Moughton (3), Sanderson (40), Sibley (42), Springett (46), Watson (15), Wilks (7).
Goalscorers: Marsh (30), Allen (16), Lazarus (16), Morgan R. (11), Keen (6), Langley (6), Sanderson (6), Wilks (5), Morgan I. (4), Leach (1), Sibley (1), 1 own goal.

FOURTH DIVISION:
1: Stockport County (64 points)
2: Southport (59)
3: Barrow (59)

Championship squad:
Allchurch (25 appearances), Allen (24), Atkins (13), East (11), Fleet (20), Goodwin (37), Harley (16), Haydock (46), Henderson (17), Holden (1), Jones (27), Kevan (15), Lister (16), Lord (18), Morrin (16), Mulhearn (26), Parry (1), Price (36), Prentis (6), Quixall (13), Sykes (15), Stuart (44), Shawcross (17), Woods (46).
Goalscorers: Lord (10), Lister (9), Price (7), Allen (6), Shawcross (5), Henderson (4), Sykes (4), Allchurch (3), East (3), Harley (3), Kevan (3), Atkins (3), Morris (2), Jones (1), Goodwin (1), Stuart (1), 2 own goals.

SCOTTISH FIRST DIVISION:
1: Celtic (58 points)
2: Rangers (55)
3: Clyde (46)

Championship squad:
Clark (34 appearances), Gemmell (34), McNeill (33), Simpson (33), Murdoch (31), Chalmers (29), Auld (27), Lennox (26), Johnstone (25), Wallace (21), Hughes (19), O'Neil (18), Craig (17), McBride (14), Gallagher (11), Cushley (1), Fallon (1), Young (1).
Goalscorers: Chalmers (24), McBride (18), Wallace (14), Lennox (13), Johnstone (12), Gemmell (9), Auld (7) Hughes (6), Murdoch (5), Gallagher (2), 1 own goal.

SCOTTISH SECOND DIVISION:
1: Morton (69 points)
2: Raith Rovers (58)
3: Arbroath (57)

FA CUP FINAL:
Tottenham Hotspur 2 *(Robertson, Saul)*
Jennings, Kinnear, Knowles, Mullery, England, Mackay, Robertson, Greaves, Gilzean, Venables, Saul. Sub: Jones.
Chelsea 1 *(Tambling)*
Bonetti, A. Harris, McCreadie, Hollins, Hinton, R. Harris, Cooke, Baldwin, Hateley, Tambling, Boyle. Sub: Kirkup.

LEAGUE CUP FINAL:
Queen's Park Rangers 3 *(R. Morgan, Marsh, Lazarus)*
Springett, Hazell, Langley, Sibley, Hunt, Keen, Lazarus, Sanderson, Allen, Marsh, R. Morgan. Sub: I. Morgan.
West Bromwich Albion 2 *(Clark 2)*
Sheppard, Cram, Williams, Collard, Clarke, Fraser, Brown, Astle, Kaye, Hope, Clark. Sub: Foggo.

SCOTTISH CUP FINAL:
Celtic 2 *(Wallace 2)*
Simpson, Craig, Gemmell, Murdoch,McNeill, Clark, Johnstone, Wallace, Chalmers, Auld, Lennox.
Aberdeen 0
Clark, Whyte, Shewan, Munro, McMillan, Pederson, Wilson, Smith, Storrie, Melrose, Johnstone.

SCOTTISH LEAGUE CUP FINAL:
Celtic 1 *(Lennox)*
Simpson, Gemmell, O'Neil, Murdoch, McNeill, Clark, Johnstone, Lennox, McBride, Auld, Hughes. Sub: Chalmers.
Rangers 0
Martin, Johansen, Provan, Greig, McKinnon, D. Smith, Henderson, Watson, McLean, A. Smith, Johnston. Sub: Wilson.

EUROPEAN CUP FINAL:
Played in Lisbon
Celtic 2 *(Gemmell, Chalmers)*
Simpson, Craig, Gemmell, Murdoch, McNeill, Clark, Johnstone, Wallace, Chalmers, Auld, Lennox.
Inter-Milan 1 *(Mazzola pen.)*
Sarti, Burgnich, Facchetti, Bedin, Guarneri, Pocchi, Domenghini, Mazzola, Cappellini, Bicicli, Corson.

EUROPEAN CUP-WINNERS' CUP FINAL:
Played at Nuremburg
Bayern Munich 1 *(Roth)*
Maier, Nowak, Kupperschmidt, Roth, Beckenbauer, Oik, Nafziger, Ohlhauser, Müller, Koulmann, Brenniger.
Rangers 0
Martin, Johansen, Provan, Jardine, McKinnon, Greig, Henderson, A. Smith, Hynd, D. Smith, Johnston.
After extra-time.

EUROPEAN FAIRS CUP FINAL:

First leg:

Dynamo Zagreb 2 *(Cercer 2)*

Skoric, Gracanin, Brnic, Belin, Ramljak, Blaskovic, Cercer, Piric, Zambata, Guomirti, Rota.

Leeds United 0

Sprake, Reaney, Cooper, Bremner, Charlton, Hunter, Lorimer, Belfitt, Bates, Gray, O'Grady.

Second leg:

Dynamo Zagreb 0

Skoric, Gracanin, Brnic, Belin, Ramljak, Blaskovic, Cercer, Piric, Zambata, Guomirti, Rota.

Leeds United 0

Sprake, Bell, Cooper, Bremner, Charlton, Hunter, Reaney, Belfitt, Greenhoff, Gray, O'Grady.

Top Football League goalscorers:

Ron Davies (Southampton)	37
Rodney Marsh (Queen's Park Rangers)	30
Geoff Hurst (West Ham United)	29
John O'Rourke (Middlesbrough)	27
Ian Towers (Oldham Athletic)	27
Don Rogers (Swindon Town)	25
Allan Clarke (Fulham)	24
Bobby Gould (Coventry City)	24
George Harris (Reading)	24
Reg Stratton (Colchester United)	24
Jimmy Greaves (Tottenham Hotspur)	23
Denis Law (Manchester United)	23
Bill Curry (Mansfield Town)	22
Arthur Horsfield (Middlesbrough)	22
Francis Lee (Bolton Wanderers)	22
Ernie Phythian (Hartlepool United)	22

Top Scottish First Division marksman:

Steve Chalmers (Celtic) 24 goals

Highest average League attendance:

Manchester United (53,984)

Footballer of the Year:

Jack Charlton (Leeds United)

Scottish Footballer of the Year:

Ronnie Simpson (Celtic)

European Footballer of the Year:

Florian Albert (Ferencvaros)

World Club Championship:

Racing Club of Argentina beat Celtic 0-1, 2-1, 1-0

1967-68: BUSBY'S FINEST HOUR

Anybody who was around in 1958 will understand why Manchester United's European Cup final against Benfica at Wembley Stadium on 29 May, 1968, had such deep significance. The whole of Britain, and the sympathies and good wishes of most of Europe, too, were behind Matt Busby and his team as they set out to fulfil at last a dream that had been shattered in the Munich air disaster ten years earlier.

Busby and his skipper Bobby Charlton were survivors of a crash that had cost the lives of eight United players. It was the day a team died, and Busby had silently vowed one day to win the premier prize of the European Cup in memory of those who had perished in Munich on the way home from a successful European Cup quarter-final match against Red Star in Belgrade.

It had taken Busby the best part of a decade to rebuild his squad to the quality and craftsmanship flourished by the pre-Munich team. The side he was sending into action against Benfica was almost in the class of the 'Busby Babes', who had been setting out a powerful argument to be recognised as the greatest British club team of all time until cruelly decimated in one of the worst tragedies ever to hit British football.

Perhaps the most important part in the Busby jigsaw as he put together a mix of outstandingly skilful and physically powerful players was his purchase in the summer of 1966 of goalkeeper Alex Stepney. Alex had started his career with Millwall and had played just one League match for Tommy Docherty's Chelsea when Busby bought him for what was then a goalkeeping transfer record of £55,000. At £500,000 he would have been a bargain.

Stepney brought stability and confidence to a United defence that had been giving away goals like a charitable organisation. This carelessness was cancelling out the creative work of a stunningly gifted attack which had three shining jewels in Irishman George Best, Scotsman Denis Law and Bobby Charlton, the favourite son of English football. A knee injury forced Law on to the sidelines for this game of a lifetime which he watched from a hospital bed following an operation. His place went to Manchester-born prodigy Brian Kidd, who would celebrate his 19th birthday on the day of the final.

Providing the passes from midfield alongside Charlton was master tactician Paddy Crerand, and operating like a mine sweeper in front of the back line of the defence was the 'Toothless Tiger' Nobby Stiles who, of course, had been one of England's heroes in the 1966 World Cup finals. His most impressive performance had come in the World Cup semi-finals when he had stifled the menace of Portugal's exceptionally talented striker Eusebio. Now United needed a repeat performance from him because Eusebio was the inspiration behind Benfica's climb to their fifth European Cup final in eight years.

Also in the Benfica team from the Portuguese side that had given England a close call in the World Cup were midfield marshal Mario Coluna and quick and clever forwards José Torres, José Augusto and sparkling left-winger Simoes. With the towering six foot four inch Torres leading the attack, the United defence was going to be tested as never before and all hearts went out to veteran United centre-half Bill Foulkes, another Munich survivor who was coming towards the end of a long and distinguished career at Old Trafford. He was flanked by Irish international full-backs Shay Brennan and Tony Dunne, and utility player David Sadler was delegated to drop back from an attacking role to fill in alongside Foulkes whenever there was pressure from Benfica.

On their way to the final, United had dismissed Hibernian of Malta, Sarajevo, Gornik Zabrze and, in a memorable semi-final, Real Madrid. Benfica had survived a scare against gallant Glentoran before eliminating St Etienne, Vasas Budapest and then, in the semi-final, Juventus.

This was how they lined up for one of the most important matches in English football history:

Manchester United: Stepney, Brennan, Foulkes, Stiles, Dunne, Crerand, Charlton, Sadler, Best, Kidd, Aston.

Benfica: Henrique, Adolfo, Humberto, Jacinto, Cruz, Graca, Coluna, Augusto, Torres, Eusebio, Simoes.

CHAMPIONS OF EUROPE

Few teams have been under such mental strain as United when they walked out on to the Wembley pitch and into a sea of emotion. The publicity spotlight had been turned on them as never before because of the link with the Munich tragedy, and the bellowing 100,000 crowd were in a frenzied grip of hope and expectation.

As could only be expected in the circumstances, both teams struggled to settle into their stride and the ball was being moved quickly from player to player as if it was an unexploded bomb. Nobody wanted the responsibility of trying to force the first opening for fear of making a mistake.

All eyes were on United wonder winger George Best, but he was taking a severe buffeting from the Portuguese defenders who recalled the way he had destroyed them almost single-handedly in a European Cup tie two years earlier. Eusebio was getting similarly harsh treatment from the unyielding Stiles, and the only forward making any sort of impression was United's unsung outside-left John Aston, whose father had won an FA Cup-winners' medal with United on this same pitch almost exactly 20 years earlier. Aston was racing past Benfica's defenders in Best fashion, but his team-mates were unable to capitalise on his stunning running in a goalless first half that was wrecked by nervous tension.

Benfica came closest to breaking the deadlock when Eusebio, free for a split second from the fervent attentions of Stiles, clipped the United crossbar with a drive from 20 yards.

The half-time break seemed to steady United's nerves and they began the second half with a spurt of the special sort of football with which this Busby team had continually lit up memorable matches during the swinging 'sixties. It was the one and only Bobby Charlton, as graceful as a gazelle, who gave them the lead that the crowd were baying for when he sprinted away from his marker to meet a left cross from Sadler with a perfectly placed glancing header.

Aston created a procession of chances for United to seal victory, but the finishing never matched the brilliance of the winger's foundation work. Nine minutes from the end you could almost hear the intake of breath from the suddenly hushed United fans when Graca equalised for Benfica in a breakaway raid.

With just seconds left and extra-time looming Eusebio looked certain to destroy United's dream. One of the deadliest marksmen in the world broke free from Stiles and had only Stepney to beat, but somehow the United goalkeeper managed to parry his rocketing shot with a sensational reaction save. United were still shaking from this heart- stopping escape when the referee blew the final whistle, and Charlton and Stiles found themselves facing the same extra-time mountain they had climbed in the 1966 World Cup final.

Matt Busby, the years suddenly heavy on his shoulders, walked urgently on to the pitch and told his players: 'You are being too careless with your passes. Just take a little care and you can win it. Don't throw it away now. Make every pass count and when you get into their box steady yourselves. You are snatching at your shots'.

It was going to take a moment of inspiration to lift the worn-out United players, and it was the irresistible Best who provided it early in the first period of extra-time. He at last managed to escape his Benfica jailers to run on to a headed through ball from Kidd following a long punt upfield by Stepney. Best side-stepped a tackle and nonchalantly dummied his way past onrushing goalkeeper Henrique before slotting the ball into the net as casually as if in a training match.

This was the goal that settled the match. The spirit and fight suddenly disappeared from Benfica like air leaving a punctured balloon, and birthday-boy Kidd put the icing on his cake with a determined smash-and-grab goal. After heading the ball against the bar he then beat everybody to the rebound to nod it into the net.

As if the match was being plotted by the great scriptwriter in the sky, it was Charlton – as an 18-year-old boy he had miraculously scrambled out of the wreckage at Munich – who provided the final telling contribution to give the game a fairy-tale finish. He volleyed a centre from Kidd high into the Benfica net from the tightest of angles.

Wembley went wild with excitement and was awash with tears as Charlton led his team-mates forward to collect the prize of the European Cup. He tried to talk Matt Busby into receiving it, but the master of managers said firmly: 'No. This is your day'.

Yes, it was Bobby's day. Or rather his night. Ask football fans to name the greatest player they have ever seen and Bobby Charlton's name is unlikely to come immediately to mind and tongue. Ask them to nominate their favourite footballer of all time ... and there is every chance that Bobby Charlton is the name offered instantly.

Bobby was the player everybody loved to love. George Best had more tricks, Denis Law had more dynamism, but Charlton had an indefinable charisma that put him ahead in the popularity polls. Football followers have three faces and three phases of Charlton deposited in their memory bank. Standing out sharpest in my mind is the teenage 'Busby Babe' of the pre-Munich air disaster with his shock of blond hair and the bombing shots from the left wing. In those days he could be unpredictable, but was the most exciting thing on two feet. His performances dipped and soared like a barometer on the English weather, sometimes hot with sunshine brilliance; other times caught in the wild wind of inconsistency. Never, ever was he dull ... all the way from his opening goals in League football in his debut against, of all teams, Charlton in 1956 and from his first match with England against Scotland at Hampden Park in 1958. He marked his international debut with a gem of a goal, crashing a shot in on the volley from a pass from one of his schoolboy idols, Tom Finney. It was in this era when I first started playing with Bobby, initially with England Under-23s and then at full level. And in those springtime days of our careers I used to think of him as a marvel. There has never since been any reason to change those first impressions.

The second Bobby Charlton face, more serious, lean and frowning under a rapidly thinning thatch, came after he had survived the Munich air crash. His game began to gather maturity, consistency and style. He had lost some of his early impudence but showed greater variety and verve as he switched to an inside-forward role.

The third and – for many people – favourite face shines in these mid-'sixties when he became a strolling midfield player. Wearing the No. 9 shirt, but rarely as a conventional centre-forward, he plotted openings for team-mates and created goals himself with sudden sprints at the heart of defences, climaxed with rifled shots from either foot.

His greatest moments came in this deep-lying role, plundering vital goals and supplying a succession of measured passes for England's 1966 World Cup-winning team, and providing the same service for the magnificent European Cup-winning United team of this golden era. It is doubtful whether either side could have succeeded without him. He is the only footballer to win the grand slam of honours in British soccer: World

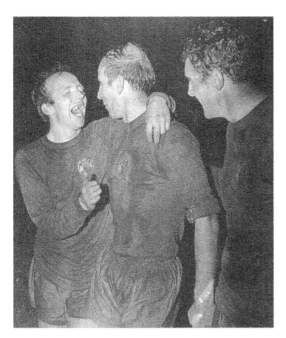 

Nobby Stiles *(left, above)* gives his famous toothless laugh as the tears start to flow for Bobby Charlton after the European Cup final victory over Benfica. Matt Busby *(right, above)* has Pat Crerand hanging round his neck as he joins in the celebrations with Bill Foulkes. Busby, Foulkes and Charlton all survived the Munich air disaster. Matt, flanked by Denis Law and Bobby Charlton *(below),* shows off the European Cup and, probably, the most powerful squad of players in United's history.

Cup, European Cup, League championship and FA Cup-winners' medals. He was European and English Footballer of the Year in 1966, and his collection of 106 England caps would be a record until eventually topped by Bobby Moore and then Peter Shilton.

Born in Ashington, Northumberland, on 11 October, 1937, Bobby came from a mining and footballing family that included the talented Milburn brothers. He and his elder brother Jackie played together for England in 35 international matches. Before he hung up his boots, Bobby would score 198 League goals for United in 606 games, and would then add eight more to his collection when playing 38 times for Preston as player-manager. He is England's top marksman with 49 goals.

His first international match was in 1958 and his last would be against West Germany in the 1970 World Cup quarter-final, when Alf Ramsey substituted him with England leading 2-0 so that he would be fresh for the semi-final. England lost the match 3-2 with Bobby looking on helplessly from the touchline bench. What a sad way to end such a glorious international career. He will always have a prominent place in any football hall of fame.

The victory over Benfica at Wembley was the pinnacle of Matt Busby's managerial career. In 22 years in charge at Old Trafford after distinguished service as a player with Manchester City and Liverpool, he managed five League championship-winning teams and captured the FA Cup twice. Every team he built played with flair and style. After the European Cup triumph the modest, quietly spoken Scot would be knighted – a fitting tribute to a man who well earned his unofficial title, 'Father of Football'.

There was not a dry eye in the house the night United beat Benfica. It was not a classic match but an unforgettable occasion, and United's victory became a wonderful memorial to those players and officials who died in the Munich air disaster. The success at Wembley could not have happened to greater footballing ambassadors than Bobby Charlton, Bill Foulkes and, of course, Matt Busby.

'We have lived with the ambition of winning the European Cup for so long that this time we knew we had to do it. When the game went to extra-time it was like the 1966 World Cup final all over again. We had to be professional and not let emotion take over, as it so easily could have done. We owed it to too many people, particularly Matt Busby, not to fail after all the club has been through. A lot of special people were in our thoughts tonight. We won this Cup for them.' –**Bobby Charlton**.

The city of Manchester was continually under the media micro-scope during the memorable 1967-68 season. While United had their eyes on the glittering prize of the European Cup, their rivals Manchester City came through on the blind side to pip them for the League championship and pre-vent them from completing a unique double.

THE LEAGUE CHAMPIONS

In an era when the game was becoming more and more dominated by ruthless defences, City managed to put a smile on the face of the game. Football was all about fluency, fun and flamboyance at Maine Road, where Joe Mercer and Malcolm Allison had been in harness since the summer of 1965. At the peak of their partnership, City captured the Second Division championship, the League title, the FA Cup, League Cup and European Cup-Winners' Cup. This stunning sequence of success came in a five-year span between 1965 and 1970. It meant that after years of standing in the shadows of Manchester United, City were suddenly no longer *the other* team from Manchester.

The alliterative reference to the fluency, fun and flamboyance of City's football could also apply to the men who masterminded City's peak performances. Manager Mercer was the wise old man of soccer, cheerful even in a crisis and accustomed to success as a tigerish player with Everton, Arsenal and England. He shrewdly selected the young, ambitious Allison as his coach after he had been 'lost' in the backwaters of Bath City and Plymouth Argyle. He had turned to coaching after tuberculosis forced him to end his playing career with West Ham at the age of 32. Big Mal was headstrong and a creator of controversy, but he had an electric personality and was one of the most inventive and imaginative thinkers in the game. Together, Mercer and Allison brought the best out of each other and out of the Manchester City players.

City's defence was not the most dominating there has ever been, chiefly because Mercer and Allison had built a 'going forward' team. Goalkeepers Harry Dowd, Ken Mulhearn and later big Joe Corrigan took turns in patrolling the goal-line at the back of a defence that could be tough and tight but which was sometimes suspect under pressure.

Tony Book was a demanding skipper at right-back. He had blossomed into an out-standing player following a late entry into League Football after impressing Malcolm Allison during his days in charge at Bath City. Tony, a decisive marker and always quick to launch counter attacks, had formed an excellent understanding with cultured left- back Glyn Pardoe, and they encouraged each other to go off on powerful over-lapping runs. The always dependable Alan Oakes had two long-running partnerships at the heart of the defence, first with George Heslop and then with Tommy Booth.

Colin Bell was the master of the midfield. He made the team tick with intelligent running, passing and positioning, and well earned his thoroughbred nickname of 'Nijinsky'. I have rarely known a player to match his energy and stamina. He had an amazing capacity for running marathon distances at sprint speed, and was equally effective as a schemer or support striker. Colin was continually doing the work of two men and it makes me wonder if he had an extra lung!

Mike Doyle's contribution in the engine-room was equally important though less creative. He had a balance of strength and skill, winning the ball with firm tackles and then using it with accuracy and speed. The elegant Neil Young was a skilful go-between, moving rapidly from a midfield position to a striking role where his left-foot shooting was a vital weapon.

City's forward line was an explosive mixture of skill, speed and power. Francis Lee and Mike Summerbee sliced through defences with rapier thrusts, and were as devastating a double act as you could find in the League. Franny, a shrewd businessman off the football field, was an expert at the goalscoring business. He could play wide on the right or as a central striker, and his willingness to make direct runs rather than across the face of the defence meant he was a handful to mark. He had good close control and packed a stunning right-foot shot. A 'boy wonder' at Bolton at the age of 16, Franny symbolised the City approach to football. He was always cheerful and bouncing with confidence, and was a born entertainer.

Mike Summerbee, the son of a professional footballer, was the first new player recruited to Manchester City by Mercer and Allison, and since moving from Swindon in 1965 had proved one of their greatest buys. He was a menace to defences whether at outside-right or centre-forward, and he played with flair and fire regardless of how tight the marking on him in this age when defenders kicked first and asked questions later. Like his sidekick Lee, he was a confident character. In fact there was a swagger going right the way through the City team. They got that from big Mal, who did not include modesty among his many qualities.

Tony Coleman was a busy, buzzing outside-left who could turn the best of full-backs when at full pace, and Neil Young continually came through from deep positions to support Coleman out on the left. In the early rise of City, Johnny Crossan and Dave Connor both served the City attack with distinction, but it was the 'Big Three' – Lee, Bell and Summerbee – who were the main architects of the City revival movement. Their synthesised talent turned a good side into a great one, and all three were rewarded by Alf Ramsey with England caps.

In the season of 1967-68 it was the combined goal power of Young (19), Lee (16), Bell (14) and Summerbee (14) that lifted City to the title in a head-to-head race with United. In a desperately close and exciting finish, City clinched the championship by beating Newcastle 4-3 at St James' Park in their last match of the season to pip Manchester United by two points, with Liverpool back in third place just ahead of Leeds.

Colin Bell *(left, above)* was the man who made Manchester City tick for the team's creators Joe Mercer *(extreme left)* and Malcolm Allison. Bell, whose shot has just been saved by Everton goalkeeper Gordon West, was nicknamed Nijinsky because of his stamina and style

'You ain't seen nothing yet. We will now murder anybody we come across in the European Cup. When we are really motoring there is not a team I would back to beat us.' – *Malcolm Allison*.

THE FA CUP WINNERS

West Bromwich Albion got quick consolation for their defeat by Queen's Park Rangers in the previous season's League Cup final when they returned to Wembley for the FA Cup final. They caused a shock of their own by beating favourites Everton 1-0 in a disappointing match that rarely rose above the mediocre.

On paper, Everton looked racing certainties to capture the Cup. But it was a different story on the pitch. West Brom hustled and harried them into making elementary errors, and Everton were never able to get into their elegant stride even though they had that magnificent trio of Alan Ball, Howard Kendall and Colin Harvey operating in midfield, and young centre-forward goliath Joe Royle thrusting at the head of the attack. Their defence was strengthened by the inclusion of anchorman John Hurst, who wore the No. 10 shirt but was mainly concerned with stopping rather than starting attacks. Adding his speed and skill up front was Jimmy Husband, a neat, upright player who liked to sprint in towards goal from wide on the right.

It is this Everton side that would become the first League champions of the 'seventies, but this Wembley Cup final had come too early for them.

Everybody who had written off West Brom before a ball had been kicked was now getting sharp reminders of what a resilient and talented team manager Alan Ashman had pieced together. John Osborne was an intelligent and reliable goalkeeper, and he had a good understanding with powerful centre-half John Talbut, who had been a wise buy from Burnley. Scottish international Doug Fraser and Welsh international Graham Williams were among the most experienced full-back pairings in the land, and were both solid in the tackle. Attacking from midfield they had Tony 'Bomber' Brown, one of the most ruthless finishers in the business, and John Kaye, who had developed into a useful utility player since switching from his role as a bustling centre-forward.

Scotsman Bobby Hope was the midfield general, who could split the tightest defence with exact passes. Ian Collard and Graham Lovett gave expert support wherever they were needed, while Clive Clark was always looking for the chance to use his speed out on the left wing. Everyone worked together with the main objective of getting the ball to either the head or the feet of Jeff Astle, who was having the greatest goal-hunting season of his career. He was the country's leading marksman going into the final, with 34 League and Cup goals to his name, and he won the FA Cup for West Brom with his 35th goal.

The match had been bogged down in midfield where there were too many players fighting for space. The game lapped over into extra-time, and it was in the 93rd minute that Astle at last got the opening he had been working for. He drove the ball in rightfooted from 15 yards, and it rebounded off Colin Harvey back into the path of Astle, who sent an instant left-foot volley into the top right-hand corner of the Everton net to provide the one memorable moment of the match.

> 'You don't stop and think about what you're going to do in moments like that. You just hit the ball and hope for the best. I was lucky to connect just right. We were really fired up for this match after our defeat by QPR in last season's League Cup final. It suited us having nearly everybody tipping Everton to win. That put all the pressure on them. We had enough experience of that sort of thing against QPR. We were happy to be the underdogs.' – **Jeff Astle**.

FOOTBALL LEAGUE CUP WINNERS

Leeds had at long last tossed away their bridesmaids' dresses! After four years of broken promises they had got a trophy in their cabinet. Admittedly it was 'only' the League Cup, the poor relation of the competitions. But it was now established as a major tournament, and Leeds saw it as just a start. I wish I could report that they had covered themselves in glory in winning the Cup by beating Arsenal 1-0 in the final, but in all honesty the two teams managed to produce a stinker of a match that was totally dominated by the defences.

Arsenal were in a similar foundation-laying situation as Leeds had been four years earlier. Manager Bertie Mee had yet to put the finishing touch to a team that contained seven of the players who would take the Gunners to a League and FA Cup double in 1970-71: Peter Storey, Bob McNab, skipper Frank McLintock, Peter Simpson, John Radford, George Graham and George Armstrong. Jim 'Fingers' Furnell was in goal before the rise of Bob Wilson, and Ian Ure, David Jenkins, Jon Sammels and substitute Terry Neill would all have moved on before Arsenal enjoyed their harvest.

Both teams were so frightened of losing that they concentrated on cancelling each

Terry Cooper *(out of shot, above)* scores the goal that at last brings Leeds United a trophy in the 1968 League Cup final against Arsenal. Jeff Astle *(below),* his right arm raised, lets fly with the shot that wins the FA Cup for West Bromwich Albion against Everton.

other out rather than searching for goals. The deadlock was finally broken by left-back Terry Cooper, a former winger who gave his team-mates a lesson in how to finish with a late winner that was angrily disputed by Arsenal.

The sterile match was an advertisement for all that was worst about football in the 'sixties, with too many niggling fouls and petty feuds to make it worthy of Wembley. Ironically, Arsenal would beat Leeds 4-3 in a thriller at Highbury in the last but one week of the season to block the Leeds bid for the League championship.

Arsenal would return to Wembley the following season for the League Cup final ... and one of the most miserable moments in their long and proud history.

*'This is the only goal I've scored this season, and it could not have come at a better time. The boss [Don Revie] is always on at me to go for goal after I've done the hard work of getting into the opposition penalty area. We've come so close in so many competitions that we were petrified of losing again against Arsenal. But now we have proved we can win when it matters we are confident that we can start mopping up the major trophies.' – **Terry Cooper.**

THE EUROPEAN CUP-WINNERS' CUP

My old club AC Milan won the European Cup-Winners' Cup at their first attempt. Their opponents in the final in Rotterdam were SV Hamburg, who had had to overcome a spirited challenge from Cardiff City in the semi-final. West Germany skipper Uwe Seeler, the spring-heeled centre-forward, had blitzed eight goals on the way to the final, but he was shut out by the massed AC Milan defence.

Kurt Hamrin, the stocky Swedish outside-right who had featured against Brazil in the 1958 World Cup final, was still fast enough to give the Hamburg defence the run around and his two first-half goals clinched a comfortable victory for the Italians.

THE FAIRS CUP FINAL

Leeds were now on an unstoppable run. Following their League Cup triumph they reached the final of the Fairs Cup for the second successive year, eliminating Rangers and Dundee on the way. A first-leg goal by Mick Jones at Elland Road was enough to give them a 1-0 aggregate victory over Ferencvaros in the final.

Peter Lorimer was the Leeds star in the competition, scoring a total of eight goals. Now Leeds, so often the runners-up, had two trophies on their sideboard. They had to wait for the Fairs Cup, with the final delayed until the start of the 1968-69 season.

GREAVSIE'S FOOTBALL DIARY 1967-68

1967

12 August: Tottenham and Manchester United draw 3-3 in the Charity Shield match at Old Trafford. Goalkeeper Pat Jennings scores our second goal with a huge clearance from the Spurs penalty area that goes first bounce over the head of Alex Stepney and into the back of the United net. The bewildered looks on the faces of the United players is one of the funniest sights I have seen on a football pitch, and I say to Alan Gilzean: 'Do you realise that makes Pat our top scorer?'.

17 August: Jimmy Hill ends a flamboyantly successful five-year reign as Coventry City manager. He has given the Sky Blues a new image, with some of the most creative public relations ideas ever introduced into the football world. Jimmy 'The Jaw', who has steered Coventry from the Third Division to the First, will switch to television and become one of the best known faces on the screen. A lot of people might disagree with his strong opinions, but you can never ignore them. His Coventry job will go to Noel Cantwell, the former West Ham, Manchester United and Eire skipper who, like Jimmy, is a former PFA chairman.

9 September: Charlton sack Bob Stokoe. He is the 30th manager to lose his job in the last 30 months. Bob has his glory days to come at Sunderland in the 'seventies. Eddie Firmani, South African-born former Charlton centre-forward, will take over as manager at The Valley. Eddie had his greatest days playing in Italy.

22 September: Leeds buy Sheffield United centre-forward Mick Jones for £100,000. He will become a key player at Elland Road.

6 October: Controversial Tommy Docherty quits as Chelsea manager after he is suspended for a month by the Football Association following incidents during a club tour of Bermuda in the close-season.

21 October: Martin Peters, Bobby Charlton and Alan Ball are the scorers as England beat Wales 3-0 on a rain-saturated pitch at Ninian Park.

23 October: Dave Sexton is named as new Chelsea manager. Don Howe will replace him as Arsenal coach.

4 November: Five players are sent for early baths as the play-off for the World Club Championship between Celtic and Racing Club of Argentina in Montevideo degenerates into a disgraceful brawl. Jimmy Johnstone, Bobby Lennox and Billy Hughes are the Celtic players ordered off, and the referee later says that he also sent off Bertie Auld but he refused to go! Hatred between the two teams built up during two legs, first in Glasgow and then in Buenos Aires. Celtic won 1-0 at Hampden and lost the return 2-1. In the match in Argentina goalkeeper Ronnie Simpson was struck on the head by a stone thrown from the crowd as he came out for the kick-off, and he was unable to play. In my view Celtic should have told Racing Club to take the trophy (and also where to stick it) after the second leg rather than risk trouble in a play-off. Celtic fine each of their players £250 for their part in the brawl.

21 November: Peterborough will be demoted to the Fourth Division at the end of this season as punishment for offering players illegal signing-on fees and bonuses. There will be a lot of knees knocking in boardrooms throughout the League. Under-the-counter payments have been commonplace.

22 November: Geoff Hurst and Bobby Charlton score second-half goals as England beat Northern Ireland – minus George Best and Derek Dougan – 2-0 at Wembley.

23 November: Tommy Docherty starts a new job a million miles away from the bright lights of King's Road, Chelsea. He takes over as manager of Rotherham United.

6 December: England and the USSR draw 2-2 on a snow carpet of a pitch at Wembley. Ray Wilson, one of the finest full-backs I have ever seen, is made to look almost ordinary by Russia's flying 'Red Rocket' right winger Chislenko, who scores both their goals. Alan Ball and Martin Peters are on the mark for England.

11 December: Jim Baxter joins Nottingham Forest from Sunderland for £100,000. Sadly, the greatest days are behind this former idol of Ibrox – one of my all-time favourite players.

12 December: A frustrating night at White Hart Lane. I score two goals as we beat Olympique Lyons 4-3 in the second leg of our second round European Cup-Winners'

Cup tie. But Tottenham go out on the away goals rule because Lyons beat us 1-0 in France.

1968

9 January: Liverpool lose 1-0 to Hungarians Ferencvaros at Anfield and go out of the Fairs Cup 2-0 on aggregate.

10 January: Martin Chivers joins Tottenham from Southampton in a British record transfer deal valued at £125,000. Frank Saul goes to The Dell as part of the deal. I will enjoy playing alongside Chiv, who for a big man is incredibly light on his feet. He will develop into one of England's greatest ever centre- forwards, before a crippling knee injury interrupts his career. Chiv will show character and courage in overcoming the injury.

22 January: Fulham sack their creative but eccentric manager Vic Buckingham. He will be succeeded by former Fulham favourite Bobby Robson.

2 February: Bobby Gould, bustling Coventry City centre-forward, joins Arsenal for £90,000.

8 February: Alan Brown, acknowledged as one of the great tacticians when in charge at Burnley, returns as boss of his old club Sunderland following the dismissal of manager Ian McColl. On the same day Sunderland sell centre-forward Neil Martin to Coventry for £90,000.

14 February: Billy Bingham, an outstanding winger in his playing days with Luton and Everton, leaves Southport to take over as manager of Plymouth Argyle.

24 February: Scotland and England draw 1-1 on a muddy pitch at Hampden. Martin Peters scores the goal that clinches a place for England in the European Nations Cup quarter-finals.

6 March: Port Vale are fined £4,000 and sentenced to expulsion from the Football League at the end of this season for making illegal payments to players. They will be reelected the following season, by which time their general manager Sir Stanley Matthews will have quit the club.

15 March: Noel Cantwell takes his spending since joining Coventry to £325,000 when he signs full-back Chris Cattlin from Huddersfield and Everton forward Ernie Hunt. He recoups £65,000 by selling winger Ronnie Rees to West Brom.

17 March: Johnny Byrne joins Fulham from Crystal Palace for £20,000. 'Budgie' will wind down his career at Craven Cottage before moving to South Africa. Alan Stephenson, Palace centre-half, moves to West Ham for £80,000.

3 April: A Bobby Charlton thunderbolt at Wembley gives England a 1-0 victory over Spain in the first leg of the European Nations Cup quarter-final.

8 May: England reach the European Nations Cup semi-finals by beating Spain 2-1 in

Madrid. The winning goal is scored by Norman Hunter, who fires the ball into the net with his right foot, which he normally uses only to stand on.

11 May: QPR clinch promotion to the First Division, making it from the Third Division in successive seasons.

15 May: Manchester United, playing on the same Madrid pitch where England beat Spain seven days ago, fight back for a 3-3 draw that gives them a 4-3 aggregate victory over Real Madrid and a place in the European Cup final.

22 May: England beat Sweden 3-1 at Wembley, and Bobby Charlton overtakes me as top England scorer with his 45th international goal.

1 June: West Germany score their first victory over England in 13 attempts. Franz Beckenbauer scores the only goal of the match in Hanover with a deflected shot.

5 June: Alan Mullery unluckily becomes the first player ever to be sent off while playing for England as Yugoslavia kick their way to a 1-0 victory in the European Nations Cup semi-final in Florence. The Yugoslavs will be beaten 2-0 by Italy in an uninspiring final.

8 June: England beat the USSR 2-0 in Rome to win the third-place play-off, with Bobby Charlton and Geoff Hurst scoring the goals.

11 June: Allan Clarke becomes England's most expensive player when he moves from Fulham to Leicester for £150,000. Frank Large joins Fulham as part of the deal. Allan is the third of three Clarke brothers to move in the space of four months. Older brother Frank has joined QPR from Shrewsbury, and younger brother Derek has moved to Wolves from Walsall.

THE CHAMPIONS OF
1967-68

FIRST DIVISION:
1: Manchester City (58 points)
2: Manchester United (56)
3: Liverpool (55)

Championship squad:
Bell (35 appearances), Book (42), Bowles (4), Clay (1), Coleman (38), Connor (10), Cheetham (2), Dowd (7), Doyle (37), Heslop (41), Horne (4), Hince (6), Jones (2), Kennedy (4), Lee (31), Mulhearne (33), Oakes (41), Ogley (2), Pardoe (41), Summerbee (41), Young (40).
Scorers: Young (19), Lee (16), Bell (14), Summerbee (14), Coleman (8), Doyle (5), Bowles (2), Hince (2), Oakes (2), Book (1), Connor (1), Heslop (1).

SECOND DIVISION:
1: Ipswich Town (59 points)
2: Queen's Park Rangers (58)
3: Blackpool (58)

Championship squad:
Baker (11 appearances), Barnard (2), Baxter (41), Bolton (5), Broadfoot (4), Brogan (36), Carroll (38), Crawford (39), Hancock (42), Harper (1), Hegan (41), Houghton (41), Hunt (8), Jefferson (28), Lea (4), McNeill (10), Mills (9), Morris (14), O'Rourke (15), Spearritt (19), Viljoen (39), Wigg (5), Woods (9), Wosahlo (1).
Goalscorers: Brogan (17), Crawford (16), O'Rourke (12), Spearritt (7), Viljoen (7), Hegan (6), Wigg (4), Baker (3), Baxter (2), Houghton (2), Carroll (1), Hunt (1), Woods (1).

THIRD DIVISION:
1: Oxford United (57 points)
2: Bury (56)
3: Shrewsbury Town (55)

Championship squad:
G. Atkinson (38 appearances), R. Atkinson (35), Barron (35), Beavon (29), Buck (1), Bullock (39), Clarke (39), Evanson (5), Hale (4), Harrington (17), Higgins (4), Jones (7), Kerr (10), Kyle (41), Lloyd (27), Lucas (1), Shuker (37), Skeen (38), Sloan (16), Sherratt (11), Smithson (29), Thornley (16).
Scorers: Bullock (13), G. Atkinson (11), Shuker (10), Clarke (9), Skeen (6), Hale (5), Jones (4), Harrington (3), Sloan (3), Thornley (3), Evanson (2), Kerr (1), Smithson (1), 1 own goal.

FOURTH DIVISION:
1: Luton Town (66 points)
2: Barnsley (61)
3: Hartlepool United (60)

Championship squad:
Allen (45 appearances), Beaven (1), Branston (46), Brown (12), Buxton (36), Denton (4), Dougan (40), French (31), Green (11), Hare (12), Jardine (41), Johnson (2), McDermott (20), Moore (45), Potter (5), Read (43), Rioch (44), Ryan (10), Slough (35), Taylor (3), Tinsley (1), Whittaker (38).
Goalscorers: Rioch (24), Allen (14), Buxton (13), Whittaker (10), Slough (6), Branston (5), French (5), Moore (4), Green (3), Brown (2), Ryan (1)

SCOTTISH FIRST DIVISION:
1: Celtic (63 points)
2: Rangers (61)
3: Hibernian (45)

Championship squad:
Gemmell (34 appearances), McNeill (34), Murdoch (34), Simpson (33), Hughes (31), Johnstone (29), Wallace (28), Lennox (27), Craig (22), Clark (18), Brogan (18), Auld (18), Chalmers (13), Gallacher (13), O'Neill (5), Cattanach (4), McMahon (2), Shelvane (2), Fallon (1).
Goalscorers: Lennox (32), Wallace (21), Chalmers (9), Hughes (7), Murdoch (6), Auld (5), Johnstone (5), McNeill (5), Gemmell (4), McBride (4), Brogan (1), Cattanach (1), McMahon (1), Quinn (1), 4 own goals.

SCOTTISH SECOND DIVISION:
1: St Mirren (62 points)
2: Arbroath (53)
3: East Fife (49)

FA CUP FINAL:
Wesf Bromwich Albion 1 (Astle)
Osborne, Fraser, Williams, Brown, Talbut, Kaye, Lovett, Collard, Astle, Hope, Clark. Sub: Clarke.
Everton 0
West, Wright, Wilson, Kendall, Labone, Harvey, Husband, Ball, Royle, Hurst, Morrissey. Sub: Kenyon.
After extra-time.

LEAGUE CUP FINAL:
Leeds United 1 (Cooper)
Sprake, Reaney, Cooper, Bremner, Charlton, Hunter, Lorimer, Greenhoff, Madeley, Giles, Gray. Sub: Belfitt.
Arsenal 0
Furnell, Storey, McNab, McLintock, Ure, Simpson, Radford, Jenkins, Graham, Sammels, Armstrong. Sub: Neill.

SCOTTISH FA CUP FINAL:
Dunfermline Athletic 3 (Gardner 2, Lister pen.)
Martin, W. Callaghan, Lunn, McGarty, Barry, T. Callaghan, Lister, Paton, Gardner, Robertson, Edwards. Sub: Thomson.
Heart of Midlothian 1 (Lunn own goal)
Cruickshank, Sneddon, Mann, Anderson, Thomson, Miller, Jensen, Townsend, Ford, Irvine, Traynor. Sub: Muller.

SCOTTISH LEAGUE CUP FINAL:
Celtic 5 (Chalmers 2, Wallace, Lennox, Hughes)
Simpson, Craig, Gemmell, Murdoch, McNeill, Clark, Chalmers, Lennox, Wallace, Auld, Hughes.
Dundee 3 (G. McLean 2, J. McLean)
Arrol, R. Wilson, Houston, Murray, Stewart, Stuart, Campbell, J. McLean, S. Wilson, G. McLean, Bryce.

EUROPEAN CUP FINAL:
Played at Wembley
Manchester United 4 (Charlton 2, Best, Kidd)
Stepney, Brennan, Dunne, Crerand, Foulkes, Stiles, Best, Kidd, Charlton, Sadler, Aston.
Benfica 1 (Graca)
Henrique, Adolfo, Humberto, Jacinto, Cruz, Graca, Coluna, Augusto, Torres, Eusebio, Simoes.
After extra-time.

EUROPEAN CUP-WINNERS' CUP FINAL:
Played in Rotterdam
AC Milan 2 (Hamrin 2)
Cudicini, Anquilletti, Schnellinger, Trapattoni, Rosato, Scala, Hamrin, Lodetti, Sormani, Rivera, Prati.
SV Hamburg 0
Ozcan, Sondemann, Kurbjohn, Dieckemann, Horst, Schulz, B. Dorfel, Kramer, Seeler, Hornig, G. Dorfel.

EUROPEAN FAIRS CUP FINAL:

First leg:

Leeds United 1 *(Jones)*

Sprake, Reaney, Cooper, Bremner, Charlton, Hunter, Lorimer Madeley, Jones, Giles, Gray. Subs: Belfitt, Greenhoff.

Ferencvaros 0

Geczi, Novak, Pancsics, Havasi, Juhasz, Szucs, Szoke, Varga, Albert, Rakosi, Fenyvesi. Sub: Balint.

Second leg:

Ferencvaros 0

Geczi, Novak, Pancsics, Havasi, Juhasz, Szucs, Szoke, Varga, Albert, Rakosi, Katona. Sub: Karaba.

Leeds United 0

Sprake, Reaney, Cooper, Bremner, Charlton, Hunter, Lorimer Madeley, Jones, Hibbitt, O'Grady. Subs: Belfitt, Bates.

Leeds win 1-0 on aggregate.

EUROPEAN NATIONS CUP FINAL:

Italy 2 (Riva, Anastasi)

Zoff, Burnich, Facchetti, Rosto, Gueneri, Salvadore, Domenghini, Mazzola, Anastasi, Desisti, Riva.

Yugoslavia 0

Pantelic, Fazlagic, Damjanovic, Pavolovic, Paunovic, Holcer, Petkovic, Hosic, Musemic, Acimovic, Dzajic.

Play-off after a 1-1 draw in Rome. Italy qualified for the final after winning the toss of a coin following a goalless draw with the USSR in Naples.

Top Football League goalscorers:

George Best (Manchester United)	28
Ron Davies (Southampton)	28
George Yardley (Tranmere Rovers)	27
Jeff Astle (West Bromwich Albion)	25
Roy Chapman (Port Vale)	25
Roger Hunt (Liverpool)	25
Les Massie (Halifax Town)	25
Bobby Owen (Bury)	25
Don Rogers (Swindon Town)	25
John Hickton (Middlesbrough)	24
Bruce Rioch (Luton Town)	24
Kit Napier (Brighton and Hove Albion)	24
Jim Fryatt (Stockport County)	22
Barry Bridges (Birmingham City)	23
Jimmy Greaves (Tottenham Hotspur)	23

Top Scottish First Division marksman:

Bobby Lennox (Celtic) 32 goals

Highest average League attendance:

Manchester United (57,759)

Footballer of the Year:

George Best (Manchester United)

Scottish Footballer of the Year:

Gordon Wallace (Raith Rovers)

European Footballer of the Year:

George Best (Manchester United)

World Club Championship:

Estudiantes beat Manchester United 1-0, 1-1

1968-69:
THE REVIE
REVOLUTION

And so we come to the final season on our journey back through the swinging 'sixties. When we came into the decade footballers were little more than slaves, handcuffed to clubs who paid them a pittance for their services. As we approached the 'seventies, the top players were earning more than Prime Minister Harold Wilson and many of them were as idolised as pop stars. That was the good news. The bad news was that the carefree spirit had been kicked out of the game, and win-at-all-costs too often seemed the order of the day.

The 'sixties had seen the rise of folk heroes like Best, Law and Charlton, Scottish and English clubs proving that 'British was Best' in Europe and, glory be, England winning the World Cup. But as we approached the end of the dizzy decade the blinkered coaches were beginning to get a grip on the game – and in my opinion it was a dead man's grip that would gradually squeeze the individual artists out of football. You can take it from me, soccer in the 'seventies would not be nearly as entertaining to watch as in the 'fifties and 'sixties.

There was, however, a blaze of light on the horizon. Brian Clough, one of the youngest managers in the League, guided Derby County to the Second Division championship with my old chum Dave Mackay masterminding things on the pitch as a cagey back-line defender. Cloughie would become one of the sensations of the 'seventies, 'eighties and 'nineties, a real man for all seasons. He and his right-hand man Peter Taylor had woken a sleeping giant, and it would not be long before Derby were challenging for – and capturing – the League championship.

This final season before the dawn of the 'seventies belonged to Leeds United. Whoever said that it's not the winning but the taking part that matters had clearly never been given listening time at Elland Road. The steam-rolling Leeds machine was now in top gear, and the label second-best had been kicked into touch. They did not always win friends but they certainly influenced results with football that was often mean and ruthless, and they set new standards of professionalism and had plenty of method to go with their muscle. It would be less than charitable for anybody not to concede that for ten years the team that Don Revie created was one of the most potent forces in football. Leeds had been struggling to survive in the Second Division when Revie took over as manager in March 1961. By the time he left Elland Road to succeed Alf Ramsey as England manager in the summer of 1974, Leeds would have established themselves as one of Europe's major clubs.

As a player, Revie had had a distinguished career that reached its peak when he was voted Footballer of the Year in 1955 while playing a revolutionary deep-lying centre-forward role with Manchester City. He had also played for Leicester, Hull, Sunderland and, finally, Leeds. His skilful, intelligent football was rewarded with six England caps and an FA Cup-winners' medal in 1956 after the heartbreak of defeat at Wembley the previous year.

As a manager, Revie was a thoughtful tactician, a great motivator of players, a master of public relations and single-minded to the point of being merciless. 'The Don' had lots of flair, could be extremely fiery and defeat to him was like poison. He had created a team in his own image ...

THE LEAGUE CHAMPIONS

Leeds made no mistake in capturing the First Division title all their years of near-misses. They clinched the championship on a memorable April night at the home of their greatest rivals, Liverpool, and the Anfield fans give them the sort of generous applause that you could only get on Merseyside as Don Revie's team earned a draw and the point that confirmed them as champions.

They finished the season with a record haul of 67 points, six ahead of Liverpool, with Everton and Arsenal trailing in third and fourth places. An indication of the Leeds supremacy was that they were unbeaten at Elland Road all season and were losers only twice away from home.

Revie's favourite combination as he drove his team on towards the title was this flexible 4-3-3 formation: Sprake, Reaney, Charlton, Hunter, Cooper, Bremner, Giles, Gray, Lorimer, Jones, O'Grady. Paul 'Mr Utility' Madeley was able to take on any job, and filled in extremly ably wherever and whenever he was wanted.

Leeds built their success on a foundation of a strong defence in which Paul Reaney and Terry Cooper were as talented a pair of full-backs as you could find anywhere in club football. Jack 'The Giraffe' Charlton and Norman 'Bites Yer Legs' Hunter stood at the centre of the defence with an air of authority that could give way to the big stick if there appeared to be any danger of somebody being foolish enough to try to plot a way past them. I had the bruises to prove it.

Billy Bremner, as explosive as a sawn-off shotgun, was a bundle of atomic energy in midfield, and as skipper was like an extension of Don Revie on the pitch. Johnny Giles, the 'Irish Imp', was full of marvellous skill mixed with mischief as he dictated the tactics with considered ball placement. Eddie Gray was one of the most gifted ball players in the land, and he could take any defence apart with controlled runs from the left side of the pitch. Other players who got brief look-ins in supporting roles during this championship season were Mick Bates, Rod Belfitt, Jimmy Greenhoff, Albert Johanneson and Terry

Goalkeeper Gary Sprake and manager Don Revie *(left, above)* have their hands full as Leeds end the 'sixties leading the football treasure hunt. Norman 'Bites Yer Legs' Hunter *(above)* was a key man in the Leeds glory march that lasted into the mid-1970s before a dramatic decline that ended with a stunning revival in the 'nineties.

Hibbitt. The Leeds squad had great strength in depth.

Mick Jones led the attack with Yorkshire grit and determination, while Peter Lorimer and Mike O'Grady were both encouraged to be positive on the flanks. 'Hot Shot' Lorimer could hit the ball with rocketing power with his right foot, and O'Grady's pace and crossing ability had earned him England recognition at Huddersfield before his switch to his home-town club of Leeds.

The fact that Jones was the top marksman with 'only' 14 goals revealed that Leeds were not exactly the most attack-minded team of the century. But winning was everything to them, and they closed up shop the moment they got a goal in front. When they did open up and blaze away with all guns they were as exciting and skilful a team as you could wish to see.

Leeds started the season by winning the Fairs Cup final left over from the previous year, and they finished it by lifting the League championship. A couple of seasons before, they had been getting neurotic about their failure to win the matches that mattered. Now there was no stopping them. It was the age of the Revie Revolution.

> 'We would have run through brick walls for the boss [Don Revie]. He was that great a manager. Our record under him speaks for itself. At one stage we were unfairly labelled a "dirty" side because we were competitive and played to win. I don't think that the team has been given nearly enough credit for its all-round skills and high quality football.' – **Billy Bremner**.

THE FA CUP WINNERS

Manchester City continued their sweep of the prizes by winning the FA Cup against a Leicester City team going down to their third Wembley defeat of the decade. It was not an easy victory for the Maine Road team. They were made to battle every inch of the way by a Leicester side coming into the match just a week after their relegation to the Second Division had been sealed. The quality of their football made you think they were a team on the way up rather on the way down. In goal they had the young Peter Shilton putting the foundations to his career as one of the all-time great goalkeepers, while in attack they had the most effective forward on the field in Allan Clarke. His polished performance would convince Leeds manager Don Revie to shell out a record £165,000 for him a month after the final.

Neil Young strikes with his trusty left foot *(above)* and Manchester City are on their way to an FA Cup final victory over Leicester City at Wembley in 1969. Skipper Tony Book *(left)* gets the chair of honour on Mike Doyle's shoulders, with Francis Lee and goalkeeper Harry Dowd in support.

Manchester City, relying on the team that had captured the League championship the previous season, won by the only goal of the match, which was created by Mike Summerbee and executed by Neil Young in the 24th minute. First Clarke and then skipper Peter Rodrigues threatened to put Leicester into the lead before the tall, elegant Young struck his golden goal. He rifled the ball into the net from 12 yards with his trusty left foot after a typically brave run down the right by Summerbee that took him past tackles by David Nish and Alan Woollett.

Young had been an unsung hero with City for several seasons, having to live in the shadow of his more illustrious colleagues Lee, Bell and Summerbee. He played with an effortless style that could deceive defenders into thinking he was lacking in concentration. How wrong they could be! He had a whiplash left-foot shot, and could also set up goals for team-mates with perfectly weighted passes.

'This is the greatest moment of my football career. To score the winner at Wembley is as much as any player could wish for. Mike Summerbee deserves credit for the way he set up the goal for me. There was a defender standing either side of Peter Shilton guarding the Leicester goal when Mike played the ball into my path, but I managed to find the only gap they had left. I have never been happier to see a ball hit the back of the net.' – **Neil Young**.

FOOTBALL LEAGUE CUP WINNERS

Swindon Town's football history had been more about taking part than winning when they travelled to Wembley for the first time to tackle aristocratic Arsenal in the League Cup final. In the previous year Arsenal had been narrowly beaten 1-0 in the final by Leeds United, and few people seriously expected the unfashionable Third Division Wiltshire club to stop the Londoners from winning the trophy at the second time of asking. But perhaps somebody should have pointed out that Arsenal would be wise to beware the Ides of March. Swindon knives had been sharpened for this 15 March showdown, and they would be buried deep into the Arsenal backs.

Swindon were not burdened with any sort of complex about their Third Division status. They took heart from the fact that just two years previously Third Division Queen's Park Rangers, inspired by the creative Rodney Marsh, had come from behind to beat West Bromwich Albion of the First Division in the first League Cup final staged at Wembley.

Swindon knew they had their West Country version of a Rodney Marsh in the shape of Don Rogers.

Arsenal were more concerned than Swindon when on the day of the match they found the famous Wembley turf looking a mudheap. Gallons of rain water had been pumped away, leaving the pitch ankle-deep in a mixture of sludge and sand. The sight did nothing to improve the mood of the Arsenal players, who were still suffering from the after-effects of a 'flu outbreak. They knew they were on a hiding to nothing and were well aware of the old football cliché that 'the mud is a great leveller'.

Anybody who had witnessed Swindon purring their way into a promotion-challenging position in the Third Division that season would have been able to warn Arsenal that they should not under-estimate a team that had had the character to survive four replays on the way to Wembley. They had conquered Torquay United and Blackburn Rovers at the first go, but needed replays before overcoming Bradford City, Coventry City, Derby County and Burnley.

Their manager Danny Williams, a former Yorkshire miner who had played his heart out for Rotherham for 20 years, encouraged Swindon to play attacking, adventurous football even though most teams were now beginning to put the emphasis on defence. He had an ace up his sleeve in Don Rogers, a West Country winger who was as free as a bird to express his skill in any way he saw fit. 'You don't tell a Goya how to paint a picture or a Caruso how to sing a song,' said Williams. 'I just tell Don to go out and play.'

This was how the two teams lined up for what would prove to be one of the most sensational and surprising matches in Wembley history:

Swindon Town: Downsborough, Thomas, Trollope, Butler, Burrows, Harland, Heath, Smart, Smith, Noble, Rogers. Sub: Penman.

Arsenal: Wilson, Storey, McNab, McLintock, Ure, Simpson, Radford, Sammels, Court, Gould, Armstrong. Sub: Graham.

For most of the 90 minutes of ordinary time Arsenal's pedigree showed as they penned Swindon in their own half with football that was as smooth as the heavy conditions would allow and was lacking only in goalmouth punch. When they were able to get past a defence in which full-backs Rod Thomas and John Trollope were outstanding they found goalkeeper Peter Downsborough in inspired form. He saved at least three possible goals before Swindon broke away to take a shock lead with a goal that had 'made by Arsenal' stamped on it. Centre-half Ian Ure made a mess of an attempted back pass to goalkeeper Bob Wilson and Roger Smart nipped in to score a gift of a goal.

Arsenal charged forward on the churned-up pitch in the second half in a desperate bid to avoid the embarrassment of defeat, but Downsborough was in an even more defiant mood and smothered and saved shot after shot. He made his one mistake of the match with just four minutes to go when he misjudged a run off his line and was way out of position as battling Bobby Gould powered through the mud to ram in an equaliser.

The Gunners were then faced with the last thing their 'flu-weakened players wanted – 30 minutes of extra-time on a pudding of a pitch that was making every step a challenge. But one player sensed that this was the time and the place for some West Country magic. Enter, stage left, Don Rogers.

He threaded the ball past a queue of outwitted Arsenal defenders to put Swindon into the lead just before the halfway point of extra-time. Then, in the closing minutes, he raced 40 yards with the ball at his feet, stopping only to look up and gauge the angle for his shot, which he duly placed wide of the oncoming Wilson.

They were two unforgettable moments of footballing genius, and shell-shocked Arsenal had been blown aside by the team that had become known as the 'Wiltshire Whirlwind'.

Born in Midsomer Norton on 27 October, 1945, Rogers had started and would end his career with Swindon, for whom he netted a total of 149 League goals. In between he played with mixed success for Crystal Palace and Queen's Park Rangers. He rarely showed his scintillating form in London, mainly because of injury problems. I am convinced that if Don had played for one of the big city clubs early in his career he would have established himself as an outstanding international. He had beautiful close skills and was deadly with his finishing. 'The Don', one of the most talented players ever to come out of the West Country, would retire in 1973 to concentrate on business interests in Swindon, the town where he would always be an idol.

Swindon completed a double in 1968-69 by winning promotion to the Second Division. Shaken by the defeat, Arsenal took stock of their situation and started a team rebuilding plan that would bear fruit with the winning of the League and FA Cup double two years later.

It was Don Rogers who had dynamited them into action.

'Arsenal treated us too lightly. They thought we were just country bumpkins, but we knew that if we could play at anything like our best we were a match for any team in the country.' – Don Rogers.

CHAMPIONS OF EUROPE

With two Manchester teams in the competition, English hopes of retaining the European Cup were high. But Manchester City were unable to live up to the boasts of coach Malcolm Allison and they fell at the first hurdle against Turkish club Fenerbahce. 'We shall return', vowed Allison, and sure enough City would capture the European Cup-Winners' Cup the following year. Matt Busby's Manchester United powered through to the semi-finals again, where they lost 2-1 on aggregate to AC Milan, going under 2-0 in the first leg the San Siro Stadium and then winning 1-0 at Old Trafford. So near, yet so far.

Milan had also accounted for Celtic in the previous round, and they proved too experienced for an emerging Ajax side in the final in Madrid. Ajax, the first Dutch team to reach the final, had produced their peak performance in the semi-final when they eliminated Benfica. They impressively won a play-off in Paris 3-0 with the front-line combination of young Johan Cruyff and Swedish international centre-forward Inge Danielsson pulling the Portuguese defence apart with their imaginative running and bewitching ball control.

AC Milan had a team of scouts watching the match and they came up with an effective plan to counter the Cruyff-Danielsson combination. Ajax were never allowed to get into their stride, and it was the turn of their defence to be teased and taunted by the passes of Gianni Rivera.

Pierino Prati, a jet-propelled utility forward, emerged as the Milan man-of-the-match. He scored two goals in the first half to give the Italians a 2-0 lead at half-time. Ajax briefly pulled themselves back into the game when Velibor Vasovic scored from the penalty spot in the 70th minute after a foul on Piet Keizer. Vasovic, a have-boots-will-travel Yugoslav, had also scored for Partizan Belgrade in the 1966 final, and again he had to be content with a runners-up medal. Dutch hopes of winning the game died with an Angelo Sormani goal, followed, six minutes from the final whistle, by a fourth goal added by hat-trick hero Prati. It was a desperate disappointment for Ajax, but the 'seventies would be their decade. The two Johans – Cruyff and Neeskens – would see to that.

THE EUROPEAN CUP-WINNERS' CUP

Politics poisoned the first round of both the European Cup and the Cup-Winners' Cup when several Eastern Bloc clubs pulled out in protest after a re-draw to keep East and West apart following Russia's invasion of Czechoslovakia. It seemed almost poetic justice when a Czech side – Slovan Bratislava – emerged as the winners of the Cup-Winners' Cup.

In the semi-final they overcame the challenge of Dunfermline, who had squeezed past West Bromwich Albion 1-0 on aggregate in the quarter-final thanks to a goal by Pat Gardner at The Hawthorns.

Slovan got off to a perfect start against Barcelona in the final in Basle, Cvelter scoring in the second minute. Left-back Hrivnak and left winger Jan Capkovic added goals to give Slovan a commanding 3-1 lead at half-time. Rexach scored direct from a corner for Barcelona, but the Slovan defence held out against fierce attacks from the Spaniards and the team from Bratislava were rewarded for their resilience with a 3-2 victory.

THE FAIRS CUP FINAL

Newcastle had not experienced football fever quite like it since the heady days in the 'fifties when they captured the FA Cup three times in five years. It was their progress in the Fairs Cup that had brought choruses of *Blaydon Races* roaring down from the packed Tyneside terraces.

It was incredible that Newcastle were in Europe at all after finishing tenth in the First Division the previous season. The 'one-club-per-city' rule blocked higher-placed Everton, Spurs and Arsenal; Manchester United and Manchester City were competing in the European Cup, while West Bromwich were contesting the Cup-Winners' Cup. For the first time four English clubs were invited into the Fairs Cup, and it was Newcastle who scraped into the fourth place. They then made the most of their luck.

Newcastle's Fairs Cup victims on the way into the two-leg final reads like a who's who of European football clubs: Feyenoord of Holland, Sporting Lisbon of Portugal, Real Zaragoza of Spain, Vitoria Setubal of Portugal and, in the semi-finals, Glasgow Rangers. The irony that they were eliminated by a goal each from Geordie Scots Jackie Sinclair and Jim Scott at St James' Park after a goalless draw at Ibrox was not lost on Rangers. Ugly scenes scarred the match at Gallowgate, with the referee having to delay play for 17 minutes in the second half following a pitch invasion by Rangers fans trying to force an abandonment.

Waiting for Newcastle in the final were Hungarians Ujpest Doza, rated by many the finest team in Eastern or Central Europe. They had proved their class by eliminating Fairs Cup-holders and First Division leaders Leeds United 3-0 on aggregate in the quarter-final.

Newcastle, with Wyn Davies and 'Pop' Robson a dynamic duo up front, produced a storming second-half display against Ujpest in the first leg at St James' in front of a heaving crowd of 60,000, proving that the north east could match Merseyside when it came to football passion. Skipper Bobby Moncur scored twice and Jim Scott also found the back of the net to give the Geordies a 3-0 lead to take into the second leg in Budapest.

The match in Hungary on 11 June, 1969, coincided with the 51st birthday of manager Joe Harvey, who had been the rock in defence for the Magpies in the Cup glory days of the 'fifties. What a present he was about to get. Newcastle fielded the same side that had won so convincingly at home: Liam McFaul, David Craig, Frank Clark, Tommy Gibb, Olly Burton, Bobby Moncur, Jim Scott, Bryan 'Pop' Robson, Wyn Davies, Ben Arentoft, Jackie Sinclair, with Alan Foggon coming on as a substitute.

Newcastle's three-goal cushion was suddenly all but snatched away from them in the first half when exceptional Hungarian international players Ferenc Bene and Janos Gorocs scored a goal each to make it 3-2. But the Magyar spirit was broken early in the second half when big-hearted Bobby Moncur – the Dave Mackay of Newcastle – hammered in a shot on the volley to make it 4-2 on aggregate. With the Hungarians having to throw everything into the attack they left themselves exposed at the back and Newcastle took full advantage of the freedom of movement with goals from the little Dane Arentoft and substitute Foggon. It was the first time in the beautiful city of Budapest that they had heard *Blaydon Races* sung. The Magpies had stolen the silver.

> *'What an unforgettable birthday! I have known some great moments in my time with Newcastle, but I have never experienced anything quite like this. Ujpest Doza are a magnificent team, but tonight we proved ourselves equal to anything they could produce. The players have done us proud.'* – **Joe Harvey.**

GREAVSIE'S FOOTBALL DIARY
1968-69

1968

10 August: This is the earliest-ever start to the season. Much earlier and we would have to play on the beach. Attendances are down 39,000 on last season's first day. It will become a continuing trend of falling gates. I put it down to a mixture of defensive football, increased prices and the growing cancer of hooliganism. Mind you, in a couple of decades' time what would they give for a total aggregate League attendance of 29,383,172, with an average 31,569 in the First Division?

20 August: Queen's Park Rangers buy Barry Bridges from Birmingham City for £50,000. It is like a home-coming for Barry, a fleet-footed striker who won an England cap while with his original club Chelsea.

24 August: Nottingham Forest's main stand is gutted by fire which forces the abandonment of their match against Leeds. They will play their home matches at neighbouring Notts County until the damage is repaired.

25 August: Willie Morgan joins Manchester United from Burnley for £100,000, and Derby sign Willie Carlin from Sheffield United for £60,000.

27 August: Birmingham City buy Jimmy Greenhoff from Leeds United for £75,000.

16 September: Alun Evans becomes British football's first £100,000 teenage footballer when he joins Liverpool from Wolves. The 18-year-old inside-forward has played only first-team matches with the Midlands club. Welsh international Barrie Hole moves from Blackburn to Aston Villa for £48,000.

18 September: West Brom centre-forward Jeff Astle is knocked out as fans invade the pitch in Bruges where Albion lose their first European Cup-Winners' Cup tie 3-1.

19 September: Centre-forward Tony Hateley is head-hunted by Coventry. He moves to Highfield Road for £80,000 just 15 months after signing for Liverpool from Chelsea for £100,000.

25 September: Nobby Stiles is ordered off as Manchester United lose a bitterly fought World Club championship first-leg match against Estudiantes in Buenos Aires.

10 October: After ten distinguished years with Tottenham, flying Welsh winger Cliff Jones moves to Fulham. He has been a magnificent servant for Spurs, and is one of the finest wingers I have ever seen.

16 October: George Best goes for an early bath during United's 1-1 draw with Estudiantes at Old Trafford. The Argentinians take the World Club title 2-1 on aggregate.

19 October: Geoff Hurst hammers in six goals for West Ham against Sunderland in a First Division match at Upton Park. He might have had ten but for some blinding saves by Sunderland goalkeeper Jim Montgomery, who will make a name for himself against Leeds at Wembley in 1973.

31 October: Rangers sign Hibs centre-forward Colin Stein for £100,000-£40,000 more than the previous record between Scottish clubs.

4 November: Alec Stock, who performed miracles guiding Queen's Park Rangers from the Third Division to the First in successive seasons, is sacked. It is the start of a crazy game of 'managerial' chairs.

6 November: Tommy Docherty resigns from Rotherham to take over as boss at QPR. Team manager Bill Dodgin is demoted to assistant manager.

6 November: I score four goals for Spurs against Sunderland – two short of Geoff Hurst's haul.

20 November: Ronnie Allen quits as manager of Wolves, and Bill McGarry leaves Ipswich to replace him at Molineux.

21 November: Bobby Robson is sacked as manager of Fulham. Johnny Haynes becomes player-manager at Craven Cottage, with Bill Dodgin moving from neighbours QPR to become his assistant.

2 December: John Carey gets the boot at Nottingham Forest. He will be replaced by Matt Gillies, who has resigned from Leicester City.

5 December: Here we go again! Tommy Docherty walks out on QPR following a row with chairman Jim Gregory. He has been at Loftus Road for just a month. Les Allen is appointed caretaker-manager.

8 December: Johnny Haynes says he has had enough of managing Fulham after just four games as boss. Bill Dodgin, son of a famous manager of the 'fifties, will take over. I reckon Haynsie has given it up because the worry is turning his Brylcreemed hair grey!

11 December: Geoff Hurst scores the goal as England draw 1-1 in a drab match with Bulgaria at Wembley.

13 December: Back to the managerial roundabout. Frank O'Farrell resigns as Torquay manager and takes over at Leicester City.

18 December: You can't keep Tommy Docherty out of the headlines. He is appointed new manager of Aston Villa following a boardroom shake-up at Villa Park.

19 December: Alec Stock re-surfaces. Allan Brown is moved aside at Luton Town so that Alec can take over.

1969

8 January: Peterborough manager Norman Rigby resigns, and will be replaced by old Sheffield United, Spurs, Nottingham Forest and New-castle favourite Jim Iley.

9 January: Les Allen is confirmed as QPR manager, Allan Brown takes over at Torquay and John Carey is appointed administrative manager of Blackburn Rovers.

14 January: Sir Matt Busby announces that he is giving up the team management of Manchester United. He will become general manager. How do you follow this legend? With great difficulty.

15 January: England 1, Rumania 1 at Wembley. It is a memorable night for the Charlton brothers. Bobby skippers England in his 90th international, and Jack scores the goal. I have hit a purple patch in my club career with Tottenham, and there is a press campaign for my recall. Sir Alf Ramsey tells the media that I have asked not to be selected, and claims that he is being crucified for leaving me out. Sorry, Alf, but you've got it wrong. What I have said privately to you is that I would rather not be considered for the England team if you are going to call me up and not play me. Alf has been getting into the habit of putting me in his squad and then leaving me kicking my heels on the touchline. I am not complaining, but there are plenty of things I can be doing rather than wasting hours at training get-togethers which, for me, have no end product. This brings up the old chestnut in the press that I have not forgiven Alf for leaving me out of the 1966 World Cup Final. What baloney! I have enormous respect for Alf and consider him the greatest of all England managers. We do not agree on the way the game should be played, but I bow to his superior tactical knowledge. He left me out of the England team against West Germany and Geoff Hurst scored a hat-trick. Ramsey 3, Greaves 0. End of argument. Alf and I have never had a cross word, and have a lot of warmth for each other. So there.

30 January: New Wolves manager Bill McGarry signs Scottish striker Hugh Curran from Norwich City for a bargain £60,000.

7 February: Spurs manager Bill Nicholson sees double. He buys winger Roger Morgan from QPR for £100,000, and his identical twin brother Ian also comes to White Hart Lane as part of the deal.

24 February: Walsall sack Ron Lewin. He is the 700th manager to move since the war. Twenty-nine changes have taken place so far this season. It is around about this time that the silly trend of managers getting more publicity than the players starts.

12 March: Geoff Hurst scores another hat-trick as England beat France 5-0 at Wembley. Mike O'Grady and Franny Lee are also on the mark. Now the press can get off Alf's back about recalling me. Despite what some people think, I loved nearly every moment of my England career and am happy with my input of 44 goals in 57 matches.

13 March: Liverpool sign defender Alec Lindsay from Bury for £60,000. Full-back Bobby Thomson moves from Wolves to Birmingham City for £60,000, and winger Mike

Kenning switches from Molineux to The Valley for a bargain £25,000. It is his second spell with Charlton.

23 March: Roger Hunt announces that he no longer wishes to be considered for England international matches. This great competitor, stunning finisher and marvellous sportsman finishes with 18 goals in 34 internationals.

28 March: George Cohen, another wonderful England servant, is forced out of football with a crippling knee injury. George had his peak moments in 1966 when he was a key defender in England's World Cup-winning team. George is a lovely bloke, and is choked to be forced out of the game when he still has so much to give. Fulham, England and football in general will miss this great character.

9 April: Wilf McGuinness, the Old Trafford trainer, is given a trial run as Manchester United team manager. He will always struggle in the shadow of Sir Matt Busby. Who wouldn't? Wilf was an exceptional midfield prospect until a broken leg ended his career at the age of 22.

10 April: Manchester City captain Tony Book and Derby County skipper Dave Mackay are elected joint Footballers of the Year. I feel this is an insult to Dave, who deserves the trophy on his own – and that is no disrespect to Book, who is having an incredible run at Maine Road. Mackay always seems to be on the wrong end of the sentimental vote. He should have collected the award in 1963, but was pipped by one vote by Stanley Matthews.

17 April: Lol Morgan is sacked by Norwich City. It's the 35th managerial change this season.

3 May: Martin Peters, Franny Lee and Geoff Hurst are the scorers as England beat Northern Ireland 3-1 in Belfast.

10 May: It's the West Ham double-act of Hurst and Peters again as England beat Scotland 4-1 at Wembley. They score two goals each.

8 June: Franny Lee and Geoff Hurst are the scorers as England beat Uruguay 2-1 in Montevideo.

12 June: A glimpse of the 'seventies. The Brazilian team that will win the 1970 World Cup in such dazzling style beat current world champions England 2-1 in Rio. Tostao and Jairzinho score for Brazil, with Colin Bell replying for England.

THE CHAMPIONS OF
1968-69

FIRST DIVISION:
1: Leeds United (67 points)
2: Liverpool (61)
3: Everton (57)

Championship squad:
Bates (3 appearances), Belfitt (6), Bremner (42), Charlton (41), Cooper (34), Giles (32), Gray (32), Greenhoff (3), Hibbitt (9), Hunter (42), Johanneson (1), Jones (40), Lorimer (24), Madeley (31), O'Grady (38), Reaney (42), Sprake (42).
Goalscorers: Jones (14), O'Grady (9), Lorimer (8), Giles (8), Bremner (6), Gray (5), Belfitt (3), Charlton (3), Hibbitt (3), Madeley (3), Cooper (1), Johanneson (1), Reaney (1), 1 own goal.

SECOND DIVISION:
1: Derby County (66 points)
2: Crystal Palace (56)
3: Charlton Athletic (50)

Championship squad:
Barker (7 appearances), Carlin (36), Daniel (2), Durban (36), Green (42), Hector (41), Hinton (41), McGovern (18), McFarland (42), Mackay (41), O'Hare (41), Richardson (4), Robson (42), Stewart (4), Walker (23), Webster (37), Wright (1), Wignall (4).
Goalscorers: Hector (16), O'Hare (10), McFarland (9), Carlin (8), Hinton (7), Durban (6), Wignall (4), Barker (2), Mackay (1), Walker (1), 1 own goal.

THIRD DIVISION:
1: Watford (64 points)
2: Swindon Town (64)
3: Luton Town (61)

Championship squad:
Dyson (18 appearances), Eddy (46), Endean (28), Garbett (39), Garvey (33), Green (12), Hale (39), Lees (14), Lewis (10), Low (6), Owen (30), Packer (1), Scullion (42), Slater (4), Sinclair (6), Walker (42), Walley (46), Welbourne (46), Williams (44).
Goalscorers: Endean (18), Garbett (11), Eddy (8), Scullion (6), Green (5), Dyson (4), Owen (4), Walley (4), Lees (3), Lewis (3), Sinclair (2), Welbourne (2), Hale (1), Low (1), 2 own goals.

FOURTH DIVISION:
1: Doncaster Rovers (59 points)
2: Halifax Town (57)
3: Rochdale (56)

Championship squad:
Aiken (5 appearances), Barrett (1), Bird (8), Briggs (17), Clish (44), Flowers (42), Gavan (14), Gilfillan (31), Gray (12), Harrity (2), Haselden (31), Jeffrey (25), Johnson (41), Morritt (1), Ogston (31), Rabjohn (28), Regan (36), Robertson (42), Stainwright (1), Usher (26), Watson (18), Webber (14), Wilcockson (36).
Goalscorers: Jeffrey (11), Regan (10), Johnson (9), Watson (8), Gilfillan (7), Briggs (3), Rabjohn (3), Robertson (3), Webber (3), Clish (2), Usher (2), Flowers (1), Haselden (1), Wilcockson (1), 1 own goal.

SCOTTISH FIRST DIVISION:

1: Celtic (54), **2:** Rangers (49), **3:** Dumfermline Athletic (45)

Championship squad: McNeill (34), Craig (32), Gemmell (31), Brogan (30), Johnstone (30), Murdoch (30), Wallace (29), Hughes (27), Lennox (27), Fallon (22), Chalmers (17), Callaghan (12), Simpson (12), Auld (9), Clark (9), Hood (7), Connelly (5), McBride (4), O'Neill (4), Cattanach (1), Macari (1).

Goalscorers: Wallace (19), Lennox (12), Chalmers (11), Hughes (10), Gemmell (8), Hood (5), Johnstone (5), Murdoch (4), Callaghan (3), McNeill (3), Brogan (2), Auld (1), Connelly (1), Craig (1), McBride (1), Macari (1), 1 own goal.

SCOTTISH SECOND DIVISION:

1: Motherwell (64 points)
2: Ayr United (53)
3: East Fife (48)

FA CUP FINAL:

Manchester City 1 (Young)
Dowd, Book, Pardoe, Doyle, Booth, Oakes, Summerbee, Bell, Lee, Young, Coleman. Sub: Connor.

Leicester City 0
Shilton, Rodrigues, Nish, Roberts, Woollett, Cross, Fern, Gibson, Lochhead, Clarke, Glover. Sub: Manley.

LEAGUE CUP FINAL:

Swindon Town 3 (Rogers 2, Smart)
Downsborough, Thomas, Trollope, Butler, Burrows, Harland, Heath, Smart, Smith, Noble, Rogers. Sub: Penman.

Arsenal 1 (Gould)
Wilson, Storey, McNab, McLintock, Ure, Simpson, Radford, Sammels, Court, Gould, Armstrong. Sub: Graham.
After extra-time.

SCOTTISH FA CUP FINAL:

Celtic 4 (McNeill, Lennox, Connelly, Chalmers)
Fallon, Craig, Gemmell, Murdoch, McNeill, Brogan, Connelly, Chalmers, Wallace, Lennox, Auld. Sub: Clark.

Rangers 0
Martin, Johansen, Mathieson, Greig, McKinnon, Smith, Henderson, Penman, Ferguson, Johnston, Person. Sub: Jardine.

SCOTTISH LEAGUE CUP FINAL:

Celtic 6 (Lennox 3, Wallace, Auld, Craig)
Fallon, Craig, Gemmell, Murdoch, McNeill, Brogan, Johnstone, Wallace, Chalmers, Auld, Lennox. Sub: Clark.

Hibernian 2 (O'Rourke, Stevenson)
Allan, Sheviane, Davis, Stanton, Madsen, Blackley, Marinello, Quinn, Cormack, O'Rourke, Stevenson. Sub: Hunter.

EUROPEAN CUP FINAL:

Played in Madrid
AC Milan 4 (Prati 3, Sormani)
Cudicini, Anquiletti, Schnellinger, Rosato, Malatrasi, Trapattoni, Hamrin, Lodetti, Sormani, Rivera, Prati.

Ajax 1 (Vasovic pen.)
Bals, Suurbier, Hulshoff, Vasovic, Van Dulvenbode, Pronk, Groot, Swart, Cruyff, Danielsson, Keizer.

EUROPEAN CUP-WINNERS' CUP FINAL:

Played at Basle
Slovan Bratislava 3 (Zvetler, Hrivnak, Jan Capkovic)
Vencel, Filo, Hrivnak, Zlocha, Horvath, Hrdlicka, Cvetler, Moder, Josef Capkovic, Jokl, Jan Capkovic. Sub: Bizon.

Barcelona 2 (Zaldua, Rexach)
Sadurni, Franch, Eladio, Rife, Olivella, Zabalza, Pellicer, Castro, Zaldua, Fuste, Rexach. Subs: Pereda, Mendoza.

EUROPEAN FAIRS CUP FINAL:

First leg:

Newcastle United 3 *(Moncur 2, Scott)*

McFaul, Craig, Clark, Gibb, Burton, Moncur, Scott, Robson, Davies, Arentoft, Sinclair. Sub: Foggon.

Ujpest Doza 0

Szentimihale, Kaposzta, Solymosi, Bankuti, Nosko, E. Dunai, Fazekas, Gorocs, Bene, A. Dunai, Zambo.

Second leg:

Ujpest Doza 2 *(Gorocs, Bene)*

Szentimihale, Kaposzta, Solymosi, Bankuti, Nosko, E. Dunai, Fazekas, Gorocs, Bene, A. Dunai, Zambo.

Newcastle United 3 *(Moncur, Arentoft, Foggon)*

McFaul, Craig, Clark, Gibb, Burton, Moncur, Scott, Robson, Davies, Arentoft, Sinclair. Sub: Foggon.

Newcastle win 6-2 on aggregate.

Top Football League goalscorers:

Jimmy Greaves (Tottenham Hotspur)	27
Geoff Hurst (West Ham United)	25
Brian Lewis (Luton Town)	22
Don Rogers (Swindon Town)	22
Joe Royle (Everton)	22
Gary Talbot (Chester City)	22
John Toshack (Cardiff City)	22
Jeff Astle (West Bromwich Albion)	21
John Galley (Bristol City)	21
Bryan Robson (Newcastle United)	21
Billy Best (Southend United)	20
Ron Davies (Southampton)	20
Jim Hall (Peterborough United)	20
Ken Wagstaff (Hull City)	20

Top Scottish First Division marksman:

John (Dixie) Deans (Motherwell) 29 goals

Highest average League attendance:

Manchester United (51,121)

Footballer of the Year:

Tony Book (Manchester City)/Dave Mackay (Derby County)

Scottish Footballer of the Year:

Bobby Murdoch (Celtic)

European Footballer of the Year:

Gianni Rivera (AC Milan)

World Club Championship:

AC Milan beat Estudiantes 3-0, 1-2

THE FINAL BOW

Come back with me to the end of 1969, to be re-united with the main characters in the cast of thousands who made the 'sixties the most memorable decade in the history of British football. This was what they were doing as the curtain fell on the decade ... and what they went on to achieve.

MALCOLM ALLISON was galvanising his Manchester City players ready for an assault on the European Cup-Winners' Cup. In 1970 they captured the trophy by beating Gornik Zabrze 2-1 in the final in Vienna. It completed a double for City, 2-1 winners of the League Cup final against West Bromwich Albion. Big Mal later tried to conquer fresh fields with Crystal Palace, Porto in Portugal, Plymouth Argyle, Middlesbrough and Fisher Athletic, and he also had a season back at Manchester City. But he never managed to recreate the magic that he and Joe Mercer had sparked at Maine Road.

JIMMY ARMFIELD hung up his boots in 1970 after 568 League appearances for Blackpool and 43 caps for England as a cultured right-back. He had three years as manager at Bolton before taking over at Elland Road following Brian Clough's short stay as Leeds manager. In 1978 Jimmy switched to his first love, journalism, and became a respected football reporter with the *Daily Expresses* well as a frequent radio broadcaster.

JEFF ASTLE won five England caps, including a nightmare match against Brazil in the 1970 World Cup finals when he came on as a substitute and missed a sitter from right in front of the goal. After scoring 137 League goals in 290 appearances for West Brom he quit in 1974 because of injury problems. He wound down his goal-packed career with Dunstable Town before starting a successful industrial cleaning business.

BERTIE AULD could not shake off the drug of football after helping Celtic win yet another League championship in 1970, and he joined the managerial roundabout with Partick Thistle, Hamilton Academicals, Dumbarton and Hibernian.

ALAN BALL was the mastermind behind Everton's League championship victory in 1969-70. In December 1971 he joined Arsenal in a record £220,000 deal. Ballie then moved to Southampton before following his father as a manager with Blackpool, Portsmouth, Stoke City and Exeter City. He won a total of 72 England caps and became a valued member of Graham Taylor's England coaching team

GORDON BANKS had his distinguished career cruelly finished by a car smash in 1972 that cost him the sight of an eye. He played for two seasons in the United States where, even with one eye, he was voted 'Most Valuable Goalkeeper'. Gordon became a respected goalkeeper coach after being in charge at Telford United, and he ran a successful public relations business, but no League club gave him the chance he would have liked as a manager. What a way to treat a hero. England caps: 73.

JIM BAXTER was back at his beloved Rangers, but he was just a shadow – a fat shadow – of the 'Slim Jim' who became the idol of Ibrox. He retired at 30 to run a pub. Like me, Jim did love a glass or three. At his peak, there were few midfield players to touch him.

COLIN BELL continued to play for Manchester City throughout the 'seventies, before retiring to concentrate on his restaurant business. A succession of injuries limited his England appearances to 48.

GEORGE BEST retired from Manchester United in 1973 following a catalogue of controversial incidents. His 137 goals in 361 League matches tells only half the story of his impact on United. He came back to play for a string of clubs, including Stockport County, Cork Celtic, Los Angeles Aztecs, Fulham, Hibernian and San José Earthquakes. The media made a meal of his battles with the booze and birds. But every time I met him George seemed as happy as a sandboy, so don't waste your sympathy.

DANNY BLANCHFLOWER was carving out a career for himself as a witty and perceptive sports columnist. He made the mistake of having a stab at club management with Chelsea. Sadly, he was handicapped by a debilitating illness in the 'nineties.

JOHN BOND was laying the foundation to a managerial career with Bournemouth. He was in harness with his old West Ham team-mate Ken Brown. The colourful Bond later hit the headlines as manager at Norwich City and Manchester City before brief associations with Burnley, Swansea and Birmingham City on the way to Shrewsbury Town.

PETER BONETTI won an FA Cup-winners' medal with Chelsea in 1970 and a European Cup-Winners' Cup medal the following year. He played more than 600 League matches for Chelsea before trying his hand at the insurance lark and then became a hotelier and postman on a remote Scottish isle. After that he became a goalkeeper coach with Chelsea and England.

TONY BOOK played on at Maine Road until 1973 before switching to the backroom staff, taking over as Manchester City manager following the brief reign of Ron Saunders.

BILLY BREMNER continued to skipper Leeds until 1976, when he switched to Hull before becoming player-manager of Doncaster in 1978. In 1985 he took over as manager of Leeds, but returned to Doncaster in 1989. Billy won massive libel damages from a national newspaper following allegations that he had got involved in match-fixing while playing for Leeds.

MATT BUSBY served his beloved Manchester United right into the 'nineties, as a director and then as club president. Following the departure of Wilf McGuinness he had another brief spell as manager before the arrival of Frank O'Farrell.

JOHNNY BYRNE had just emigrated to South Africa where he became an influential

Three players who took the sparkle of the 'sixties into the 'seventies: *(above)* Tommy Smith (left) and Alan Ball go their separate ways as they lead Liverpool and Everton out for a Merseyside derby, and *(left)* Peter Shilton saves for Leicester City. By the end of the 'sixties he was still waiting for the first of his world record 125 England caps.

force in football down there. The next time I saw him John – who at his playing peak was as thin as a rake – weighed something over 16 stone, and he was just as chirpy as in the good old days.

IAN CALLAGHAN became an even bigger Anfield hero during the 'seventies. He took his honours haul to five First Division championship medals as well as two FA Cup and two European Cup medals, and a UEFA Cup and a Super Cup-winners' medal. Then, in 1978, he joined his old Liverpool chum John Toshack at Swansea and helped them to promotion from the Third Division. He was elected Footballer of the Year in 1974. Some career.

NOEL CANTWELL was fired by Coventry City in 1972 and then returned to League football for two spells in charge of Peterborough.

HARRY CATTERICK had his proudest moment as a manager when Everton lifted the League championship in style in 1970. He then suffered a heart attack, and became a consultant at the club to make way for Billy Bingham to take over as manager. Harry had a spell as Preston manager before sadly going to the great dressing-room in the sky. Football missed one of its most successful managers.

MIKE CHANNON became a favourite footballing son of the 'seventies, scoring lots of goals and entertaining fans with his direct running for Southampton and Manchester City before returning to The Dell, where he took his club scoring record to 185 goals. Mike then played briefly for Newcastle United, Bristol Rovers and Norwich City, and had a spell in Hong Kong before switching full-time to his hobby of training race-horses. He scored 21 goals in 46 England appearances.

BOBBY CHARLTON closed his glorious Manchester United career in 1973 after 606 League matches, and he held just about every honour the game has to offer. He lifted his League goals tally to 206 when operating briefly as player-manager of Preston. Bobby then retired to go into the travel and promotions business, and continued to be closely involved with his beloved United as a director.

JACK CHARLTON retired as a Leeds player in 1973 and then started a successful career as a manager, first with Middlesbrough and later with Sheffield Wednesday and Newcastle United. But his greatest days came as a Messiah figure in Irish football, leading the Republic of Ireland to the finest sequence of performances in their history.

MARTIN CHIVERS made a marvellous recovery from a knee injury that could easily have finished his career, and enjoyed success in Switzerland after leaving Tottenham. He wound down his League career with Norwich before switching to non-League foot-ball and becoming a pub owner.

ALLAN CLARKE made his England debut in 1970, and scored ten goals in 19 international appearances. He got bitten by the manager bug after winning League championship, FA Cup and Fairs Cup-winners' medals with Leeds in the 'seventies. Following a spell as player-manager of Barnsley, he returned to Leeds as manager. Allan then had a spell at Scunthorpe before a second run at Barnsley and then on to

Lincoln City where he continued his love affair with football.

RONNIE CLAYTON became a representative for a tie firm when he hung up his boots in 1968 after 577 League appearances for Blackburn and 35 England caps.

BRIAN CLOUGH won the League championship with Derby County in 1972, and then arrived at Nottingham Forest via Brighton and a 44-day stay at Leeds. At Forest he twice captured the European Cup and became one of the legendary characters of the game.

GEORGE COHEN became a successful property developer, and showed tremendous character in conquering cancer. George has been a fighter all his life.

BOBBY COLLINS was about to pass on his great knowledge of the game as a player-coach with Oldham at the age of 41, following an extension to his playing career with Bury and Morton. Not bad for a man who was written off after breaking a thigh bone while playing for Leeds in Turin back in 1965. He later managed at Barnsley, Huddersfield and Hull.

CHARLIE COOKE helped Chelsea win the FA Cup in 1970 and the European Cup-Winners' Cup in 1971, and then had a season at Crystal Palace before returning to Chelsea. He married an American girl, and was attracted to soccer in the States.

RAY CRAWFORD wound down his goal-hunting career at Colchester after travelling the football trail with Portsmouth, Ipswich, Wolves, West Brom and Charlton.

PAT CRERAND hung up his boots in 1970, and became a popular World Cup television panellist. He was briefly Tommy Docherty's assistant manager at Old Trafford, and then had a season in charge at Northampton before concentrating on running a successful pub.

TOMMY DOCHERTY was hardly out of the headlines throughout the 'seventies and into the 'eighties. After leaving Aston Villa in 1970 he managed in Portugal before returning to British football with Hull City and then took over as Scottish team manager. He had four years with Manchester United, an up-and-down association that ended when he fell in love with the wife of the United physiotherapist. The Doc's road show then moved on to Derby County, followed by a return visit to Queen's Park Rangers, and he took in spells Down Under in Sydney and as manager at Preston and Wolves. In the 'nineties he is established as one of the most in-demand speakers on the after-dinner circuit.

DEREK DOUGAN became one of the most eloquent of all PFA chairmen before playing the final shots of his career with Wolves in 1974. He managed Kettering Town, and retained his links with the PFA as a special enterprises director. In the mid-1980s he put together a rescue deal to save hard-up Wolves and had three years as chairman and chief executive at Molineux.

BRYAN DOUGLAS, who had run shops and stalls even during his playing days, became a successful businessman after scoring 102 goals in 438 League games for Blackburn Rovers.

MIKE DOYLE played five times for England during the 'seventies before switching from Manchester City to Stoke City in 1978.

GEORGE EASTHAM netted the winning goal for Stoke in the 1972 League Cup final, and had a spell as manager of the Potteries club before continuing his career in South Africa.

MIKE ENGLAND left Tottenham in 1974 to wind down his career with Cardiff City after spreading the football gospel in the United States. He had a successful period as Welsh international team manager.

RON FLOWERS was just deciding that management at Northampton Town was not for him, so he concentrated on building up his sports shop business.

BILL FOULKES retired in 1970 and became the youth team coach at Old Trafford. He then headed for the United States where he managed first the Chicago Stings and then the Tulsa Roughnecks.

JOHNNY GILES became West Brom player-manager and was later in charge of Shamrock Rovers and the Republic of Ireland team before a stint in Vancouver. He returned to the Hawthorns for a second brief spell as manager, and subsequently launched a successful career as a football columnist with the *Daily Express.*

ALAN GILZEAN helped Spurs win two League Cup finals in 1971 and 1973, and also the Fairs Cup in 1972, before retiring after scoring 94 goals for Spurs. He won 23 Scotland caps, and he remains one of my all-time favourite players.

GEORGE GRAHAM helped Arsenal win the League and Cup double in 1970-71, and moved on to Manchester United, Portsmouth and Crystal Palace before joining QPR as coach under manager Terry Venables, his closest friend. George served his managerial apprenticeship at Millwall before becoming an astonishingly successful manager at his old club, Arsenal.

JIMMY GREAVES. I was into my last season with Spurs before joining West Ham as the makeweight in a £200,000 transfer deal involving Martin Peters. It was one of my dafter mistakes. I should have listened to approaches being made to me on behalf of dynamic Derby manager Brian Clough. I retired in 1971 at the age of 31 with 357 First Division goals to my name, and I concentrated on business interests while foolishly spending five years looking at life through the bottom of a glass. I had some happy times in non-League football, particularly with Barnet, before sobering up and starting a new career in television. It's a funny old life.

RON GREENWOOD gradually handed over control at West Ham to his assistant John Lyall, before succeeding Don Revie as a reasonably successful and extremely conscientious England manager.

JOHN GREIG set a Rangers record of 496 League appearances before his final game for the Ibrox club in 1978. He had a spell in charge at Ibrox in between Jock Wallace's two periods as Rangers manager.

RON HARRIS skippered the Chelsea team that won the FA Cup and European Cup-Winners' Cup at the start of the 'seventies, and he set a club appearances record of 655 League games before switching to Brentford. In 1984 he became general manager of Aldershot for a season and then made a million selling a golf course, which he had previously bought, at an enormous profit.

COLIN HARVEY was a key midfield player in Everton's 1970 League championship team. He switched to Sheffield Wednesday for a season, but returned to the backroom staff at Goodison where he had three seasons as manager before becoming Howard Kendall's assistant.

TONY HATELEY completed his have-boots-will-travel journey with Birmingham City, his first club Notts County and then Oldham. He passed his knowledge on to his son, Mark, who became an England international

JOHNNY HAYNES became a successful manager in South Africa after leaving Fulham. In the 'eighties he returned to Britain, setting up home and business in Scotland where, in his great playing days, he had been the scourge of the Scots.

WILLIE HENDERSON had one season on the wing with Sheffield Wednesday in 1972-73 after winning 29 Scottish caps while with Rangers.

JIMMY HILL crossed channels from ITV to become the voice of football for the BBC. He also had football connections with the United States and the Middle East, and became chairman of Fulham.

JOHN HOLLINS won FA Cup and European Cup-Winners' Cup medals with Chelsea in 1970 and 1971. He would become a popular player with QPR and then Arsenal after leaving Stamford Bridge in 1975. John would manage Chelsea for three seasons, and would then become a players' adviser.

DON HOWE became the brains behind Arsenal's League and Cup double success in 1970-71. He later managed West Bromwich Albion and coached in Turkey and at Leeds before returning to Arsenal as assistant manager before becoming manager. He worked as England boss Bobby Robson's right-hand man and managed QPR and then Coventry City. In 1992 he became coach of Chelsea.

ROGER HUNT had moved to Bolton Wanderers for the final two seasons of his career. In 1972 he switched full-time to his family road haulage business, which he had helped build up throughout his playing days at Anfield.

NORMAN HUNTER continued as the backbone of the Leeds defence until 1976, when he moved to Bristol City and then to Barnsley as player-manager. He joined Johnny Giles at West Brom as coach and later managed Rotherham.

GEOFF HURST took his West Ham goals total to 180 in 409 League matches before joining Stoke in 1972. He had a wind-down season with West Bromwich before serving his managerial apprenticeship with Telford. Geoff worked closely with England manager

Ron Greenwood, and then had a crack at League management with Chelsea, succeeding Danny Blanchflower to whom he had been coach. He was somewhat disillusioned when he left Stamford Bridge, and started a successful insurance-selling business with Martin Peters.

PAT JENNINGS played a then world record 119 times for Northern Ireland before retiring at the grand old age of 41. Tottenham inexplicably let him move to North London rivals Arsenal in 1978, and he used his giant hands to help them reach three successive FA Cup finals.

JIMMY JOHNSTONE spent a season in England with Sheffield United in 1975-76, after winning 23 Scotland caps while dazzling on the right wing with Celtic.

CLIFF JONES was about to hang up his boots after a distinguished career during which he had won 59 caps with Wales and scored 182 League goals, an incredible output for a winger. He later coached schoolboys, and had some business adventures.

HOWARD KENDALL was one of the midfield driving forces in Everton's 1970 title team. He later played for Birmingham and Stoke before becoming player-manager at Blackburn Rovers. Howard returned in triumph to Goodison, guided Everton to the League title and FA Cup and, more important, out of the shadow of Merseyside rivals Liverpool. He had a couple of successful seasons in Spain before a brief stop off at Maine Road on his way back to Everton.

CYRIL KNOWLES retired as a phenomenally popular player with Tottenham in 1975, and then coached at Doncaster and Middlesbrough before cheerfully travelling on the managerial roundabout with Darlington, Torquay United and Hartlepool. Alight went out on the football stage when Cyril died following a brain operation in 1991.

BRIAN LABONE played for England in the 1970 World Cup finals after skippering the championship-winning Everton team. He astonished everybody by prematurely retiring in 1971 to concentrate on the family business.

DENIS LAW was given a free transfer from Manchester United by Tommy Docherty, and moved down the road to his old hunting ground at Maine Road. It was Denis who scored the goal for Manchester City that doomed United to relegation in 1973-74. He became an energetic businessman and a popular broadcaster on radio and television.

FRANCIS LEE moved from Manchester City in 1974 for a final fling with Derby, before retiring to build up his waste-paper business in Bolton. It made him a wealthy man, and he then became a successful racehorse trainer. What a life. Of all the players I have known, Franny really cracked it.

PETER LORIMER was a 'hot shot' for Leeds throughout the 'seventies, and continued shooting for them in the 'eighties after playing in Toronto and with York City. He took his club scoring record to 168 League goals.

EDDIE McCREADIE won FA Cup and European Cup-Winners' Cup medals with

Chelsea in 1970, and became manager at Stamford Bridge in 1975 after Dave Sexton moved to Manchester United. He quit in disgust following a row over money after steering Chelsea to promotion from the Second Division. Eddie was in demand in the United States.

JIMMY McILROY coached at Stoke and managed Oldham and Bolton before he put his intelligent mind to writing about the game of football that he had played better than most. He based himself in his adopted home town of Burnley, where he had been a master of the soccer arts.

DAVE MACKAY moved to Swindon in 1971 to lay the foundation of an eventful managerial career. He moved on to Nottingham Forest in 1972, and was summoned back to his old club, Derby, following the shock departure of Brian Clough. In 1974-75 he led Derby to the League championship, and had a season in charge at Walsall before a long stint in the Middle East. Dave, the most inspiring footballer I ever played with, returned to the British stage with Doncaster and then managed Birmingham City.

FRANK McLINTOCK led Arsenal to the FA Cup and League double in 1970-71, and then took his leadership qualities to Queen's Park Rangers. Frank managed at Leicester and Brentford and coached at Millwall, and he also got involved in several business enterprises. He became a regular radio and television broadcaster and acted as a representative for leading players.

BILLY McNEILL switched successfully to a managerial career after playing a club record 486 League matches for Celtic. He managed at Aberdeen, and had two headline- hitting spells in charge at Celtic. Billy was tempted south for three years with Manchester City, and he had a year at Aston Villa before Graham Taylor's arrival as manager at Villa Park.

PAUL MADELEY was a key man for Leeds throughout the 'seventies before retiring from the world of football to concentrate on making a fortune from a family wallpaper business.

RODNEY MARSH joined Manchester City in 1971 and entertained the Maine Road fans with his box of tricks before heading for the United States, where he became an influential player-coach. He lined up with George Best for a magical spell with Fulham and then settled in Florida.

BOBBY MONCUR moved from Tyneside to Wearside to join Sunderland miracle-worker Bob Stokoe before becoming player-manager at Carlisle. He travelled the long and winding managerial road with Hartlepool, Hearts and Plymouth Argyle.

BOBBY MOORE moved from West Ham to Fulham in 1974, and at the end of his first season at Craven Cottage lined up with Alan Mullery against the Hammers in the FA Cup final at Wembley. He played in the United States, had a couple of business disasters and coached in Hong Kong and at Oxford City before a spell as chief executive and then manager of Southend United. Bobby later switched to a career in sports journalism and broadcasting, and battled with typical character against a rough bout of ill health. 'Mr Cool' was the best defender that I ever played with.

STANLEY MATTHEWS travelled the world coaching and even occasionally playing, through into his 60s. He settled first in Malta and then Canada before returning home to his beloved Stoke, where they put up a statue to mark the memorable exploits of the legendary 'Wizard of Dribble'.

JOE MERCER became general manager of Coventry City after leaving Maine Road in 1972, and was a successful temporary manager of England. It was a sad day for football when dear old Joe passed on in 1990. He will always be remembered as one of the game's great characters.

ALAN MULLERY returned to Fulham in 1972 and skippered them when they reached the FA Cup final in 1974. He managed Crystal Palace for a couple of seasons in between two spells in charge at Brighton, and he was also briefly in charge at Queen's Park Rangers and Charlton. Alan is an experienced broadcaster.

TERRY NEILL became player-manager of Hull City in 1970, and on leaving Booth-ferry Park in 1974 he managed first Tottenham and then Arsenal. He later became an eloquent radio broadcaster and took his coaching skills to the Middle East.

BILL NICHOLSON was shamefully sacked by Spurs in 1974, but after a short period scouting for West Ham he returned to his beloved Tottenham in an advisory capacity. He was made club president and they named the main new stand after him. Bill Nick will always be 'Mr Spurs'.

PETER OSGOOD helped Chelsea win the FA Cup and the European Cup-Winners' Cup at the start of the 'seventies, and collected an FA Cup-Winners' medal with South-ampton before a loan spell with Norwich and then a final bow with Chelsea. He displayed his talent on the United States circuit and later became involved with former Chelsea team-mate Ian Hutchinson in a pub-restaurant business that ran into problems.

TERRY PAINE extended his long-playing record to 713 League games after joining Hereford from Southampton. He later ran a pub before emigrating to South Africa.

MARTIN PETERS joined Tottenham from West Ham in 1970, and was a big influence in helping Spurs win two League Cup finals and the UEFA Cup. He played for Norwich and then became player-coach and, briefly, manager of Sheffield United. Martin lifted his League goals tally to 169, a tremendous collection for a midfield player. He later started a successful car insurance operation with his old West Ham United and England team-mate Geoff Hurst.

ALF RAMSEY got kicked out of his job by the blinkered FA in 1974 after England's failure to qualify for the World Cup finals. Sir Alf paid for his poor public relations rather than his record as manager, which clearly showed him to be the most success-ful England manager of all time. He returned to the game with Birmingham City, but didn't reveal his old motivating powers.

DON REVIE succeeded Alf Ramsey as England manager after his glorious reign at Leeds. He was greeted with a thunder *of* criticism when he secretly negotiated a job for himself as soccer supremo in the United Arab Emirates in 1977. The Football Association did not take lightly to his desertion of his post, and banned him from British football for ten years. A lot of dirty washing was exposed in a sour court case when Revie got the ban squashed. 'The Don', who always attracted the unswerving loyalty of his Leeds United players, returned to Britain where he died tragically in 1989 of motor neurone disease. There have been few more masterly club managers.

BOBBY ROBSON was starting a highly successful association with Ipswich after a brief and bruising introduction to League management with his old club Fulham. After steering Ipswich to the FA Cup and the UEFA Cup he was selected as the man to follow Ron Greenwood as England manager. He guided England to the 1990 World Cup semifinals, and then continued his managing career with PSV Eindhoven in Holland before moving on to Portugal.

IAN St JOHN wound down his playing career with Coventry and then Tranmere, and had a spell in South Africa before trying his hand at management with Motherwell and Portsmouth. He was Jack Charlton's coach at Sheffield Wednesday and later became an enormously popular football presenter on ITV, despite the ramblings of his scruffy partner.

BILL SHANKLY stunned the world of football by retiring from his job as Liverpool manager in 1974. It ended one of the greatest managerial reigns of all time. Merseyside in particular and football in general was plunged into mourning when Shanks died in 1981. He had seemed indestructible. Apart from all the titles he had won while at Liverpool there is a permanent reminder of the great Scot at Anfield where the Bill Shankly Gates have been erected.

PETER SHILTON took over from Pat Jennings as the world's most capped footballer with 125 England appearances, and after joining Nottingham Forest from Stoke City helped them win the League title and two European Cup finals. He then moved on to continue his marathon career with Southampton and later Derby County. He was into his 40s when he became Plymouth player-manager.

BOBBY SMITH drifted away from football after his magnificent haul of 217 League goals from 376 matches with Chelsea, Tottenham and Brighton. Bobby was one of my favourite of all partners, and he was never given the credit he deserved for his high level of skill.

TOMMY SMITH took his appearances tally with Liverpool to 467 League games before he played out his career at Swansea. The highlight of the 'seventies came for Tommy when he headed a crucial goal for Liverpool that helped them win the European Cup for the first time in 1977. He became a successful pub owner in his beloved Liverpool.

JOCK STEIN continued to cast his spell at Celtic, becoming general manager before agreeing to take over at Leeds United. He was at Elland Road only three months before leaving to become manager of the Scottish national team. Jock survived a car crash and a heart attack, but tragically died 'in harness' in 1985 at the age of 62. He collapsed and died just moments after seeing Scotland beat Wales in a vital World Cup qualifying match in Cardiff. Football had lost one of its finest servants.

ALEX STEPNEY continued to play a vital role for Manchester United through the managements of Wilf McGuinness, Frank O'Farrell, Tommy Docherty and Dave Sexton. He played 433 League games in goal for United, and for a while in 1973-74 he was even United's top goalscorer after netting two penalties.

NOBBY STILES joined Middlesbrough from Manchester United for £20,000 in 1971 before joining his pal Bobby Charlton at Preston, where he became manager for three years. Nobby was a coach at West Bromwich Albion when his brother-in-law Johnny Giles was in charge, and then returned to Old Trafford to pass on his considerable knowledge to the United youngsters.

MIKE SUMMERBEE left Maine Road for Burnley in 1975 before adding his experience in midfield at Blackpool. He was appointed player-manager of Stockport County, and later concentrated full-time on the shirt-tailoring business that he used to run in his spare time at Manchester City. Mike always had plenty of neck.

PETER THOMPSON closed his career with Bolton after scoring 42 goals in 322 League appearances with Liverpool. Peter became something of a dinosaur when wingers disappeared from the game, but he deserves a place in the Anfield hall of fame for artistry that was rewarded with 16 England caps.

TERRY VENABLES played for Queen's Park Rangers and Crystal Palace before managing first Palace and then Rangers. In partnership with writer Gordon Williams, he created the television character James Hazell. Terry was always on the look out for a challenge, and jumped at the chance to manage Barcelona. After steering them to the Spanish League championship he returned to Tottenham and later became co-owner of the club when he put together a mega-money rescue package in partnership with businessman Alan Sugar. Terry liked the club so much that he bought it!

ROY VERNON wound down his League playing career with Halifax Town before taking his shooting boots to the United States. In 398 League games Roy scored 171 goals.

RAY WILSON played briefly with Oldham and Bradford City before leaving football to join his father-in-law as a funeral director. It makes me wonder exactly what Ray meant when he used to tell me that I was good in the box!

RON YEATS left Liverpool in December 1971 to take over as player-manager of Tranmere Rovers. He will always be associated with Liverpool, and that wonderful quote from Bill Shankly when introducing Ron to the press for the first time: 'The man is a colossus. Let me show you around him'.

ALEX YOUNG hung up his boots after holding a passing out parade with Glentoran and Stockport. For me, he was one of the brightest Scottish stars of the decade with Hearts and Everton. He collected what I always considered the most imaginative nickname of the 'sixties: 'The Golden Vision'.

And that was the 'sixties revisited. I hope you enjoyed the journey, and that as we return to the 'nineties you are not too disappointed to find that football is not the game it used to be. It's fitting to finish with the famous Kenneth Wolstenholme commentary line at the climax of England's finest hour in the 1966 World Cup final: 'They think it's all over ... it is now!'

This is where you get off the time machine. Thanks for your company.

THE LEAGUE TABLES

1959-60

FIRST DIVISION

	P	W	D	L	F	A	Pts
Burnley	42	24	7	11	85	61	55
Wolves	42	24	6	12	106	67	54
Tottenham	42	21	11	10	86	50	53
WBA	42	19	11	12	83	57	49
Sheff Wed	42	19	11	12	80	59	49
Bolton	42	20	8	14	59	51	48
Man United	42	19	7	16	102	80	45
Newcastle	42	18	8	16	82	78	44
Preston	42	16	12	14	79	76	44
Fulham	42	17	10	15	73	80	44
Blackpool	42	15	10	17	59	71	40
Leicester	42	13	13	16	66	75	39
Arsenal	42	15	9	18	68	80	39
West Ham	42	16	6	20	75	91	38
Man City	42	17	3	22	78	84	37
Everton	42	13	11	18	73	78	37
Blackburn	42	16	5	21	60	70	37
Chelsea	42	14	9	19	76	91	37
Birmingham	42	13	10	19	63	80	36
Nottm Forest	42	13	9	20	50	74	35
Leeds United	42	12	10	20	65	92	34
Luton Town	42	9	12	21	50	73	30

SECOND DIVISION

	P	W	D	L	F	A	Pts
Aston Villa	42	25	9	8	89	43	59
Cardiff	42	23	12	7	90	62	58
Liverpool	42	20	10	12	90	66	50
Sheff United	42	19	12	11	68	51	50
Middlesbro'	42	19	10	13	90	64	48
Huddersfield	42	19	9	14	73	52	47
Charlton	42	17	13	12	90	87	47
Rotherham	42	17	13	12	61	60	47
Bristol Rovers	42	18	11	13	72	78	47
Leyton Orient	42	15	14	13	76	61	44
Ipswich Town	42	19	6	17	78	68	44
Swansea	42	15	10	17	82	84	40
Lincoln	42	16	7	19	75	78	39
Brighton	42	13	12	17	67	76	38
Scunthorpe	42	13	10	19	57	71	36
Sunderland	42	12	12	18	52	65	36
Stoke City	42	14	7	21	66	83	35
Derby County	42	14	7	21	61	77	35
Plymouth	42	13	9	20	61	89	35
Portsmouth	42	10	12	20	59	77	32
Hull City	42	10	10	22	48	76	30
Bristol City	42	11	5	26	60	97	27

THIRD DIVISION

	P	W	D	L	F	A	Pts
Southampton	46	26	9	11	106	75	61
Norwich City	46	24	11	11	82	54	59
Shrewsbury	46	18	16	12	97	75	52
Coventry City	46	21	10	15	78	63	52
Grimsby Town	46	18	16	12	87	70	52
Brentford	46	21	9	16	78	61	51
Bury	46	21	9	16	64	51	51
QPR	46	18	13	15	73	54	49
Colchester	46	18	11	17	83	74	47
Bournemouth	46	17	13	16	72	72	47
Reading	46	18	10	18	84	77	46
Southend	46	19	8	19	76	74	46
Newport	46	20	6	20	80	79	46
Port Vale	46	19	8	19	80	79	46
Halifax	46	18	10	18	70	72	46
Swindon	46	19	8	19	69	78	46
Barnsley	46	15	14	17	65	66	44
Chesterfield	46	18	7	21	71	84	43
Bradford City	46	15	12	19	66	74	42
Tranmere	46	14	13	19	72	75	41
York City	46	13	12	21	57	73	38
Mansfield	46	15	6	25	81	112	36
Wrexham	46	14	8	24	68	101	36
Accrington	46	11	5	30	57	123	27

FOURTH DIVISION

	P	W	D	L	F	A	Pts
Walsall	46	28	9	9	102	60	65
Notts County	46	26	8	12	107	69	60
Torquay	46	26	8	12	84	58	60
Watford	46	24	9	13	92	67	57
Millwall	46	18	17	11	84	61	53
Northampton	46	22	9	15	85	63	53
Gillingham	46	21	10	15	74	69	52
Crystal Palace	46	19	12	15	84	64	50
Exeter City	46	19	11	16	80	70	49
Stockport	46	19	11	16	58	54	49
Bradford PA	46	17	15	14	70	68	49
Rochdale	46	18	10	18	65	60	46
Aldershot	46	18	9	19	77	74	45
Crewe	46	18	9	19	79	88	45
Darlington	46	17	9	20	63	73	43
Workington	46	14	14	18	68	60	42
Doncaster	46	16	10	20	69	76	42
Barrow	46	15	11	20	77	87	41
Carlisle	46	15	11	20	51	66	41
Chester	46	14	12	20	59	77	40
Southport	46	10	14	22	48	92	34
Gateshead	46	12	9	25	58	86	33
Oldham	46	8	12	26	41	83	28
Hartlepool	46	10	7	29	59	109	27

1960-61

FIRST DIVISION

	P	W	D	L	F	A	Pts
Tottenham	42	31	4	7	115	55	66
Sheff Wed	42	23	12	7	78	47	58
Wolves	42	25	7	10	103	75	57
Burnley	42	22	7	13	102	77	51
Everton	42	22	6	14	87	69	50
Leicester	42	18	9	15	87	70	45
Man United	42	18	9	15	88	76	45
Blackburn	42	15	13	14	77	76	43
Aston Villa	42	17	9	16	78	77	43
WBA	42	18	5	19	67	71	41
Arsenal	42	15	11	16	77	85	41
Chelsea	42	15	7	20	98	100	37
Man City	42	13	11	18	79	90	37
Nottm Forest	42	14	9	19	62	78	37
Cardiff	42	13	11	18	60	85	37
West Ham	42	13	10	19	77	88	36
Fulham	42	14	8	20	72	95	36
Bolton	42	12	11	19	58	73	35
Birmingham	42	14	6	22	62	84	34
Blackpool	42	12	9	21	68	73	33
Newcastle	42	11	10	21	86	109	32
Preston	42	10	10	22	43	71	30

SECOND DIVISION

	P	W	D	L	F	A	Pts
Ipswich Town	42	26	7	9	100	55	59
Sheff United	42	26	6	10	81	51	58
Liverpool	42	21	10	11	87	58	52
Norwich City	42	20	9	13	70	53	49
Middlesbro'	42	18	12	12	83	74	48
Sunderland	42	17	13	12	75	60	47
Swansea	42	18	11	13	77	73	47
Southampton	42	18	8	16	84	81	44
Scunthorpe	42	14	15	13	69	64	43
Charlton	42	16	11	15	97	91	43
Plymouth .	42	17	8	17	81	82	42
Derby County	42	15	10	17	80	80	40
Luton Town	42	15	9	18	71	70	39
Leeds United	42	14	10	18	75	83	38
Rotherham	42	12	13	17	65	64	37
Brighton	42	14	9	19	61	75	37
Bristol Rovers	42	15	7	20	73	92	37
Stoke City	42	12	12	18	51	59	36
Leyton Orient	42	14	8	20	55	78	36
Huddersfield	42	13	9	20	62	71	35
Portsmouth	42	11	11	20	64	91	33
Lincoln City	42	8	8	26	48	95	24

THIRD DIVISION

	P	W	D	L	F	A	Pts
Bury	46	30	8	8	108	45	68
Walsall	46	28	6	12	98	60	62
QPR	46	25	10	11	93	60	60
Watford	46	20	12	14	85	72	52
Notts County	46	21	9	16	82	77	51
Grimsby	46	20	10	16	77	69	50
Port Vale	46	17	15	14	96	79	49
Barnsley	46	21	7	18	83	80	49
Halifax	46	16	17	13	71	78	49
Shrewsbury	46	15	16	15	83	75	46
Hull	46	17	12	17	73	73	46
Torquay	46	14	17	15	75	83	45
Newport	46	17	11	18	81	90	45
Bristol City	46	17	10	19	70	68	44
Coventry City	46	16	12	18	80	83	44
Swindon	46	14	15	17	62	55	43
Brentford	46	13	17	16	56	70	43
Reading	46	14	12	20	72	83	40
Bournemouth	46	15	10	21	58	76	40
Southend	46	14	11	21	60	76	39
Tranmere	46	15	8	23	79	115	38
Bradford City	46	11	14	21	65	87	36
Colchester	46	11	11	24	68	101	33
Chesterfield	46	10	12	24	67	87	32

FOURTH DIVISION

	P	W	D	L	F	A	Pts
Peterborough	46	28	10	8	134	65	66
Crystal Palace	46	29	6	11	110	69	64
Northampton	46	25	10	11	90	62	60
Bradford PA	46	26	8	12	84	74	60
York	46	21	9	16	80	60	51
Millwall	46	21	8	17	97	86	50
Darlington	46	18	13	15	78	70	49
Workington	46	21	7	18	74	76	49
Crewe	46	20	9	17	61	67	49
Aldershot	46	18	9	19	79	69	45
Doncaster	46	19	7	20	76	78	45
Oldham	46	19	7	20	79	88	45
Stockport	46	18	9	19	57	66	45
Southport	46	19	6	21	69	67	44
Gillingham	46	15	13	18	64	66	43
Wrexham	46	17	8	21	62	56	42
Rochdale	46	17	8	21	60	66	42
Accrington	46	16	8	22	74	88	40
Carlisle	46	13	13	20	61	79	39
Mansfield	46	16	6	24	71	78	38
Exeter	46	14	10	22	66	94	38
Barrow	46	13	11	22	52	79	37
Hartlepool	46	12	8	26	71	103	32
Chester	46	11	9	26	61	104	31

1961-62

FIRST DIVISION

	P	W	D	L	F	A	Pts
Ipswich Town							

SECOND DIVISION

	P	W	D	L	F	A	Pts

THIRD DIVISION

	P	W	D	L	F	A	Pts

FOURTH DIVISION

	P	W	D	L	F	A	Pts

1962-63

FIRST DIVISION

	P	W	D	L	F	A	Pts
Everton	42	25	11	6	84	42	61
Tottenham	42	23	9	10	111	62	55
Burnley	42	22	10	10	78	57	54
Leicester	42	20	12	10	79	53	52
Wolves	42	20	10	12	93	65	50
Sheff Wed	42	19	10	13	77	63	48
Arsenal	42	18	10	14	86	77	46
Liverpool	42	17	10	15	71	59	44
Nottm Forest	42	17	10	15	67	69	44
Sheff United	42	16	12	14	58	60	44
Blackburn	42	15	12	15	79	71	42
West Ham	42	14	12	16	73	69	40
Blackpool	42	13	14	15	58	64	40
WBA	42	16	7	19	71	79	39
Aston Villa	42	15	8	19	62	68	38
Fulham	42	14	10	18	50	71	38
Ipswich Town	42	12	11	19	59	78	35
Bolton	42	15	5	22	55	75	35
Man United	42	12	10	20	67	81	34
Birmingham	42	10	13	19	63	90	33
Man City	42	10	11	21	58	102	31
Leyton Orient	42	6	9	27	37	81	21

SECOND DIVISION

	P	W	D	L	F	A	Pts
Stoke City	42	20	13	9	73	50	53
Chelsea	42	24	4	14	81	42	52
Sunderland	42	20	12	10	84	55	52
Middlesbro'	42	20	9	13	86	85	49
Leeds United	42	19	10	13	79	53	48
Huddersfield	42	17	14	11	63	50	48
Newcastle	42	18	11	13	79	59	47
Bury	42	18	11	13	51	47	47
Scunthorpe	42	16	12	14	57	59	44
Cardiff	42	18	7	17	83	73	43
Southampton	42	17	8	17	72	67	42
Plymouth	42	15	12	15	76	73	42
Norwich City	42	17	8	17	80	79	42
Rotherham	42	17	6	19	67	74	40
Swansea	42	15	9	18	51	72	39
Portsmouth	42	13	11	18	63	79	37
Preston	42	13	11	18	59	74	37
Derby County	42	12	12	18	61	72	36
Grimsby Town	42	11	13	18	55	66	35
Charlton	42	13	5	24	62	94	31
Walsall	42	11	9	22	53	89	31
Luton Town	42	11	7	24	61	84	29

THIRD DIVISION

	P	W	D	L	F	A	Pts
Northampton	46	26	10	10	109	60	62
Swindon	46	22	14	10	87	56	58
Port Vale	46	23	8	15	72	58	54
Coventry City	46	18	17	11	83	69	53
Bournemouth	46	18	16	12	63	46	52
Peterborough	46	20	11	15	93	75	51
Notts County	46	19	13	14	73	74	51
Southend	46	19	12	15	75	77	50
Wrexham	46	20	9	17	84	83	49
Hull City	46	19	10	17	74	69	48
Crystal Palace	46	17	13	16	68	58	47
Colchester	46	18	11	17	73	93	47
QPR	46	17	11	18	85	76	45
Bristol City	46	16	13	17	100	92	45
Shrewsbury	46	16	12	18	83	81	44
Millwall	46	15	13	18	82	87	43
Watford	46	17	8	21	82	85	42
Barnsley	46	15	11	20	63	74	41
Bristol Rovers	46	15	11	20	70	88	41
Reading	46	16	8	22	74	78	40
Bradford PA	46	14	12	20	79	97	40
Brighton	46	12	12	22	58	84	36
Carlisle	46	13	9	24	61	89	35
Halifax	46	9	12	25	64	106	30

FOURTH DIVISION

	P	W	D	L	F	A	Pts
Brentford	46	27	8	11	98	64	62
Oldham	46	24	11	11	95	60	59
Crewe	46	24	11	11	86	58	59
Mansfield	46	24	9	13	108	69	57
Gillingham	46	22	13	11	71	49	57
Torquay	46	20	16	10	75	56	56
Rochdale	46	20	11	15	67	59	51
Tranmere	46	20	10	16	81	67	50
Barrow	46	19	12	15	82	80	50
Workington	46	17	13	16	76	68	47
Aldershot	46	15	17	14	73	69	47
Darlington	46	19	6	21	72	87	44
Southport	46	15	14	17	72	106	44
York City	46	16	11	19	67	62	43
Chesterfield	46	13	16	17	70	64	42
Doncaster	46	14	14	18	64	77	42
Exeter City	46	16	10	20	57	77	42
Oxford	46	13	15	18	70	71	41
Stockport	46	15	11	20	56	70	41
Newport	46	14	11	21	76	90	39
Chester	46	15	9	22	51	66	39
Lincoln	46	13	9	24	68	89	35
Bradford City	46	11	10	25	64	93	32
Hartlepool	46	7	11	28	56	104	25

1963-64

FIRST DIVISION

	P	W	D	L	F	A	Pts
Liverpool	42	26	5	11	92	45	57
Man United	42	23	7	12	90	62	53
Everton	42	21	10	11	84	64	52
Tottenham	42	22	7	13	97	81	51
Chelsea	42	20	10	12	72	56	50
Sheff Wed	42	19	11	12	84	67	49
Blackburn	42	18	10	14	89	65	46
Arsenal	42	17	11	14	90	82	45
Burnley	42	17	10	15	71	64	44
WBA	42	16	11	15	70	61	43
Leicester	42	16	11	15	61	58	43
Sheff United	42	16	11	15	61	64	43
Nottm Forest	42	16	9	17	64	68	41
West Ham	42	14	12	16	69	74	40
Fulham	42	13	13	16	58	65	39
Wolves	42	12	15	15	70	80	39
Stoke City	42	14	10	18	77	78	38
Blackpool	42	13	9	20	52	73	35
Aston Villa	42	11	12	19	62	71	34
Birmingham	42	11	7	24	54	92	29
Bolton	42	10	8	24	48	80	28
Ipswich Town	42	9	7	26	56	121	25

SECOND DIVISION

	P	W	D	L	F	A	Pts
Leeds United	42	24	15	3	71	34	63
Sunderland	42	25	11	6	81	37	61
Preston	42	23	10	9	79	54	56
Charlton	42	19	10	13	76	70	48
Southampton	42	19	9	14	100	73	47
Man City	42	18	10	14	84	66	46
Rotherham	42	19	7	16	90	78	45
Newcastle	42	20	5	17	74	69	45
Portsmouth	42	16	11	15	79	70	43
Middlesbro	42	15	11	16	67	52	41
Northampton	42	16	9	17	58	60	41
Huddersfield	42	15	10	17	57	64	40
Derby County	42	14	11	17	56	67	39
Swindon	42	14	10	18	57	69	38
Cardiff	42	14	10	18	56	81	38
Leyton Orient	42	13	10	19	54	72	36
Norwich City	42	11	13	18	64	80	35
Bury	42	13	9	20	57	73	35
Swansea	42	12	9	21	63	74	33
Plymouth	42	8	16	18	45	67	32
Grimsby Town	42	9	14	19	47	75	32
Scunthorpe	42	10	10	22	52	82	30

THIRD DIVISION

	P	W	D	L	F	A	Pts
Coventry City	46	22	16	8	98	61	60
Crystal Palace	46	23	14	9	73	51	60
Watford	46	23	12	11	79	59	58
Bournemouth	46	24	8	14	79	58	56
Bristol City	46	20	15	11	84	64	55
Reading	46	21	10	15	79	62	52
Mansfield	46	20	11	15	76	62	51
Hull City	46	16	17	13	73	68	49
Oldham	46	20	8	18	73	70	48
Peterborough	46	18	11	17	75	70	47
Shrewsbury	46	18	11	17	73	80	47
Bristol Rovers	46	19	8	19	91	79	46
Port Vale	46	16	14	16	53	49	46
Southend	46	15	15	16	77	78	45
QPR	46	18	9	19	76	78	45
Brentford	46	15	14	17	87	80	44
Colchester	46	12	19	15	70	68	43
Luton Town	46	16	10	20	64	80	42
Walsall	46	13	14	19	59	76	40
Barnsley	46	12	15	19	68	94	39
Millwall	46	14	10	22	53	67	38
Crewe	46	11	12	23	50	77	34
Wrexham	46	13	6	27	75	107	32
Notts County	46	9	9	28	45	92	27

FOURTH DIVISION

	P	W	D	L	F	A	Pts
Gillingham	46	23	14	9	59	30	60
Carlisle	46	25	10	11	113	58	60
Workington	46	24	11	11	76	52	59
Exeter City	46	20	18	8	62	37	58
Bradford City	46	25	6	15	76	62	56
Torquay	46	20	11	15	80	54	51
Tranmere	46	20	11	15	85	73	51
Brighton	46	19	12	15	71	52	50
Aldershot	46	19	10	17	83	78	48
Halifax	46	17	14	15	77	77	48
Lincoln	46	19	9	18	67	75	47
Chester	46	19	8	19	65	60	46
Bradford PA	46	18	9	19	75	81	45
Doncaster	46	15	12	19	70	75	42
Newport	46	17	8	21	64	73	42
Chesterfield	46	15	12	19	57	71	42
Stockport	46	15	12	19	50	68	42
Oxford	46	14	13	19	59	63	41
Darlington	46	14	12	20	66	93	40
Rochdale	46	12	15	19	56	59	39
Southport	46	15	9	22	63	88	39
York City	46	14	7	25	52	66	35
Hartlepool	46	12	9	25	54	93	33
Barrow	46	6	18	22	51	93	30

1964-65

FIRST DIVISION

	P	W	D	L	F	A	Pts
Man United	42	26	9	7	89	39	61
Leeds United	42	26	9	7	83	52	61
Chelsea	42	24	8	10	89	54	56
Everton	42	17	15	10	69	60	49
Nottm Forest	42	17	13	12	71	67	47
Tottenham	42	19	7	16	87	71	45
Liverpool	42	17	10	15	67	73	44
Sheff Wed	42	16	11	15	57	55	43
West Ham	42	19	4	19	82	71	42
Blackburn	42	16	10	16	83	79	42
Stoke City	42	16	10	16	67	66	42
Burnley	42	16	10	16	70	70	42
Arsenal	42	17	7	18	69	75	41
WBA	42	13	13	16	70	65	39
Sunderland	42	14	9	19	64	74	37
Aston Villa	42	16	5	21	57	82	37
Blackpool	42	12	11	19	67	78	35
Leicester	42	11	13	18	69	85	35
Sheff United	42	12	11	19	50	64	35
Fulham	42	11	12	19	60	78	34
Wolves	42	13	4	25	59	89	30
Birmingham	42	8	11	23	64	96	27

SECOND DIVISION

	P	W	D	L	F	A	Pts
Newcastle	42	24	9	9	81	45	57
Northampton	42	20	16	6	66	50	56
Bolton	42	20	10	12	80	58	50
Southampton	42	17	14	11	83	63	48
Ipswich Town	42	15	17	10	74	67	47
Norwich City	42	20	7	15	61	57	47
Crystal Palace	42	16	13	13	55	51	45
Huddersfield	42	17	10	15	53	51	44
Derby County	42	16	11	15	84	79	43
Coventry City	42	17	9	16	72	70	43
Man City	42	16	9	17	63	62	41
Preston	42	14	13	15	76	81	41
Cardiff	42	13	14	15	64	57	40
Rotherham	42	14	12	16	70	69	40
Plymouth	42	16	8	18	63	79	40
Bury	42	14	10	18	60	66	38
Middlesbro'	42	13	9	20	70	76	35
Charlton	42	13	9	20	64	75	35
Leyton Orient	42	12	11	19	50	72	35
Portsmouth	42	12	10	20	56	77	34
Swindon	42	14	5	23	63	81	33
Swansea	42	11	10	21	62	84	32

THIRD DIVISION

	P	W	D	L	F	A	Pts
Carlisle	46	25	10	11	76	53	60
Bristol City	46	24	11	11	92	55	59
Mansfield	46	24	11	11	95	61	59
Hull City	46	23	12	11	91	57	58
Brentford	46	24	9	13	83	55	57
Bristol Rovers	46	20	15	11	82	58	55
Gillingham	46	23	9	14	70	50	55
Peterborough	46	22	7	17	85	74	51
Watford	46	17	16	13	71	64	50
Grimsby Town	46	16	17	13	68	67	49
Bournemouth	46	18	11	17	72	63	47
Southend	46	19	8	19	78	71	46
Reading	46	16	14	16	70	70	46
QPR	46	17	12	17	72	80	46
Workington	46	17	12	17	58	69	46
Shrewsbury	46	15	12	19	76	84	42
Exeter City	46	12	17	17	51	52	41
Scunthorpe	46	14	12	20	65	72	40
Walsall	46	15	7	24	55	80	37
Oldham	46	13	10	23	61	83	36
Luton Town	46	11	11	24	51	94	33
Port Vale	46	9	14	23	41	76	32
Colchester	46	10	10	26	50	89	30
Barnsley	46	9	11	26	54	90	29

FOURTH DIVISION

	P	W	D	L	F	A	Pts
Brighton	46	26	11	9	102	57	63
Millwall	46	23	16	7	78	45	62
York City	46	28	6	12	91	56	62
Oxford	46	23	15	8	87	44	61
Tranmere	46	27	6	13	99	56	60
Rochdale	46	22	14	10	74	53	58
Bradford PA	46	20	17	9	86	62	57
Chester	46	25	6	15	119	81	56
Doncaster	46	20	11	15	84	72	51
Crewe	46	18	13	15	90	81	49
Torquay	46	21	7	18	70	70	49
Chesterfield	46	20	8	18	58	70	48
Notts County	46	15	14	17	61	73	44
Wrexham	46	17	9	20	84	92	43
Hartlepool	46	15	13	18	61	85	43
Newport	46	17	8	21	85	81	42
Darlington	46	18	6	22	84	87	42
Aldershot	46	15	7	24	64	84	37
Bradford City	46	12	8	26	70	88	32
Southport	46	8	16	22	58	89	32
Barrow	46	12	6	28	59	105	30
Lincoln	46	11	6	29	58	99	28
Halifax	46	11	6	29	54	103	28
Stockport	46	10	7	29	44	87	27

1965-66

FIRST DIVISION

	P	W	D	L	F	A	Pts
Liverpool	42	26	9	7	79	34	61
Leeds United	42	23	9	10	79	38	55
Burnley	42	24	7	11	79	47	55
Man United	42	18	15	9	84	59	51
Chelsea	42	22	7	13	65	53	51
WBA	42	19	12	11	91	69	50
Leicester	42	21	7	14	80	65	49
Tottenham	42	16	12	14	75	66	44
Sheff United	42	16	11	15	56	59	43
Stoke City	42	15	12	15	65	64	42
Everton	42	15	11	16	56	62	41
West Ham	42	15	9	18	70	83	39
Blackpool	42	14	9	19	55	65	37
Arsenal	42	12	13	17	62	75	37
Newcastle	42	14	9	19	50	63	37
Aston Villa	42	15	6	21	69	80	36
Sheff Wed	42	14	8	20	56	66	36
Nottm Forest	42	14	8	20	56	72	36
Sunderland	42	14	8	20	51	72	36
Fulham	42	14	7	21	67	85	35
Northampton	42	10	13	19	55	92	33
Blackburn	42	8	4	30	57	88	20

SECOND DIVISION

	P	W	D	L	F	A	Pts
Man City	42	22	15	5	76	44	59
Southampton	42	22	10	10	85	56	54
Coventry City	42	20	13	9	73	53	53
Huddersfield	42	19	13	10	62	36	51
Bristol City	42	17	17	8	63	48	51
Wolves	42	20	10	12	87	61	50
Rotherham	42	16	14	12	75	74	46
Derby County	42	16	11	15	71	68	43
Bolton	42	16	9	17	62	59	41
Birmingham	42	16	9	17	70	75	41
Crystal Palace	42	14	13	15	47	52	41
Portsmouth	42	16	8	18	74	78	40
Norwich City	42	12	15	15	52	52	39
Carlisle	42	17	5	20	60	63	39
Ipswich Town	42	15	9	18	58	66	39
Charlton	42	12	14	16	61	70	38
Preston	42	11	15	16	62	70	37
Plymouth	42	12	13	17	54	63	37
Bury	42	14	7	21	62	76	35
Cardiff	42	12	10	20	71	91	34
Middlesbro'	42	10	13	19	58	86	33
Leyton Orient	42	5	13	24	38	80	23

THIRD DIVISION

	P	W	D	L	F	A	Pts
Hull City	46	31	7	8	109	62	69
Millwall	46	27	11	8	76	43	65
QPR	46	24	9	13	95	65	57
Scunthorpe	46	21	11	14	80	67	53
Workington	46	19	14	13	67	57	52
Gillingham	46	22	8	16	62	54	52
Swindon	46	19	13	14	74	48	51
Reading	46	19	13	14	70	63	51
Walsall	46	20	10	16	77	64	50
Shrewsbury	46	19	11	16	73	64	49
Grimsby Town	46	17	13	16	68	62	47
Watford	46	17	13	16	55	51	47
Peterborough	46	17	12	17	80	66	46
Oxford	46	19	8	19	70	74	46
Brighton	46	16	11	19	67	65	43
Bristol Rovers	46	14	14	18	64	64	42
Swansea	46	15	11	20	81	96	41
Bournemouth	46	13	12	21	38	56	38
Mansfield	46	15	8	23	59	89	38
Oldham	46	12	13	21	55	81	37
Southend	46	16	4	26	54	83	36
Exeter City	46	12	11	23	53	79	35
Brentford	46	10	12	24	48	69	32
York City	46	9	9	28	53	106	27

FOURTH DIVISION

	P	W	D	L	F	A	Pts
Doncaster	46	24	11	11	85	54	59
Darlington	46	25	9	12	72	53	59
Torquay	46	24	10	12	72	49	58
Colchester	46	23	10	13	70	47	56
Tranmere	46	24	8	14	93	66	56
Luton Town	46	24	8	14	90	70	56
Chester	46	20	12	14	79	70	52
Notts County	46	19	12	15	61	53	50
Newport	46	18	12	16	75	75	48
Southport	46	18	12	16	68	69	48
Bradford PA	46	21	5	20	102	92	47
Barrow	46	16	15	15	72	76	47
Stockport	46	18	6	22	71	70	42
Crewe	46	16	9	21	61	63	41
Halifax	46	15	11	20	67	75	41
Barnsley	46	15	10	21	74	78	40
Aldershot	46	15	10	21	75	84	40
Hartlepool	46	16	8	22	63	75	40
Port Vale	46	15	9	22	48	59	39
Chesterfield	46	13	13	20	62	78	39
Rochdale	46	16	5	25	71	87	37
Lincoln	46	13	11	22	57	82	37
Bradford City	46	12	13	21	63	94	37
Wrexham	46	13	9	24	72	104	35

1966-67

FIRST DIVISION

	P	W	D	L	F	A	Pts
Man United	42	24	12	6	84	45	60
Nottm Forest	42	23	10	9	64	41	56
Tottenham	42	24	8	10	71	48	56
Leeds United	42	22	11	9	62	42	55
Liverpool	42	19	13	10	64	47	51
Everton	42	19	10	13	65	46	48
Arsenal	42	16	14	12	58	47	46
Leicester	42	18	8	16	78	71	44
Chelsea	42	15	14	13	67	62	44
Sheff United	42	16	10	16	52	59	42
Sheff Wed	42	14	13	15	56	47	41
Stoke City	42	17	7	18	63	58	41
WBA	42	16	7	19	77	73	39
Burnley	42	15	9	18	66	76	39
Man City	42	12	15	15	43	52	39
West Ham	42	14	8	20	80	84	36
Sunderland	42	14	8	20	58	72	36
Fulham	42	11	12	19	71	83	34
Southampton	42	14	6	22	74	92	34
Newcastle	42	12	9	21	39	81	33
Aston Villa	42	11	7	24	54	85	29
Blackpool	42	6	9	27	41	76	21

SECOND DIVISION

	P	W	D	L	F	A	Pts
Coventry City	42	23	13	6	74	43	59
Wolves	42	25	8	9	88	48	58
Carlisle	42	23	6	13	71	54	52
Blackburn	42	19	13	10	56	46	51
Ipswich Town	42	17	16	9	70	54	50
Huddersfield	42	20	9	13	58	46	49
Crystal Palace	42	19	10	13	61	55	48
Millwall	42	18	9	15	49	58	45
Bolton	42	14	14	14	64	58	42
Birmingham	42	16	8	18	70	66	40
Norwich City	42	13	14	15	49	55	40
Hull City	42	16	7	19	77	72	39
Preston	42	16	7	19	65	67	39
Portsmouth	42	13	13	16	59	70	39
Bristol City	42	12	14	16	56	62	38
Plymouth	42	14	9	19	59	58	37
Derby County	42	12	12	18	68	72	36
Rotherham	42	13	10	19	61	70	36
Charlton	42	13	9	20	49	53	35
Cardiff	42	12	9	21	61	87	33
Northampton	42	12	6	24	47	84	30
Bury	42	11	6	25	49	83	28

THIRD DIVISION

	P	W	D	L	F	A	Pts
QPR	46	26	15	5	103	38	67
Middlesbro'	46	23	9	14	87	64	55
Watford	46	20	14	12	61	46	54
Reading	46	22	9	15	76	57	53
Bristol Rovers	46	20	13	13	76	67	53
Shrewsbury	46	20	12	14	77	62	52
Torquay	46	21	9	16	73	54	51
Swindon	46	20	10	16	81	59	50
Mansfield	46	20	9	17	84	79	49
Oldham	46	19	10	17	80	63	48
Gillingham	46	15	16	15	58	62	46
Walsall	46	18	10	18	65	72	46
Colchester	46	17	10	19	76	73	44
Leyton Orient	46	13	18	15	58	68	44
Peterborough	46	14	15	17	66	71	43
Oxford	46	15	13	18	61	66	43
Grimsby Town	46	17	9	20	61	68	43
Scunthorpe	46	17	8	21	58	73	42
Brighton	46	13	15	18	61	71	41
Bournemouth	46	12	17	17	39	57	41
Swansea	46	12	15	19	85	89	39
Darlington	46	13	11	22	47	81	37
Doncaster	46	12	8	26	58	117	32
Workington	46	12	7	27	55	89	31

FOURTH DIVISION

	P	W	D	L	F	A	Pts
Stockport	46	26	12	8	69	42	64
Southport	46	23	13	10	69	42	59
Barrow	46	24	11	11	76	54	59
Tranmere	46	22	14	10	66	43	58
Crewe	46	21	12	13	70	55	54
Southend	46	22	9	15	70	49	53
Wrexham	46	16	20	10	76	62	52
Hartlepool	46	22	7	17	66	64	51
Brentford	46	18	13	15	58	56	49
Aldershot	46	18	12	16	72	57	48
Bradford City	46	19	10	17	74	62	48
Halifax	46	15	14	17	59	68	44
Port Vale	46	14	15	17	55	58	43
Exeter	46	14	15	17	50	60	43
Chesterfield	46	17	8	21	60	63	42
Barnsley	46	13	15	18	60	64	41
Luton Town	46	16	9	21	59	73	41
Newport	46	12	16	18	56	63	40
Chester	46	15	10	21	54	78	40
Notts County	46	13	11	22	53	72	37
Rochdale	46	13	11	22	53	75	37
York City	46	12	11	23	65	79	35
Bradford PA	46	11	13	22	52	79	35
Lincoln	46	9	13	24	58	82	31

1967-68

FIRST DIVISION

	P	W	D	L	F	A	Pts
Man City	42	26	6	10	86	43	58
Man United	42	24	8	10	89	55	56
Liverpool	42	22	11	9	71	40	55
Leeds United	42	22	9	11	71	41	53
Everton	42	23	6	13	67	40	52
Chelsea	42	18	12	12	62	68	48
Tottenham	42	19	9	14	70	59	47
WBA	42	17	12	13	75	62	46
Arsenal	42	17	10	15	60	56	44
Newcastle	42	13	15	14	54	67	41
Nottm Forest	42	14	11	17	52	64	39
West Ham	42	14	10	18	73	69	38
Leicester	42	13	12	17	64	69	38
Burnley	42	14	10	18	64	71	38
Sunderland	42	13	11	18	51	61	37
Southampton	42	13	11	18	66	83	37
Wolves	42	14	8	20	66	75	36
Stoke City	42	14	7	21	50	73	35
Sheff Wed	42	11	12	19	51	63	34
Coventry City	42	9	15	18	51	71	33
Sheff United	42	11	10	21	49	70	32
Fulham	42	10	7	25	56	98	27

SECOND DIVISION

	P	W	D	L	F	A	Pts
Ipswich Town	42	22	15	5	79	44	59
QPR	42	25	8	9	67	36	58
Blackpool	42	24	10	8	71	43	58
Birmingham	42	19	14	9	83	51	52
Portsmouth	42	18	13	11	68	55	49
Middlesbro'	42	17	12	13	60	54	46
Millwall	42	14	17	11	62	50	45
Blackburn	42	16	11	15	56	49	43
Norwich City	42	16	11	15	60	65	43
Carlisle	42	14	13	15	58	52	41
Crystal Palace	42	14	11	17	56	56	39
Bolton	42	13	13	16	60	63	39
Cardiff	42	13	12	17	60	66	38
Huddersfield	42	13	12	17	46	61	38
Charlton	42	12	13	17	63	68	37
Aston Villa	42	15	7	20	54	64	37
Hull City	42	12	13	17	58	73	37
Derby County	42	13	10	19	71	78	36
Bristol City	42	13	10	19	48	62	36
Preston	42	12	11	19	43	65	35
Rotherham	42	10	11	21	42	76	31
Plymouth	42	9	9	24	38	72	27

THIRD DIVISION

	P	W	D	L	F	A	Pts
Oxford	46	22	13	11	69	47	57
Bury	46	24	8	14	91	66	56
Shrewsbury	46	20	15	11	61	49	55
Torquay	46	21	11	14	60	56	53
Reading	46	21	9	16	70	60	51
Watford	46	21	8	17	74	50	50
Walsall	46	19	12	15	74	61	50
Barrow	46	21	8	17	65	54	50
Peterborough	46	20	10	16	79	67	50
Swindon	46	16	17	13	74	51	49
Brighton	46	16	16	14	57	55	48
Gillingham	46	18	12	16	59	63	48
Bournemouth	46	16	15	15	56	51	47
Stockport	46	19	9	18	70	75	47
Southport	46	17	12	17	65	65	46
Bristol Rovers	46	17	9	20	72	78	43
Oldham	46	18	7	21	60	65	43
Northampton	46	14	13	19	58	72	41
Leyton Orient	46	12	17	17	46	62	41
Tranmere	46	14	12	20	62	74	40
Mansfield	46	12	13	21	51	67	37
Grimsby Town	46	14	9	23	52	69	37
Colchester	46	9	15	22	50	87	33
Scunthorpe	46	10	12	24	56	87	32

FOURTH DIVISION

	P	W	D	L	F	A	Pts
Luton Town	46	27	12	7	87	44	66
Barnsley	46	24	13	9	68	46	61
Hartlepool	46	25	10	11	60	46	60
Crewe	46	20	18	8	74	49	58
Bradford City	46	23	11	12	72	51	57
Southend	46	20	14	12	77	58	54
Chesterfield	46	21	11	14	71	50	53
Wrexham	46	20	13	13	72	53	53
Aldershot	46	18	17	11	70	55	53
Doncaster	46	18	15	13	66	56	51
Halifax	46	15	16	15	52	49	46
Newport	46	16	13	17	58	63	45
Lincoln	46	17	9	20	71	68	43
Brentford	46	18	7	21	61	64	43
Swansea	46	16	10	20	63	77	42
Darlington	46	12	17	17	47	53	41
Notts County	46	15	11	20	53	79	41
Port Vale	46	12	15	19	61	72	39
Rochdale	46	12	14	20	51	72	38
Exeter	46	11	16	19	45	65	38
York City	46	11	14	21	65	68	36
Chester	46	9	14	23	57	78	32
Workington	46	10	11	25	54	87	31
Bradford PA	46	4	15	27	30	82	23

1968-69

FIRST DIVISION

	P	W	D	L	F	A	Pts
Leeds United	42	27	13	2	66	26	67
Liverpool	42	25	11	6	63	24	61
Everton	42	21	15	6	77	36	57
Arsenal	42	22	12	8	56	27	56
Chelsea	42	20	10	12	73	53	50
Tottenham	42	14	17	11	61	51	45
Southampton	42	16	13	13	57	48	45
West Ham	42	13	18	11	66	50	44
Newcastle	42	15	14	13	61	55	44
WBA	42	16	11	15	64	67	43
Man United	42	15	12	15	57	53	42
Ipswich Town	42	15	11	16	59	60	41
Man City	42	15	10	17	64	55	40
Burnley	42	15	9	18	55	82	39
Sheff Wed	42	10	16	16	41	54	36
Wolves	42	10	15	17	41	58	35
Sunderland	42	11	12	19	43	67	34
Nottm Forest	42	10	13	19	45	57	33
Stoke City	42	9	15	18	40	63	33
Coventry City	42	10	11	21	46	64	31
Leicester	42	9	12	21	39	68	30
QPR	42	4	10	28	39	95	18

SECOND DIVISION

	P	W	D	L	F	A	Pts
Derby County	42	26	11	5	65	32	63
Crystal Palace	42	22	12	8	70	47	56
Charlton	42	18	14	10	61	52	50
Middlesbro'	42	19	11	12	58	49	49
Cardiff	42	20	7	15	67	54	47
Huddersfield	42	17	12	13	53	46	46
Birmingham	42	18	8	16	73	59	44
Blackpool	42	14	15	13	51	41	43
Sheff United	42	16	11	15	61	50	43
Millwall	42	17	9	16	57	49	43
Hull City	42	13	16	13	59	52	42
Carlisle	42	16	10	16	46	49	42
Norwich City	42	15	10	17	53	56	40
Preston	42'	12	15	15	38	44	39
Portsmouth	42	12	14	16	58	58	38
Bristol City	42	11	16	15	46	53	38
Bolton	42	12	14	16	55	67	38
Aston Villa	42	12	14	16	37	48	38
Blackburn	42	13	11	18	52	63	37
Oxford	42	12	9	21	34	55	33
Bury	42	11	8	23	51	80	30
Fulham	42	7	11	24	40	81	25

THIRD DIVISION

	P	W	D	L	F	A	Pts
Watford	46	27	10	9	74	34	64
Swindon	46	27	10	9	71	35	64
Luton Town	46	25	11	10	74	38	61
Bournemouth	46	21	9	16	60	45	51
Plymouth	46	17	15	14	53	49	49
Torquay	46	18	12	16	54	46	48
Tranmere	46	19	10	17	70	68	48
Southport	46	17	13	16	71	64	47
Stockport	46	16	14	16	67	68	46
Barnsley	46	16	14	16	58	63	46
Rotherham	46	16	13	17	56	50	45
Brighton	46	16	13	17	72	65	45
Walsall	46	14	16	16	50	49	44
Reading	46	15	13	18	67	66	43
Mansfield	46	16	11	19	58	62	43
Bristol Rovers	46	16	11	19	63	71	43
Shrewsbury	46	16	11	19	51	67	43
Orient	46	14	14	18	51	58	42
Barrow	46	17	8	21	56	75	42
Gillingham	46	13	15	18	54	63	41
Northampton	46	14	12	20	54	61	40
Hartlepool	46	10	19	17	40	70	39
Crewe	46	13	9	24	52	76	35
Oldham	46	13	9	24	50	83	35

FOURTH DIVISION

	P	W	D	L	F	A	Pts
Doncaster	46	21	17	8	65	38	59
Halifax	46	20	17	9	53	37	57
Rochdale	46	18	20	8	68	35	56
Bradford City	46	18	20	8	65	46	56
Darlington	46	17	18	11	62	45	52
Colchester	46	20	12	14	57	53	52
Southend	46	19	13	14	78	61	51
Lincoln	46	17	17	12	54	52	51
Wrexham	46	18	14	14	61	52	50
Swansea	46	19	11	16	58	54	49
Brentford	46	18	12	16	64	65	48
Workington	46	15	17	14	40	43	47
Port Vale	46	16	14	16	46	46	46
Chester	46	16	13	17	76	66	45
Aldershot	46	19	7	20	66	66	45
Scunthorpe	46	18	8	20	61	60	44
Exeter	46	16	11	19	66	65	43
Peterborough	46	13	16	17	60	57	42
Notts County	46	12	18	16	48	57	42
Chesterfield	46	13	15	18	43	50	41
York City	46	14	11	21	53	75	39
Newport	46	11	14	21	49	74	36
Grimsby Town	46	9	15	22	47	69	33
Bradford PA	46	5	10	31	32	106	20

THE POLL OF THE DECADE

My co-author Norman Giller conducted a poll among the Football League's leading managers, coaches and players at the end of the 'sixties. They were asked to name the outstanding Football League club of the decade, and also the individual players they considered made the greatest impact. It is fascinating to look back more than 20 years later at the results of that poll. I have marked with a star my choice in each category.

TOP CLUB

1. MANCHESTER UNITED (Manager: Sir Matt Busby)*
2. TOTTENHAM HOTSPUR (Manager: Bill Nicholson)
3. LEEDS UNITED (Manager: Don Revie)
4. LIVERPOOL (Manager: Bill Shankly)
5. WEST HAM UNITED (Manager: Ron Greenwood)
6. EVERTON (Manager: Harry Catterick)

GOALKEEPERS

1. GORDON BANKS (Leicester City and Stoke City)
2. PAT JENNINGS (Tottenham Hotspur)*
3. PETER BONETTI (Chelsea)
4. PETER SHILTON (Leicester City)
5. ALEX STEPNEY (Millwall and Manchester United)
6. RON SPRINGETT (Sheffield Wednesday and QPR)

FULL BACKS

1. RAY WILSON (Huddersfield and Everton)*
2. JIMMY ARMFIELD (Blackpool)
3. GEORGE COHEN (Fulham)
4. TERRY COOPER (Leeds United)
5. EDDIE McCREADIE (Chelsea)
6. ALEX ELDER (Burnley and Stoke City)

DEFENSIVE WING HALVES

1. BOBBY MOORE (West Ham United)*
2. DAVE MACKAY (Tottenham Hotspur)
3. NOBBY STILES (Manchester United)
4. NORMAN HUNTER (Leeds United)
5. TOMMY SMITH (Liverpool)
6. RON HARRIS (Chelsea)

CENTRE HALVES

1. JACK CHARLTON (Leeds United)
2. MIKE ENGLAND (Blackburn Rovers and Tottenham)*
3. BRIAN LABONE (Everton)
4. MAURICE NORMAN (Tottenham Hotspur)
5. RON YEATS (Liverpool)
6. CHARLIE HURLEY (Sunderland)

ATTACKING WING HALVES

1. BILLY BREMNER (Leeds United)
2. DANNY BLANCHFLOWER (Tottenham Hotspur)*
3. PAT CRERAND (Manchester United)
4. BOBBY ROBSON (West Bromwich Albion and Fulham)
5. ALAN MULLERY (Fulham and Tottenham)
6. GORDON MILNE (Preston and Liverpool)

WINGERS

1. GEORGE BEST (Manchester United)*
2. PETER THOMPSON (Liverpool)
3. CLIFF JONES (Tottenham Hotspur)
4. JOHN CONNELLY (Burnley and Manchester United)
5. IAN CALLAGHAN (Liverpool)
6. TERRY PAINE (Southampton)

SCHEMERS

1. BOBBY CHARLTON (Manchester United)
2. COLIN BELL (Manchester City)*
3. JOHN WHITE (Tottenham Hotspur)
4. JOHNNY GILES (Leeds United)
5. ALAN BALL (Blackpool and Everton)
6. MARTIN PETERS (West Ham United)

STRIKERS

1. JIMMY GREAVES (Tottenham Hotspur)
2. DENIS LAW (Manchester United)*
3. GEOFF HURST (West Ham United)
4. ROGER HUNT (Liverpool)
5. FRANCIS LEE (Manchester City)
6. ALLAN CLARKE (Fulham, Leicester City and Leeds)

REFEREES*

1. JIM FINNEY (Hereford)*
2. GORDON HILL (Leicester)
3. JACK TAYLOR (Wolverhampton)
4. LEO CALLAGHAN (Merthyr)
5. KEVIN HOWLEY (Billingham, Co Durham)
6. DAVID SMITH (Stonehouse, Gloucestershire)

*You will have found in the previous pages that I have given few mentions to referees. They have never been my favourite animals, and I have always considered the best are those that you do not notice. The six named here are as good as any I played under, and all earned respect with their firm but fair handling of matches. Players were unquestionably more respectful of referees in the 'sixties, but too many tended to treat us like schoolchildren rather than adults. Generally speaking I think the referees of the 'sixties met and maintained a better standard than today's officials, who too often wave red and yellow cards around like demented magicians.

THE MAJOR TRANSFER DEALS

Here are the major Football League transfer deals of the 'sixties as they happened through the decade. An asterisk signifies a part-exchange:

Player	From	To	Date	Fee
Roy Vernon	Blackburn	Everton	Feb.'60	£27,000
Denis Law	Huddersfield	Manchester City	Mar.'60	£55,000
George Eastham	Newcastle	Arsenal	Nov.'60	£47,500
Alex Young	Hearts	Everton	Nov.'60	£41,000
Noel Cantwell	West Ham	Manchester Utd	Nov.'60	£29,500
John McGrath	Bury	Newcastle	Feb.'61	£30,000
George Herd	Clyde	Sunderland	Apl.'61	£42,500
Ian St John	Motherwell	Liverpool	May '61	£35,000
John McLeod	Hibernian	Arsenal	June '61	£40,000
Brian Clough	Middlesbro'	Sunderland	July '61	£42,000
Peter Dobing	Blackburn	Manchester City	July '61	£37,000
Bobby Kennedy	Kilmarnock	Manchester City	July '61	£40,000
David Herd	Arsenal	Manchester Utd	July '61	£35,000
Stanley Matthews	Blackpool	Stoke	Oct.'61	£2,800
Jimmy Greaves	AC Milan	Spurs	Nov.'61	£99,999
Graham Moore	Cardiff	Chelsea	Dec.'61	£35,000
Chris Crowe	Blackburn	Wolves	Jan.'62	£28,000
Denis Viollet	Manchester Utd	Stoke	Jan.'62	£25,000
Mike Stringfellow	Mansfield	Leicester	Jan.'62	£25,000
Davie Gibson	Hibernian	Leicester	Jan.'62	£25,000
Mel Charles	Arsenal	Cardiff	Feb.'62	£28,000
Gordon West	Blackpool	Everton	Mar.'62	£27,500
Denis Stevens	Bolton	Everton	Mar.'62	£30,000

Player	From	To	Date	Fee
Bobby Collins	Everton	Leeds	Mar.'62	£25,000
Johnny Byrne	Crystal Palace	West Ham	Mar.'62	£58,000
Denis Law	Torino	Manchester Utd	July '62	£116,000
Joe Baker	Torino	Arsenal	July '62	£70,000
John Charles	Juventus	Leeds	Aug.'62	£53,000
Ivor Allchurch	Newcastle	Cardiff	Aug.'62	£18,000
Peter Brabrook	Chelsea	West Ham	Oct.'62	£35,000
Willie Stevenson	Rangers	Liverpool	Oct.'62	£20,000
Tony Kay	Sheffield W	Everton	Dec.'62	£55,000
Pat Crerand	Celtic	Manchester Utd	Feb.'63	£56,000
Alex Scott	Rangers	Everton	Feb.'63	£39,000
Jimmy McIlroy	Burnley	Stoke	Mar.'63	£26,000
Derek Kevan	WBA	Chelsea	Mar.'63	£40,000
John Kaye	Scunthorpe	WBA	May '63	£45,000
Ian Ure	Dundee	Arsenal	Aug.'63	£62,500
Peter Thompson	Preston	Liverpool	Aug.'63	£40,000
Ray Crawford	Ipswich	Wolves	Sep.'63	£55,000
Alan Peacock	Middlesbro'	Leeds	Feb.'64	£53,000
Jimmy Melia	Liverpool	Wolves	Mar.'64	£50,000
Fred Pickering	Blackburn	Everton	Mar.'64	£80,000
Alan Mullery	Fulham	Spurs	Mar.'64	£72,500
Don Howe	WBA	Arsenal	Apl.'64	£45,000
Pat Jennings	Watford	Spurs	June '64	£27,000
Cyril Knowles	Middlesbro'	Spurs	July '64	£45,000
Ray Wilson	Huddersfield	Everton	July '64	£40,000
Frank McLintock	Leicester	Arsenal	Oct '64	£80,000
Alan Gilzean	Dundee	Spurs	Dec.'64	£72,500
Ken Wagstaff	Mansfield	Hull	Nov.'64	£40,000
Johnny Crossan	Sunderland	Manchester City	Jan.'65	£40,000

Player	From	To	Date	Fee
Ian Butler	Rotherham	Hull	Jan.'65	£40,000
Ken Houghton	Rotherham	Hull	Jan.'65	£40,000
Jim Baxter	Rangers	Sunderland	May '65	£70,000
Mike Summerbee	Swindon	Manchester City	Aug.'65	£32,000
Terry Hennessey	Birmingham	Nott'm Forest	Nov.'65	£50,000
Peter Rodrigues	Cardiff	Leicester	Dec.'65	£40,000
Mike Trebilcock	Plymouth	Everton	Dec.'65	£23,000
Allan Clarke	Walsall	Fulham	Mar.'66	£35,000
Charlie Cooke	Dundee	Chelsea	Apl.'66	£72,000
Terry Venables	Chelsea	Spurs	Apl.'66	£80,000
Colin Bell	Bury	Manchester City	Mar.'66	£45,000
Barry Bridges	Chelsea	Birmingham	May '66	£55,000
Ian Gibson	Middlesbro'	Coventry	July '66	£50,000
Alan Ball	Blackpool	Everton	Aug.'66	£110,000
Mike England	Blackburn	Spurs	Aug.'66	£95,000
Ron Davies	Norwich	Southampton	Aug.'66	£50,000
Alex Stepney	Chelsea	Manchester Utd	Sep.'66	£55,000
George Graham	Chelsea	Arsenal*	Sep.'66	£75,000
Tony Hateley	Aston Villa	Chelsea	Oct.'66	£100,000
Wyn Davies	Bolton	Newcastle	Oct.'66	£85,000
Bob McNab	Huddersfield	Arsenal	Oct.'66	£50,000
John Ritchie	Stoke	Sheffield W	Nov.'66	£70,000
Emlyn Hughes	Blackpool	Liverpool	Feb.'67	£65,000
Howard Kendall	Preston	Everton	Mar.'67	£80,000
Derek Dougan	Leicester	Wolves	Mar.'67	£50,000
Gordon Banks	Leicester	Stoke	Apl.'67	£52,500
Billy Bonds	Charlton	West Ham*	May '67	£50,000
Bobby Ferguson	Kilmarnock	West Ham	May '67	£67,000
Tony Hateley	Chelsea	Liverpool	June '67	£96,000

Player	From	To	Date	Fee
Mick Jones	Sheff Utd	Leeds	Sep.'67	£100,000
Ernie Hunt	Wolves	Everton	Sep.'67	£80,000
Francis Lee	Bolton	Man City	Oct.'67	£60,000
Len Glover	Charlton	Leicester	Nov.'67	£80,000
Allan Birchenall	Sheffield Utd	Chelsea	Nov.'67	£100,000
Jim Baxter	Sunderland	Nott'm Forest	Dec.'67	£100,000
Martin Chivers	Southampton	Spurs	Jan.'68	£125,000
Geoff Butler	Chelsea	Sunderland	Jan.'68	£60,000
Bobby Gould	Coventry	Arsenal	Feb.'68	£90,000
Derek Parkin	Huddersfield	Wolves	Feb.'68	£80,000
David Webb	Southampton	Chelsea	Feb.'68	£60,000
Alan Stephenson	Crystal Palace	West Ham	Mar.'68	£80,000
Ernie Hunt	Everton	Coventry	Mar.'68	£65,000
Chris Cattlin	Huddersfield	Coventry	Mar.'68	£70,000
Allan Clarke	Fulham	Leicester	June '68	£150,000
Willie Morgan	Burnley	Manchester Utd	Aug.'68	£100,000
Jimmy Greenhoff	Leeds	Birmingham	Aug.'68	£75,000
Alun Evans	Wolves	Liverpool	Sep.'68	£100,000
Arthur Mann	Hearts	Manchester City	Nov.'68	£65,000
Will Carlin	Sheffield Utd	Derby	Jan.'69	£60,000
Hugh Curran	Norwich	Wolves	Jan.'69	£60,000
Roger Morgan	QPR	Spurs	Feb.'69	£100,000
Tommy Craig	Aberdeen	Sheffield W	May '69	£100,000
Allan Clarke	Leicester	Leeds	June '69	£165,000
Colin Suggett	Sunderland	WBA	June '69	£100,000
Bruce Rioch	Luton	Aston Villa	July '69	£100,000
Jim Smith	Aberdeen	Newcastle	July '69	£100,000
Jim McCalliog	Sheffield W	Wolves	July '69	£70,000
Ian Ure	Arsenal	Manchester Utd	Aug.'69	£80,000

Player	From	To	Date	Fee
Jimmy Greenhoff	Birmingham	Stoke	Aug.'69	£100,000
Mike O'Grady	Leeds	Wolves	Sep.'69	£80,000
John O'Rourke	Ipswich	Coventry	Nov.'69	£80,000
Tommy Jenkins	Reading	Southampton	Dec.'69	£60,000
Keith Newton	Blackburn	Everton	Dec.'69	£80,000

ACKNOWLEDGEMENTS

The authors, Jimmy Greaves and Norman Giller, wish to express their gratitude to their many footballing friends who searched their memories to make sure they covered the territory of the 'sixties as thoroughly as possible. In particular they thank the secretaries of the Football League and Scottish League clubs who were so helpful in providing statistical details, and also to the editors of the *News of the World* and *Playfair* annuals, which were a mine of information. Other sources for background facts included *One Hundred Years of Scottish Football* by John Rafferty, *The Book of Football* (Marshall Cavendish), *The Rothman's Book of Football League Players Records* edited by Barry Hugman, and *The Guinness Book of Facts and Feats* edited by Jack Rollin. Thanks, too, to Michael Giller for his Apple-a-day computer skills, Linda Silverman for her diligent picture research, the photo libraries, Harry Blackshaw for allowing us access to his programme collection, and also to Caroline North for laying the foundation to the book before being Maxwelled. Most of all, the authors wish to thank the bold Adrian Stephenson, the new supremo of Queen Anne Press, for having the confidence to take us on board after we thought the book had drowned along with Cap'n Bob. Finally, to all the players of the golden 'sixties - thanks for the memories.

PICTURE ACKNOWLEDGEMENTS

The authors and publishers wish to thank the following sources for their permission to reproduce copyright material. Where there is more than one picture on a page the photographs are numbered a, b, c from the top and from left to right:

Colorsport: 17c, 39a, 39b, 42a, 42b, 59b, 75b, 95b, 101a, 115b, 133b, 157a, 157b, 175c, 182b, 193 a, 193b, 195a, 195b, 211b

The Hulton-Deutsch Collection: 25a, 79b, 153a, 161a, 175b

Popperfoto: 63a, 87b, 161b

S & G Press Agency: 17a, 17b, 21a, 21b, 25b, 35a, 35b, 49a, 49b, 59a, 63b, 69a, 69b, 75a, 79a, 87a, 95a, 101b, 107a, 107b, 115a, 121a, 125a, 125b, 137a, 137b, 141b, 179a, 179b, 179c, 182a

Steve Hale: 131a, 131b, 133a, 211a

Syndication International: 121b, 141a, 153b, 175a

Jacket photographs:

Front: TV-am (top), S & G Press Agency (middle), Syndication International (bottom).

Back: (clockwise from top left) S & G Press Agency, Steve Hale, Steve Hale, S & G Press Agency, Colorsport, S & G Press Agency.

Malcolm Allison

Alan Ball

Gordon Banks

George Best

Derek Dougan

George Eastham

Pat Jennings

Howard Kendall

Peter Osgood

Bobby Robson

Peter Shilton

Bobby Smith

Mike Channon

Bobby Charlton

Brian Clough

Tommy Docherty

Denis Law

James McIlroy

Bobby Moore

Terry Neill

Mike Summerbee

Terry Venables

Ron Yeats

Alex Young

Lightning Source UK Ltd.
Milton Keynes UK
UKOW05f1147250216

269065UK00001B/18/P

9 781909 040250